Second Edition

SALES FORECASTING MANAGEMENT

Second Edition

SALES FORECASTING MANAGEMENT
A Demand Management Approach

John T. Mentzer ✦ Mark A. Moon
University of Tennessee

SAGE Publications
Thousand Oaks ▪ London

For information:

Sage Publications, Inc.
2455 Teller Road
Thousand Oaks, California 91320
E-mail: order@sagepub.com

Sage Publications Ltd.
1 Oliver's Yard
55 City Road
London EC1Y 1SP
United Kingdom

Sage Publications India Pvt. Ltd.
B-42, Panchsheel Enclave
Post Box 4109
New Delhi 110 017 India

Printed in the United States of America

Library of Congress Cataloging-in-Publication Data

Mentzer, John T.
Sales forecasting management : A demand management approach / John
T. Mentzer and Mark A. Moon.—2nd ed.
    p. cm.
Includes bibliographical references and index.
ISBN 1-4129-0571-0 (pbk.)
   1. Sales forecasting—Management. 2. Marketing research—Management.
I. Moon, Mark A., 1955- II. Title.
HF5415.2.M393 2005
658.8'18—dc22

                                    2004016438

This book is printed on acid-free paper.

04   05   06   07   08   10 9 8 7 6 5 4 3 2 1

Acquisitions Editor:	Al Bruckner
Editorial Assistant:	MaryAnn Vail
Production Editor:	Laureen A. Shea
Copy Editor:	Judy Wilson
Typesetter:	C&M Digitals (P) Ltd.
Indexer:	Michael Ferreira
Cover Designer:	Edgar Abarca

Contents

Preface

Our research with companies in the area of sales forecasting management began back in the early 1970s with Whirlpool, Johnson & Johnson, and Union Carbide. From that point on, we have worked with over 400 companies in the areas of sales forecasting technique development and application, sales forecasting systems, and sales forecasting management and demand management processes.

The early work led to the first of what has become four phases of sales forecasting benchmarking research. Phase 1 was a survey in the early 1980s of sales forecasting technique usage and satisfaction, and accuracy achieved, in 157 companies. Phase 2 broadened this survey 10 years later to include sales forecasting techniques, systems, and management practices in 208 companies. Phase 3 was an in-depth analysis of the sales forecasting management practices of 20 top performing companies. Phase 4, which is still on-going today, applies what we learned in the first three phases to improve the sales forecasting performance of specific companies. We call this last phase Sales Forecasting Audits, and collectively refer to all four phases as the Benchmark Studies.

In addition to the Benchmark Studies and our applied work with specific companies, we have also worked with many companies to develop sales forecasting software systems. This stream of work has culminated in a sales forecasting system, called MULTICASTER, which is used by many companies to develop their quantitative sales forecasts. A demonstration version of this powerful software is available in the Profiles section of the web site, www.jtmassociates.com.

We have tried to bring the results of all this research and experience into this book. As such, this book is designed to give sales forecasting analysts more of an understanding of the role their function plays in the organization **and** to give managers of the sales forecasting function more of an understanding of the technical aspects of developing and analyzing sales forecasts.

In addition, the book is designed to give users of the sales forecast (marketing, finance/accounting, sales, production/purchasing, and logistics managers) a better understanding of how forecasts are developed and the sales forecasting needs of all the business functions. *Thus, readers of this book should include new and experienced forecast analysts, new and experienced managers of the sales forecasting function, and those who work in functions that contribute to, or use, sales forecasts.*

In addition, this book is designed to serve as a text for the stand-alone sales forecasting course or as a required reading for the sales forecasting section of other business undergraduate or graduate courses. *Thus, readers of this book should also include undergraduate and graduate students in business schools.*

Therefore, the book is intended to be a tool for both students and practitioners of sales forecasting management. The demand histories of actual products from real companies are included with the software on the web site to provide the basis for realistic sales forecasting projects and assignments. Instructors in courses using this book are encouraged to not only assign the products that accompany the software as class projects, but also have the students gather their own data from local companies to make projects more interesting.

For practitioners, the software is intended to provide a readily available environment in which to test what you have just learned in reading the book in your company. The products already loaded in the software can be used, or we encourage practitioners to load their own demand history and apply the forecasting concepts learned in the book to see the immediate impact on their sales forecasts.

The combined key objectives of the book and the software are:

- To prepare sales forecasting analysts to understand the uses of their sales forecasts in their companies.
- To provide sales forecasting managers with a technical foundation in the techniques, approaches, and systems used to develop sales forecasts.
- To provide managers of functions that use the sales forecast with an understanding of how the forecasts are developed and the limitations of these forecasts.
- To provide managers of functions that contribute information to sales forecasts with an understanding of the critical role those forecasts play, and how their participation in that process can be improved.

- To provide undergraduate and graduate business students with an appreciation of all four previous points.
- To expose all these groups to the "state of the art" in sales forecasting today, based upon experience gathered by the authors with over 400 companies.
- To give all these groups a chance to apply what they have learned to their own data with a "state of the art" sales forecasting system designed to provide relevant sales forecasts to all the user functions in a variety of company sizes and types.

As with any effort of this sort, it is not the work of just the authors, but also the input, guidance, efforts, and understanding of a legion of colleagues. We would like to thank all those who have provided this support to us in writing this book. In general, we would like to thank the many undergraduate and graduate students we have had in our sales forecasting classes over the years for challenging us to think more thoroughly about the topics and issues involved in sales forecasting.

We would also like to thank the many people with whom we have interacted on the topic of sales forecasting. In particular, we would like to thank the many individuals who provided us with their insight while we were working with the following companies:

AET Films	ConAgra
AT&T	Continental Tire
Advance Auto	Corning
AlliedSignal	Courtlauds Performance Films
Anheuser-Busch	U.S. Defense Logistics Agency
Applied Micro Circuits	DG Products
Corporation	DJR Products
Avery Dennison	Du Pont Corporation
Bacardi	Eastman Chemical
Becton-Dickinson	Essex Chemical
Brake Parts, Inc.	Ethicon
Canadian Tire Company	Exxon
Carter-Wallace	Federal Express
CBIS Federal	Federal-Mogul
Coca Cola	Gallo Wineries
Colgate Palmolive	General Mills
Computer Data Systems, Inc.	General Motors

Gordon's Furniture
W. R. Grace
Greyhound
Heritage Healthcare
Hershey Corporation
The IJ Company
U.S. Internal Revenue Service
International Brake
    Industries
James River Limestone
John Deere
Johnson and Johnson
Kelsan Company
Kimberly Clark
Litton Industries
The Longaberger Company
Lucent Technologies
Lykes Pasco
MAC Group
Magnetek
Martin Brower Corporation
Martin Processing
Mary Kay Cosmetics
Metro and Company
    Realtors
Michelin
Midlab Corporation
Motorola
Nabisco

O'Connor Products
Owens-Corning Fiberglas
J.C. Penney
Pfizer
Pharmavite
Philips Consumer Electronics
Pillsbury
Planters LifeSavers Company
ProSource
Reckitt Colman
Red Lobster
Resource Optimization
    Corporation
Sandoz
Sara Lee
Schering Plough
SeaLand
Slimfast Foods
Smith & Nephew
Steelwedge
Sysco
Tropicana
Union Pacific Railroad
United Telecom
Warner Lambert
Westwood Squibb
Weyerhauser
Whirlpool Corporation
Williamson-Dickie

Our special thanks go to the following individuals for their insight, dedication, and guidance on the book:

Kenneth B. Kahn, Associate Professor of Marketing, The University of Tennessee

Dianne Marshall, Managing Director of the Sales Forecasting Management Forum, The University of Tennessee

Donna Davis, Assistant Professor of Marketing, Texas Tech University

Susan Golicic, Assistant Professor of Marketing, The University of Oregon

Teresa McCarthy, Assistant Professor of Marketing, Lehigh University

Finally, this book would not have been possible without the understanding, love, and support of our families. For the many hours in the evenings and on weekends that we had to work on the manuscript, and received understanding in return, we most sincerely want to thank Brenda, Ashley, and Erin Mentzer, and Colin and David Moon. Special thanks goes to Carol Ann Moon, because without her love and encouragement, the second author never would have made it.

To
Brenda, Ashley, and Erin
and
Colin and David, and to Carol

1

Managing the Sales Forecasting Process

❖   ❖   ❖

A company thought it had a forecasting problem. Many of its products were "slow movers, with spikes." This is that daunting forecasting problem where 4 units sell one week, 3 the next, 5 the next, 10,000 the next, 3 the next, 6 the next, 20,000 the next, 1 the next, and so on. The spikes seem to be impossible to forecast (come in different-size spikes, at irregular times, not related to promotional events) and cause huge supply chain disruptions (expedited production and overtime or excessive inventory to meet the order; disruption to supplier operations resulting in higher procurement costs; or outsourcing the large orders resulting in lost margins).

This company manufactures numerous lighting products, but one of its slow movers with spikes is called a ballast. A ballast is a little transformer that takes electrical energy and converts it into an energy beam that passes through a fluorescent bulb. Without the ballast, a fluorescent bulb does not work.

One source of independent demand (defined later in this chapter) is the individual "do-it-yourselfer," who replaces ballasts when they wear out at home. We now have a slow mover that sells one at a time as a replacement for ballasts already in use as they wear out. As this independent demand impacts the ordering policies of the various home supply stores in this company's supply chain, we get the fairly smooth, slow-moving component of derived demand (also defined later in this chapter) that the company experiences.

However, there is another source of independent demand for ballasts. The owners of a large office building decide to retrofit all the ballasts in their building. This is a return on investment (ROI) decision, because old ballasts use more electricity to light the fluorescent bulb than new ballasts do; that is, at some point, the cost of replacing the ballasts can be justified on the basis of the savings in electric bills. The office building in question has 10,000 ballasts that need to be replaced. When the building owner decides to retrofit the ballasts in the building (generally in connection with some other renovations), an electrical contractor is chosen to do the job, who then works with the other contractors involved in the renovation to decide when to start the ballast retrofitting part of the overall project, usually weeks or months in the future.

Unfortunately, the electrical contractor does not tell the company about the independent demand for 10,000 ballasts until the week before they are needed. Because it typically takes this company 3 weeks to fill an order of this size, the company incurs higher supply chain costs (expedited production costs, costs of higher inventory levels, spot market procurement costs, outsourcing production to higher cost alternatives) associated with expediting a large order, and the company makes far less (if any) money on this large order.

By recognizing that the demand impacting this company was derived demand (derived from the contractor's ordering policies), not independent demand, the company shifted its emphasis from forecasting the spikes in independent demand to demand planning for the derived demand. The result was a new demand planning policy in this supply chain; the company now offers contractors a 3% price discount on any orders in excess of 10,000 that are placed with the company five or more weeks before they are needed. This is a considerable savings for the contractors (3% off an order of 10,000 units, each of which typically costs more than $20!) and results in increased sales for the company.

More importantly, however, this company turned the unplanned large spikes hitting their operations systems into demand that could be planned weeks before needed. Under the new demand planning system, the company knows about spikes (that take 3 weeks to fill) 5 weeks in advance. This means that instead of expedited production, overtime, higher procurement costs, and unwanted, expensive outsourcing of production, the company can actually produce the products to fill the order anytime during the 5 week window, usually in slack production times. This "smoothing out" of the production scheduling system saves this company millions of dollars every year—all with increased market share among the contractors. This would not have been possible without the realization that the demand the company was trying to forecast was actually derived demand that could be planned.

❖ INTRODUCTION

Much like the example just given, this book is about much more than just techniques. In fact, it is about more than just sales forecasting. It is about three management activities in any supply chain: demand management, demand planning, and sales forecasting management.

❖ A DEMAND MANAGEMENT
APPROACH TO SALES FORECASTING

The role of sales forecasting changes depending upon the position in the supply chain that a company occupies. Any supply chain has only one point of **independent demand:** *the amount of product demanded (by time and location) by the end-use customer of the supply chain.* Whether this end-use customer is a consumer shopping in a retail establishment or online (B2C), or a business buying products for consumption in the process of conducting its business operations (B2B), these end-use customers determine the true demand for the product that will flow through the supply chain.

The company in the supply chain that directly serves this end-use customer directly experiences this independent demand. All subsequent companies in the supply chain experience a demand that is tempered by the order fulfillment and purchasing policies of other companies in the supply chain. This second type of supply chain demand is called **derived demand**, because it is not the independent demand of the end-use customer, but rather a *demand that is derived from what other companies in the supply chain do to meet their demand from their immediate customer (i.e., the company that orders from them).*

The derived demand for one company is often the dependent demand of their customers. **Dependent demand** is the *demand for the component parts that go into a product.* Often called bill of materials (BOM) forecasting, this is usually demand that is dependent upon the demand for the product in which it is a component. The exception is when different amounts of a component part go into different versions of the product and is, thus, a special kind of forecasting called statistical BOM forecasting. For example, the manufacturer of a large telecommunications switch may have 50 different component parts that can go in each switch, with the number of each component included varying from 0 to 5, depending upon the customer order. Thus, the independent demand of customers for the switch, and the independent demand of customers for various switch configurations (and their resulting BOM), must be forecast to determine the dependent demand for each component part.

It is important to note that only one company in any given supply chain is directly impacted by independent demand. The rest of the companies in the supply chain are impacted by derived and/or dependent demand. Equally important, the techniques, systems, and processes necessary to deal with derived and dependent demand are quite different from those of independent demand.

Recognizing the differences between independent, dependent, and derived demand, recognizing which type of demand impacts a particular company, and developing techniques, systems, and processes to deal with that company's particular type of demand can have a profound impact on supply chain costs and customer service levels. We first explore the implications of independent and derived demand, followed by a model of the demand management function in supply chain management. We will then move on to the topic of sales forecasting management.

Derived Versus Independent Demand

Figure 1.1 depicts a traditional supply chain, with a retailer serving the end-use customer, a wholesaler supplying the retailer, a manufacturer supplying the wholesaler, and a supplier providing raw materials to the manufacturer. The source of independent demand for this supply chain is 1,000 units for the planning period. However, the retailer (as is typically the case) does not know this with certainty. In fact, the retailer has a reasonably good forecasting process and forecasts end-use customer demand to be 1,000 units for the planning period. Because the forecast has typically experienced +/−10% error in the past, the retailer places an order to its supplier (the wholesaler) for 1,100 units (i.e., 1,000 units for expected demand and 100 units for safety stock to meet expected forecasting error). It is critical to notice in this simple example of a typical, *unmanaged* supply chain that the demand the wholesaler experiences is **1,100 units, not 1,000.**

The wholesaler, in turn, has a reasonable forecasting system (note that the wholesaler is not forecasting end-use customer independent demand, but is inadvertently forecasting retailer-derived demand), and forecasts the demand impacting the wholesaler at 1,100 units. Again, the wholesaler believes the forecasting error to be approximately

Figure 1.1   Demand Error in a Traditional Supply Chain

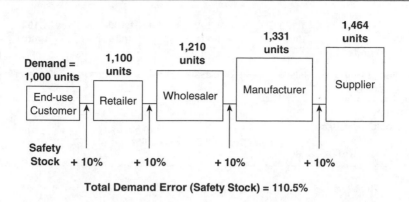

Total Demand Error (Safety Stock) = 110.5%

+/− 10%, so the wholesaler orders 1,100 plus 10% (or 1,210 units) from the manufacturer. If the manufacturer and the supplier both assume the same +/− 10% forecasting error, then each adds 10% to its orders to their suppliers. Note that we are assuming here, for simplicity's sake, that there is no BOM. If there were, the logic would still hold, but the illustration would become unnecessarily complicated.

As Figure 1.1 illustrates, simple failure to recognize the difference between independent demand (which needs to be forecast) and derived demand (which can be derived and planned)—even in a supply chain where forecasting error is only +/− 10%—adds greatly to the safety stock carried in the supply chain. In fact, because each member of the supply chain only needed 1,000 units to meet the actual demand, plus 100 units for the potential forecasting error, this particular supply chain is carrying 705 too much inventory ((210–100) + (331–100) + (464–100) = 705), or a 16.0% supply chain wide inventory overstock ((705/4,400) = 16.0%) for the actual end-use customer demand. Inventory carried for Total Demand Error (Safety Stock) in this supply chain is 1,105 (100+210+331+464), or 110.5% of actual end-use customer demand!

This example allows us to introduce the supply chain concept of **demand planning**, which is *the coordinated flow of derived and dependent demand through companies in the supply chain.* Demand planning is illustrated in the Figure 1.2 supply chain. End-use customer demand is the same as in Figure 1.1, and the retailer's faith in its forecast (+/− 10%) is unchanged. What has changed, however, is that the other companies in

Figure 1.2   Demand Error in a Demand Planning Supply Chain

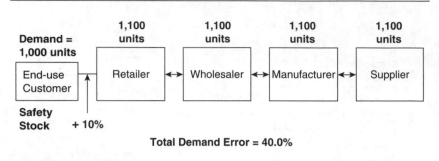

Total Demand Error = 40.0%

the supply chain are no longer even attempting to forecast the demand of their customers. Rather, each member of the supply chain receives point-of-sale (POS) demand information from the retailer, and the retailer's planned ordering based upon this demand. Combined with knowledge of the time-related order flows through this supply chain, each company can plan its processes (including orders to its suppliers). The result is that each member of the supply chain carries 1,100 units in inventory—a system-wide reduction in inventory of 13.81% from 5,105 (i.e., 1,100 for the retailer, 1,210 for the wholesaler, 1,331 for the manufacturer, and 1,464 for the supplier) to 4,400 (i.e., 1,100 each for the retailer, wholesaler, manufacturer, and supplier). More importantly, the inventory carried for forecasting error (safety stock) drops from 1,105 to 400 (from total demand error of 110.5% to 40.0%)—for a reduction of total demand error inventory (safety stock) of 63.8% ((1,105–400)/1,105).

Notice, however, that the inventory reductions are not uniform across the supply chain. Whereas the supplier has a reduction in safety stock of 78.4% (from 464 to 100), the retailer experiences no reduction. In fact, the further up the supply chain, the greater the safety stock reduction. This illustrates a paradox of demand planning in any supply chain—the very companies that are most needed to implement supply chain demand planning (i.e., implementation of systems to share with suppliers real-time POS information held by retailers) have the least economic motivation (i.e., inventory reduction) to cooperate. This leads us to the concept of demand management.

Demand management is *the creation across the supply chain and its markets of a coordinated flow of demand*. Much is implied in this seemingly simple definition. First, the traditional function of marketing creates demand for various products, but often does not share these demand creating plans (such as promotional programs) with other functions within the company (forecasting, in particular), much less with other companies in the supply chain.

Second, the role of demand management is often to decrease demand. This may sound counter-intuitive, but demand often exists for company products at a level management cannot realistically (or profitably) fulfill. Demand management implies an assessment of the profit contribution of various products and customers (all with capacity constraints in mind—including the capacity of all components in the BOM), emphasizing demand for the profitable ones, and decreasing demand (by lessening marketing efforts) for the unprofitable ones.

Finally, as we mentioned earlier, considerable supply chain savings can result from demand planning, but the rewards are not always consistent with the need to obtain collaboration from all companies in the supply chain. Thus, an aspect of demand management is **supply chain relationship management,** which is *the management of relationships with supply chain partners to match performance with measurements and rewards so that all companies in the supply chain are fairly rewarded for overall supply success (measured as cost reduction and increased customer satisfaction).*

A Model of Supply Chain Demand Management

This leads us to an overall model of the role of demand management, demand planning, and sales forecasting management in the supply chain. Figure 1.3 illustrates these roles. Supply chain management has many aspects, only one of which is demand management. As previously illustrated, demand management encompasses the traditional marketing functions, along with the coordination of marketing activities with other functions in the company and the supply chain. However, the traditional demand creation role of marketing is tempered in demand management by a desire to coordinate the flow of demand across the supply chain (demand planning) and creating incentives for supply chain partners to help manage those flows (supply chain relationship management). Demand planning is concerned with the coordination across the supply chain of derived and dependent demand. Sales forecasting management (which is the primary focus of this book, but within the overall perspective of Figure 1.3) is concerned with the independent demand that occurs in any supply chain.

Figure 1.3   Demand Management in Supply Chain Management

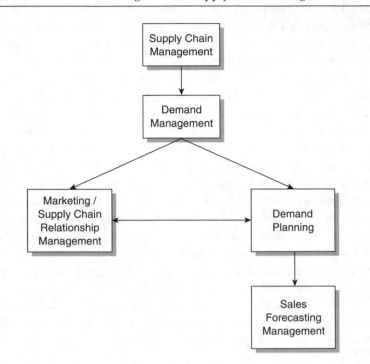

❖ SALES FORECASTING MANAGEMENT

Sales forecasting management is about the management of the sales forecasting function within an organization. It is about recognizing that, although the function is typically called sales forecasting, we are really trying to forecast *demand*—that is, we want to know what our customers demand so we can plan on achieving sales at or near that level.

Sales forecasting involves the proper use of various techniques, both qualitative and quantitative, within the context of corporate information systems, to meet the myriad of needs of the sales forecast users and to manage this entire process. To manage these multidimensional aspects, we have to understand each in turn and the management structures in which sales forecasting must operate. These will be the topics of this book. Before going any further, however, we should understand exactly what we mean by sales forecasting and the area with which it is often confused, planning.

❖ FORECASTS VERSUS PLANS VERSUS TARGETS

For the purposes of this book, we will define a *sales forecast* as **a projection into the future of expected demand, given a stated set of environmental conditions**. This should be distinguished from *operational plans*, which we will define as **a set of specified managerial actions to be undertaken to meet or exceed the sales forecast**. Examples of operational plans include production plans, procurement plans, and distribution plans. Both the sales forecast and the operational plans should be distinguished from the *sales target*, which we will define as **sales goals that are established to provide motivation for sales and marketing personnel**.

Notice that our definition of a sales forecast does not specify the technique (quantitative or qualitative), does not specify who develops the forecast within the company, nor does it include managerial plans. The reason for this is **many companies confuse the functions of forecasting, planning, and target-setting**. Operational plans for the level of sales to be achieved should be based upon the forecast of demand, but the two management functions should be kept separate. Similarly, target-setting should be done with a realistic assessment of expected future demand in mind, and this assessment comes from the sales forecast. In other words, the functions of planning and target-setting should be informed by forecasts of demand, but should not be confused with sales forecasting.

Notice that these definitions imply different performance measures for sales forecasts than for operational plans. Because the purpose of sales forecasting is to make projections of demand given a set of specified environmental assumptions, one of the key measures of sales forecasting performance is accuracy of the forecast, and one of the key methods to explain variances in accuracy is how the environment varied from the one defined. This explanation is not intended to excuse forecast inaccuracy; rather, it is meant to help us understand the business environment and forecast more accurately in the future.

In contrast, the goal of operational plans is not accuracy, but rather to effectively and efficiently meet forecasted demand. In addition, while forecasts are meant to be accurate, targets are meant to be met or exceeded. A mistake made by many companies is to confuse the sales forecast, where the objective is accuracy, with the sales target, where the objective is to at least meet, and hopefully exceed, the goal or quota. In other words, companies should never be guilty of confusing forecasting with the firm's motivational strategy.

❖ THE ROLE OF SALES FORECASTING
    IN SALES AND OPERATIONS PLANNING (S&OP)

In many companies, sales forecasting is an integral part of a critical process for matching demand and supply that is sometimes referred to as Sales and Operations Planning (S&OP). Figure 1.4 offers a simplified picture of how sales forecasting contributes to the S&OP process. As seen in Figure 1.4, an enterprise can be thought of as consisting of two primary functions: a demand function and a supply function. Demand is the responsibility of sales and marketing. In many companies, the sales organization is responsible for generating and maintaining demand from large end-user customers, or from wholesale or retail channel partners. Marketing is usually responsible for generating and maintaining demand from end consumers. Supply is the responsibility of a number of functions, including manufacturing, procurement, logistics or distribution, human resources, and finance. It is also the responsibility of a variety of suppliers, who must provide raw materials, component parts, and packaging. The S&OP process provides a "junction box" where information can flow between the demand side and the supply side of an enterprise.

As shown in Figure 1.4, critical input to the S&OP process is the **sales forecast**, which is, as defined above, the projection into the future of expected demand. The sales forecast should originate in the demand side of the enterprise, because it is the demand side of the enterprise (i.e., sales and marketing) that is responsible for generating demand and that should have the best perspective on what future demand will be. In addition to the sales forecast, which originates in the demand side of the company, another critical input to the S&OP process is a **capacity plan**. A **capacity plan** is a projection into the future about what supply capabilities will be, given a set of environmental assumptions. This input is provided by the supply side of the enterprise and documents both long- and short-term supply capabilities. The process that occurs inside the S&OP process—the junction box—is the matching of future demand projections (i.e., the sales forecast) with future supply projections (i.e., the capacity plan).

Out of the S&OP process come two critical plans, the operational plan and the demand plan. As discussed above, the operational plan consists of manufacturing plans, procurement plans, distribution plans, and human resource plans. These various operational plans can be short-term in nature, such as a monthly production schedule. They

Figure 1.4   S&OP: The Junction Box

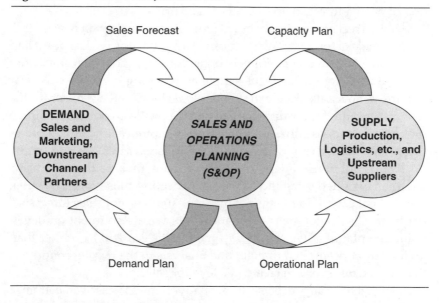

Sales Forecast   Capacity Plan

DEMAND
Sales and Marketing, Downstream Channel Partners

SALES AND OPERATIONS PLANNING (S&OP)

SUPPLY
Production, Logistics, etc., and Upstream Suppliers

Demand Plan   Operational Plan

can be long-term in nature, such as extended contracts for raw materials, or even plans to expand manufacturing capacity. The other critical plan that emerges from the S&OP process is the demand plan, which involves sales and marketing making plans about what should be sold and marketed and when, given the supply capabilities of the firm. As mentioned above, demand plans may involve suppressing demand for products or services that are capacity constrained, or shifting demand from low-margin products to high-margin items.

Other authors have discussed how to effectively manage the S&OP process within organizations (see, for example, Lapide 2002), and such discussion is beyond the scope of this book. It is important, however, to understand the critical role that sales forecasting plays in the overall planning activities of the firm. Without accurate and credible estimates of future demand, it is impossible for organizations to effectively manage their supply chains.

❖ WHY IS A SALES FORECAST NEEDED?

If we can simply set a sales goal and expect marketing and sales to exceed it, why do we even need a sales forecast in the first place? This is a question many managers ask and often answer incorrectly (i.e., we do not need a forecast), to their eventual sorrow.

The correct answer is that every time we develop a plan of any kind, we first make a forecast. This is true of individuals, as well as profit and non-profit companies, government organizations, and in fact, any entity that makes a plan. It can be as simple as planning what we will wear tomorrow. When we decide to lay out wool slacks and a sweater for the next day, we are forecasting that the weather will be cool. If we add an umbrella to our ensemble, we are forecasting rain. The plan was predicated upon the forecast, whether we consciously thought about it or not.

This is not much different from a company making financial plans based on expected sales and the costs of meeting those sales. The trick is to not get caught in the trap of making "inadvertent sales forecasts." Inadvertent sales forecasts are made when we are so intent on developing the plan that we simply assume what sales will be, rather than giving any concentrated thought and analysis to the market conditions that will be necessary to create this level of sales.

One great example of such an inadvertent forecast came from a manufacturer in the grocery products industry. The owner of the company explained to us that the sales plan called for an increase in sales of 5% for the next year. However, we had also been told that this industry in this country was not growing and that any attempt to grab market share from the competition was only met by counter moves that caused greater promotional expenditures, but no shift in market share. "Wait a minute," we said to the owner. "How can industry size not change, market share not change, but sales grow? It does not take a math major to figure out that this is not going to work." The answer was that management would simply have to motivate everyone to work harder to achieve the (mathematically impossible) plan. Of course, it is obvious what happened—no amount of motivation can overcome an impossible situation, and the sales plan was not achieved. It was not achieved because it was based on an inadvertent and uninformed forecast. This is also a classic example of management confusing forecasting, planning, and target-setting. In this case, no reasonable *forecast* would predict a 5% increase in sales. The 5% increase should have been seen for what it was—a stretch *goal*.

Let's look at one more example. A large regional distributor of food products to restaurants develops an elaborate annual profit plan. Hundreds of person-days go into the development of this plan, but it always starts with such comments as, "We need profits to increase next year by 6%. Let's figure out how much sales have to be to achieve that goal." Notice that the term "goal" sneaked into that quote. Where these executives should have started was to ask about market and environmental conditions facing the company during the planning horizon and what levels of sales could be expected based upon these conditions. The plan then becomes one of determining what marketing and sales efforts will be necessary to meet and exceed these projections to a level necessary to achieve the profit plan. The plan cannot drive the forecast; it has to be the other way around.

Thus, one of our goals in this book it to help managers see the importance of the sales forecast as *input* to their plans and to understand how these sales forecasts can and should be developed. To do this, as a first step we should talk about the sales forecast needs of the primary managerial functions within an organization. In other words, what do marketing, sales, finance/accounting, production/purchasing, and logistics each need from the sales forecast as input to their plans? To answer this question, we will first define the related concepts of sales forecasting level, time horizon, time interval, and form—mainly because different management functions require different levels, horizons, intervals, and forms of sales forecasts.

The *sales forecasting level* is the focal point in the corporate hierarchy where the forecast is needed. A corporate forecast, for instance, is a forecast of overall sales for the corporation. The *sales forecasting time horizon* generally coincides with the time frame of the plan for which it was developed. If, for instance, we continue the example just given, a corporate plan may be for the next two years and, thus, we need a sales forecast for that two-year time horizon. The *sales forecasting time interval* generally coincides with how often the plan is updated. If our two-year corporate sales plan must be updated every three months (not an unusual scenario), we can say the level is corporate, the horizon is two years, and the interval is quarterly. The *sales forecasting form* is what needs to be forecast or planned. Some functions need to know what physical units are to be produced and/or shipped, while other functions need to know the dollar equivalents of these units, and other functions need to plan based upon total pounds or cubic volume. These constitute the *forms* a sales forecast (and a plan) can take.

Sales Forecasting Needs of Marketing

Marketing is typically concerned with the success of individual products and product lines the company offers to its customers. This concern usually manifests itself in annual plans (updated monthly or quarterly) of marketing efforts for new and existing products. The marketing plans, in turn, usually involve projected product changes, promotional efforts, channel placement, and pricing. To develop these plans, marketing needs sales forecasts that take these various efforts into account and project sales (typically in dollars) at the product and product line level for an annual time horizon and with monthly or quarterly intervals.

Sales Forecasting Needs of Sales

Sales, as a management function, is typically concerned with setting goals for the individual members of the sales force and motivating those salespeople to exceed these goals. The territories of salespeople can be defined in numerous ways (geographically, by industry, by customer, by product, and so on), and it is this definition that helps define the sales forecasting level for a particular sales function.

The horizon and interval are largely defined by the time frame of the compensation plan. If, for instance, certain salespeople receive their commissions based upon quarterly sales and the sales manager must plan for the next four quarters, the horizon will be one year and the interval will be quarterly. At the very least, most companies' sales management functions need sales forecasts (in dollars) at the territory level, with typical horizons of one or two years and monthly or quarterly intervals.

Sales Forecasting Needs of Finance/Accounting

Among other responsibilities, finance (with input from the accounting function) is charged with the job of projecting cost and profit levels and capital needs, based upon a given sales forecast. These "profit plans" are typically annual intervals and can extend anywhere from 1 year to 5 years. Although individual product sales are an input to this planning process (because costs of different products may vary), the concern with the profit plan is typically at the corporate or divisional level. Thus, the sales forecasting needs of finance are typically dollar sales at the corporate, to division, to product line level; the horizon is typically one to five years; and the interval is quarterly or monthly (depending on how often the plan is updated).

Sales Forecasting Needs of Production/Purchasing

Production and purchasing must concern themselves with two very different unit forecasts, one long term and one very short term. The long-term forecast is used for planning the development of suppliers and plant and equipment, which can take several years. Because these long-term plans are dependent upon the mixture of sales of products to be made in the plant, the forecast must be at the individual product level (often in forecasting terminology referred to as stock keeping units [SKUs]). The horizon is dependent upon the time it takes to bring new suppliers, plant, and equipment on line and, thus, can range from one to three years. The interval for updating these forecasts is typically quarterly.

The short-term production/purchasing forecast is based upon the needs of the production planning schedule, which can range from one to six months (depending upon the raw materials purchasing order cycle) and needs a specific detail of which products to produce. Thus, this short-term production/purchasing sales forecast is at the SKU level, has a horizon seldom greater than six months, and has intervals ranging from daily to monthly.

Sales Forecasting Needs of Logistics

Because it is the responsibility of logistics to move the products (SKUs) that production creates to the specific locations where they will be demanded, logistics needs sales forecasts at the SKU by location (often termed SKUL) forecast level. The horizons for these forecasts are also two-fold: one for the long-term plan and one for the short-term plan. The long-term plan is needed to develop the storage facilities in various locations (thus, forecasts in units and cubic volume) and the transportation equipment to move the products between these facilities (thus, forecasts in weight). Again, the horizon is determined by the time it takes to bring these facilities on line. A large chemical company, for instance, needs an 18-month planning horizon to contract the construction of new rail cars to move its various products. Thus, the long-term logistics plan has as input a forecast with an 18-month horizon.

Across companies, these long-term horizons can range from monthly for rented facilities or contract carriage to several years for customized facilities or transportation equipment built specifically for the company. Because both are often used, the interval is typically monthly. Because the plans are influenced by specifically what is moved and where, the level is product by location (SKUL).

Short-term logistics plans are concerned with specific decisions of what products to move (expressed in units, cube, and weight) to what locations and when. Thus, the sales forecast has a horizon defined by the order cycle time from the plant to the facility and, thus, can be extremely short-term (often monthly, weekly, or in some extreme cases, daily forecasts). The intervals for updating these forecasts are also typically at the monthly or weekly (and sometimes even daily) level.

❖ SUMMARY: ORGANIZATIONAL SALES FORECASTING NEEDS

As Table 1.1 illustrates, not only are sales forecasts needed as input to all the plans of the organization, but different functions within the organization have very different needs from the sales forecast as input to their plans. It is the purpose of the book to help the reader understand these different needs and how advanced companies solve these disparate needs through the sales forecasting management tools of techniques, systems, management approaches, and performance measurement.

❖ THE TOOLS OF SALES FORECASTING MANAGEMENT

Just as any modern management function must use state-of-the-art techniques to get the job done, such as available information systems, the latest in managerial processes and approaches to managing the function, and methods of measuring and rewarding performance, so must sales forecasting management. Although we briefly review each of these areas here, we devote much more attention to each in later chapters.

Sales Forecasting Techniques

A myriad of forecasting techniques exists and is available to the sales forecasting manager. In fact, it often seems that too many techniques are available and that the choice decision can border on information overload (at last count, there were over 70 different time series techniques

Table 1.1 Forecasting Requirements of Various Managerial Functions

	Marketing	Sales	Finance/Accounting	Production/Purchasing: Long Term	Production/Purchasing: Short Term	Logistics: Long Term	Logistics: Short Term
Needs	Annual plans (updated monthly or quarterly) for new and existing products or product changes, promotional efforts, channel placement, and pricing	Setting goals for the sales force and motivating salespeople to exceed those goals	Projecting cost and profit levels and capital needs	Planning the development of plant and equipment	Planning specific production runs	Planning the development of storage facilities and transportation equipment	Specific decisions of what products to move to what locations and when
Level	Product or product line	Territory and/or customer	Corporate, division, product line	Product (SKU)	Product (SKU)	Product by location (SKUL)	Product by location (SKUL)
Horizon	Annual	1–2 years	1–5 years	1–3 years	1–6 months	Monthly to several years	Daily, weekly, monthly
Interval	Monthly or quarterly	Monthly or quarterly	Monthly or quarterly	Quarterly	Daily, weekly, monthly	Monthly	Daily, weekly, monthly
Form	Dollars	Dollars	Dollars	Units	Units	Units/Weight/Cube	Units/Weight/Cube

alone). Such a scenario often causes decision makers to give up any hope of understanding the full field of techniques and consistently use only one or two with which they are familiar, whether those techniques are appropriate for the forecasting situation or not.

Fortunately, this scenario can be considerably simplified. To understand the sales forecasting technique selection process, the sales forecasting manager needs to understand the characteristics of a relatively small set of groups of techniques, and realize in what situations each group of techniques works best. Once the technique group has been chosen, selection of the specific technique to use is a much more straightforward decision—a decision that can be influenced by a great deal of research that has looked at which techniques are most often used and when they work best (Mentzer & Kahn, 1995).

The common categories for sales forecasting techniques are based upon whether the technique uses subjective or statistical analysis; whether endogenous data (a forecasting term that means only using the history of sales, not any other factors that may explain changes in sales) or exogenous (a forecasting term meaning the use of other data, such as price or promotional changes, competitive actions, or economic measures, to explain the changes in sales) data are analyzed; and whether these data are actually analyzed by the forecaster or simply input to a technique for calculation of the forecast. These characteristics of forecasting techniques lead to three broad categories of sales forecasting techniques: time series (both fixed-model and open-model technique categories), regression (also called correlation, and incorrectly called causal, techniques), and judgmental (also called qualitative or subjective techniques). We will briefly discuss each here, but much more detail on each category and the specific techniques within each category will be discussed in later chapters.

Open-Model Time Series Techniques. Open-model time series (OMTS) techniques—Box-Jenkins, for example—build a forecast model after analyzing sales history data to identify its existing patterns (because only sales history is examined, OMTS are considered endogenous techniques). OMTS techniques are based on the interrelationship of four data patterns: level, trend, seasonality, and noise. *Level* is a horizontal sales history, or what sales patterns would be if there was no trend, seasonality, or noise. *Trend* is a continuing pattern of a sales increase or decrease, and that pattern can be a straight line or a curve. *Seasonality* is a repeating pattern of sales increases and decreases, such as high sales every summer for air conditioners, high sales of agricultural chemicals in the spring, or high sales of toys in the fall. The point is that the pattern of high sales in certain periods and low sales in other periods repeats itself every year. *Noise* is random fluctuation—that part of the sales history that a time-series technique cannot explain. This does not mean that the fluctuation could not be explained by regression analysis or judgment, it means that the pattern has not happened consistently in the past, so the time series technique cannot pick it up and forecast it.

OMTS techniques analyze the data to determine which patterns exist and then build an appropriate forecast equation. This is in contrast to fixed-model time series (FMTS) techniques that have fixed equations that are based upon *a priori* assumptions that certain patterns do or do not exist in the data. Although much academic research has been conducted with OMTS, these techniques have been of little use in business because of their complexity and limited incremental accuracy over FMTS or subjective techniques (Mentzer & Kahn, 1995).

Most OMTS forecasting techniques require extensive training and considerable analysis time. Throughout the analysis, numerous subjective decisions must serve as input to the model. Thus, the accuracy of the forecast is largely influenced by the abilities of the user. Many periods of sales history (often more than 48 data periods) are required to obtain usable results. Because of these factors, OMTS techniques are used when substantial sales history, but little exogenous data, is available, personnel are well trained in the use of the technique, and only when a limited number of forecasts are to be made. Because, for these reasons, OMTS techniques have seen so little applicability in sales forecasting, we will spend little time discussing them later in the book.

Fixed-Model Time Series Techniques. In short-range (horizons of less than six months) product forecasting, rapid changes in sales and the large number of forecasts needed often dictate the use of a simple, yet adaptable, technique. Fixed-model time series (FMTS) forecasting techniques can be effectively used in such instances. FMTS techniques use the same four patterns (level, trend, seasonality, and noise) as OMTS techniques. However, FMTS techniques arrive at a forecast by assuming that one or more of these patterns exist in a previous sales history and by projecting these patterns into the future. Exponential smoothing is a common FMTS technique.

FMTS techniques are often simple and inexpensive to use and require little data storage. Many of the techniques also adjust very quickly to changes in sales conditions and, thus, are appropriate for short-term forecasting. FMTS techniques, however, will probably be less accurate than correlation analysis if the forecaster uses a FMTS technique that assumes data patterns do not exist that are, in fact, in the sales history. Simple exponential smoothing assumes, for example, that the sales history consists of only level and noise. If trend and seasonality exist in the sales history, simple exponential smoothing will consistently err in its forecast.

As we mentioned earlier, more than 70 different FMTS techniques exist. However, a discussion of less than ten of these techniques will give the manager the necessary grasp of how these techniques work and which to use in any given situation. We concentrate on these representative techniques in Chapter 3, *Time Series Techniques*.

Regression (Correlation) Analysis. Correlation analysis is a statistical approach to forecasting that seeks to establish a relationship between sales and exogenous variables that affect sales, such as advertising, product quality, price, logistics service quality, and/or the economy. Past data on exogenous variables and sales data are analyzed to determine the strength of their relationship (for instance, every time the price goes up, sales of the product go down is a strong negative relationship). If a strong relationship is found, the exogenous variables can then be used to forecast future sales. Corporate, competitive, and economic variables can be used together in a correlation analysis forecast, thus giving it a broad environmental perspective. Correlation analysis can also provide statistical value estimates of each variable. Thus, variables contributing little to the forecast can be dropped.

Correlation analysis is potentially one of the most accurate forecasting techniques available, but it requires a large amount of data. These large data demands also make correlation analysis slow to respond to changing conditions. Understanding the advantages and disadvantages of correlation analysis helps to clarify when it is more useful, as in longer-range (greater than six-month time horizon) corporate-level forecasts for which a large amount of data on exogenous variables is readily available.

Qualitative (Subjective) Techniques. The previously discussed techniques (open-model time series, fixed-model time series, and correlation analysis) are based upon the idea that historical demand may follow some patterns, and the goal of the technique is to identify and numerically document those patterns, then project those patterns into the future. However, it is often the case that the future will not look exactly like the past. For example, there may be no historical demand data available, as is the case with new products. There may also be new conditions that arise, such as a changing competitive landscape or changes in distribution patterns, that make previous demand patterns less relevant. Thus, there is a need for qualitative, or subjective, forecasting techniques. Subjective techniques are procedures that turn the opinions of experienced personnel (e.g., marketing planners, salespeople, corporate executives, and outside experts) into formal forecasts. An advantage of subjective techniques is that they take into account the full wealth of key personnel experience and require little formal data. They are also valuable when little or no historical data are available, such as in new product introductions.

Subjective forecasting, however, takes a considerable amount of key personnel time. Because of this drawback, subjective techniques are typically used as a part of long-range, corporate-level forecasting, or for adjustment purposes in short-range, product forecasting. For example, the forecast committee of one auto parts manufacturer with whom we have worked meets once a quarter to subjectively generate a three-year forecast and once a month to subjectively adjust the product forecasts by product line (for instance, all product forecasts in a particular product line may be raised by 3%). Individual product forecasts by inventory location, however, are left to an appropriate FMTS technique determined by the forecast managers. Individual product forecasts by the forecast committee would be a waste of valuable executive time.

Sales Forecasting Systems

This dimension of sales forecasting management encompasses the computer and electronic communications hardware and software used to develop, analyze, and distribute sales forecasts. It includes the storage, retrieval, and transfer of all information related to sales forecasting.

Systems sophistication can range from individual analyses of isolated databases, often called "islands of analysis," to fully electronically, integrated analysis and communication tools that facilitate development of the sales forecast. At the lower end of this scale, companies have a number of separate information systems that are not interconnected. As a result, information that is transferred from one functional area to another is transferred via printed reports and often is not in a format nor sufficiently complete for what is needed by the receiving area. This information must be manually input to the receiving function's computer system and augmented by additional information from numerous sources. Because the systems are disjointed and complex, few people outside the information technology (IT) function understand the functionality of the systems.

At the more sophisticated end of this scale are companies with system-user interfaces that access a common data warehouse and where users in the various functional areas developing and using the sales forecasts have a complete understanding of the functionality of the systems. Companies at this end of the scale have implemented data exchange protocols, ranging from simple EDI to web-enabled interfaces, that facilitate forecasting collaboration with both key customers and suppliers.

Sales Forecasting Managerial Process and Approaches

The management of sales forecasting is concerned with how we organize and how we efficiently and effectively conduct the business of developing and using sales forecasts.

The Sales Forecasting Process. Figure 1.5 illustrates the components of the sales forecasting process. Linking the **environment** in which the sales forecasting process exists and the resultant **sales forecasting performance** are **sales forecasting management, systems**, and **techniques**. Sales forecasting management encompasses the approach taken to manage the sales forecasting process (discussed later in this section). Sales forecasting techniques encompass the selection between the time series, regression, and qualitative alternatives discussed in Chapters 3, 4, and 5, respectively. Sales forecasting systems (discussed in Chapter 6) are the analysis and communications templates that are laid over the sales forecasting management processes. How skillfully a company coordinates this sales forecasting process ultimately determines the success of the sales forecasting function.

On the outer ring of Figure 1.5 is the environment in which the demand for the company's products—and, consequently, the uncertainty faced by the sales forecasting function—exists. As one of the

Figure 1.5   The Sales Forecasting Process

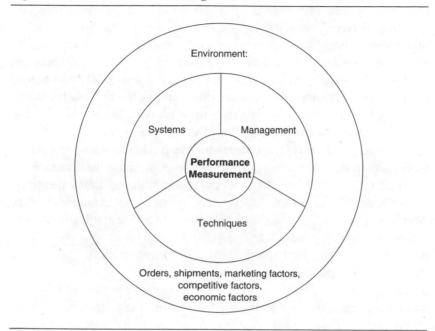

questions that we address later in this chapter indicates, this environment also encompasses the availability of a history of orders, shipments, or demand—that is, the data that can be used to help determine sales forecasts. The state of the economy and the level of competition in the industry and the supply chain, as well as possible competitive responses to company marketing policies (e.g., advertising) are also factors that impact the sales forecasting process.

Sales Forecasting Management Approaches. Based on our research and experience with hundreds of companies, we have found that companies typically organize their sales forecasting function in one of four ways: the **independent approach**, the **concentrated approach**, the **negotiated approach**, or the **consensus approach** to sales forecasting management.

Furthermore, we have also found that the efficiency and effectiveness of a company's sales forecasting organization depends on the degree of functional integration that exists within the company. The components of functional integration are defined as Forecasting C^3— Communication, Coordination, and Collaboration. Communication is the written, verbal, and electronic information shared between the functional areas. Coordination is the formal structure and required meetings between two or more functional areas. Collaboration is an orientation among functional areas, and between a company and its key customers, toward common goal setting (in this case, common sales forecasting performance goals). The four managerial approaches, along with the degree of functional integration each approach entails, will now be discussed regarding the implications of these two concepts for the success of a company's sales forecasting function.

Companies that use the *independent* approach to sales forecasting tend to be quite naïve in their approach to organizing their sales forecasting function. Each functional department in the company develops a sales forecast geared to its specific requirements; for example, finance develops a corporate-level dollar forecast 1 to 5 years out; production develops 6-month product item (SKU) forecasts for production scheduling; logistics develops monthly product/location (SKUL) forecasts for distribution planning; and so forth.

The problem with this approach is not necessarily that each department develops a forecast in the format that fits its particular requirements; rather the problem is the lack of functional integration that characterizes this approach. With the independent approach to sales forecasting management, there is little, if any, communication, no coordination, and no collaboration among the functional areas regarding the forecasting process. The lack of communication prevents input into each department's forecasting process from perspectives other than their own, thereby hindering each department's effort to develop an accurate forecast. How can production or logistics possibly develop an accurate forecast for their production or distribution planning without being aware of marketing's promotional schedule? Even more important, however, is the fact that the absence of coordination and collaboration among the departments developing separate forecasts hinders the departmental sales forecasts from being used as a contribution to the planning functions in various departments and as an aid to corporate-level planning.

The *concentrated* form of sales forecasting organization assigns forecasting responsibility to one department, e.g., logistics or marketing. This managerial approach at least partially addresses the communication and coordination aspects of functional integration more effectively than the independent managerial approach. Oral, written, and, sometimes, electronic communications generally take place among the various departmental users of the sales forecast developed by the responsible department, and these communications provide information that can be incorporated into the official forecast. Furthermore, formal meetings are frequently scheduled, or there is some structure in place for distributing the official forecast to all departments. However, this managerial approach does not address the collaboration aspect of functional integration, as evidenced by the fact that the forecast developed by the responsible department is heavily biased by that department's forecasting and planning requirements. If logistics is the department responsible for developing the sales forecasts, the forecasts will be at the SKUL level, with a time horizon of one month to several years, and daily, weekly, or monthly updating intervals. If marketing develops the sales forecasts, they will be in product/brand dollars or product line dollars, with a yearly time horizon and monthly or quarterly updates.

Furthermore, we have found that sales forecasting concentrated in marketing tends to lead to capacity unconstrained forecasts. In other words, marketing tends to develop forecasts that are solely based on market demands and does not consider the capacity constraints of the production and/or logistics systems. Conversely, sales forecasting concentrated in an operations area (production or logistics) tends to develop forecasts that are based upon capacity constraints and ignores the demands of the company's markets. The problem with either form of concentration is that, because of the lack of collaboration among departments, the orientation of the sales forecasts tends to ignore information from other departments, and the form of the official sales forecast ignores the requirements of some departments. Therefore, this managerial approach seldom provides effective input to all the planning processes.

A company that uses a *negotiated* approach to manage its sales forecasting process develops sales forecasts in each functional department, then assembles representatives from each department during each forecasting interval to negotiate an official sales forecast for each forecasting level and horizon. In terms of functional integration, the negotiated approach overcomes some of the bias problems of the concentrated approach by encouraging communication and, particularly, coordination among departments. However, because each department initially develops its own sales forecasts to bring to the negotiation process, there is no real collaboration in terms of the forecasting process; that is, the development of the sales forecasts is not guided by common goals and information, but by the separate goals, information, and requirements of each individual department.

In addition, the negotiation process intrinsic to this approach is plagued with political pressures among departments that can bias the negotiated forecast. Remember, each department brings its own forecast to the negotiation process, a forecast that was developed on the basis of its own requirements. Particularly when there is a power imbalance among departments that allows one or more departments to dominate the negotiation process, these separate orientations can bias the final forecasts.

In the *consensus* form of sales forecasting organization, a committee consisting of representatives from each functional department, as well as a member designated to be in charge of the forecasting committee, is responsible for developing sales forecasts using input from each department. A genuine consensus forecasting approach incorporates high levels of Forecasting C^3—communication, coordination, and collaboration—by asking the forecasting committee to develop a common forecast (one that is based not on the individual forecasts of different departments, but rather on informational input from each department to develop a common forecast). This degree of functional integration can assist in overcoming the biased forecasts produced by the focus on individual departmental requirements in the concentrated form of sales forecasting organization. If commitment to common goals, i.e., collaboration, is sufficiently evolved, this can aid in overcoming the political problems that tend to bias forecasts developed under the negotiated form of sales forecasting organization. Companies contemplating this managerial approach should understand that it is resource intensive, in terms of both time and personnel. However, if a company has the resources to encourage the necessary functional integration, the consensus form of organization can result in superior sales forecasts.

Processes and Systems. Many companies with which we have worked have asked us to advise them on the sales forecasting system they should use. Invariably, when we are asked this question, we ask them to describe the management process by which the sales forecasts are developed. Often, there is no answer—the company is trying to develop a systems solution without an understanding of the management process! This is a backward approach to sales forecasting management.

In many companies, there is no one person who understands the entire sales forecasting process. Many individuals understand bits and pieces of the process, but few understand the *entire* process. Without such an understanding, it is not possible to design and implement a system to augment this process.

In fact, the sales forecasting system should be a communication and analysis framework (template) that can be laid over the sales forecasting management process. The company has to define the process first. An example should help illustrate this concept.

One global manufacturer of industrial products with which we have worked has multiple product lines sold all over the world by a direct sales force. Many of these products are sold to customers in numerous industries. Thus, we may have a product that is sold by one salesperson in Australia to a particular industry and another salesperson in Europe who sells the same product for a different use in another industry. This has led to a worldwide sales force that specializes in certain products, in certain industries, and in certain geographic areas.

Given this multifaceted complexity of the sales forecasting environment, the company wanted a system that allowed development of a quantitative forecast, with qualitative adjustment by geographic territory by industry by the sales force, with adjustment by product line by marketing managers, and with overall planning adjustments by upper management. This led to a definition of their sales forecasting process that is illustrated in Figure 1.6. The process starts with a computer model-generated forecast. These sales forecasts are broken down by product, industry, and geographic territory and sent electronically to the sales force. Each salesperson is provided with a quarterly report of economic and market trends in their industry and asked to make adjustments to the quantitative forecasts. When adjustments are made, the salesperson is asked to electronically record the logic behind their adjustments.

The total of all sales force adjustments is electronically transmitted back to the forecasting group, where the totals are combined. Each marketing manager then receives the adjusted forecasts for his or her product lines and markets. Again, the marketing managers are asked to qualitatively adjust these forecasts and record their logic.

These forecast adjustments are received and compiled by the forecasting group and transmitted to management for adjustment at the division level. Once the upper management adjustments are received, the forecasts are broken down to the level and horizon appropriate for each functional planning area and transmitted electronically for use in planning.

Figure 1.6   Example Sales Forecasting Process

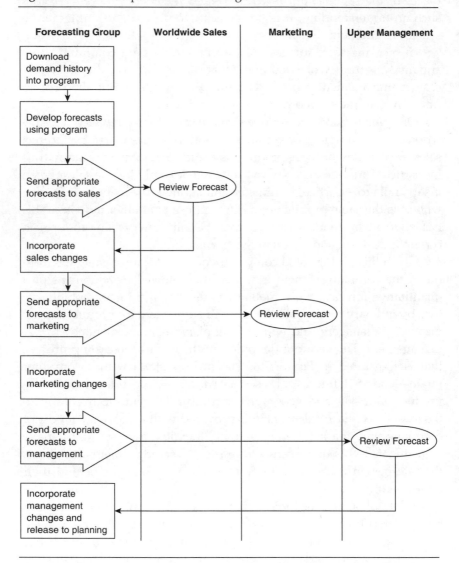

Notice that this process has laid over it the systems template to:

- Transmit all information electronically,
- Pull information necessary for the computer model forecasts from appropriate data sources within the company and the supply chain,

- aggregate and disaggregate to the level and horizon needed at each step, and
- compare each forecast and adjustment with the actual demand once it is received.

Sales Forecasting Performance Measurements

Just what are the relevant performance measurements for the sales forecasting function? The obvious answer is accuracy, and the advantages and disadvantages of various forms of measuring forecasting accuracy will be discussed in Chapter 2. However, Chapter 2 will also address the concept of multidimensional metrics of sales forecasting performance measurement. There is more to sales forecasting performance than just accuracy. For example, what about the inexpensive product that holds a monopoly position in its market (i.e., customers cannot get it anywhere else)? The cost of overstocking this product is low, and the potential to lose customers due to temporary unavailability is also low. Why should we spend much money on accurately forecasting this product, when the penalties for inaccuracy do not exist? Although this example is rather extreme to make the point, the fact still remains that desired accuracy in sales forecasting should be weighed against the dimensions of the supply chain costs, the revenue-generating potential, and the customer satisfaction implications of inaccuracy. In the next chapter we will explore this topic further to provide clear-cut measures of all the dimensions of sales forecasting performance.

❖ SALES FORECASTING MANAGEMENT QUESTIONS

Before we address any more aspects of sales forecasting management, however, there are numerous questions (listed in Table 1.2) that you should ask yourself about your company. How to find the answers to these questions is largely contained in the experience of the people within the company and in the remaining chapters of this book, but they must be answered for each company in its unique way, and they should be constantly re-examined while reading the remainder of this book. The answers to these questions should tell you much about how the sales forecasting function should operate to efficiently and effectively help your company conduct the business of developing and using sales forecasts.

Table 1.2   Sales Forecasting Management Questions

1. Customer base narrow or broad?
2. Data characteristics (shipments/sales/demand, age, detail, external data, quality)?
3. Number of forecasts (horizons and intervals, products, channels, locations)?
4. Number of new products?
5. Regional differences?
6. Seasonality?
7. Sophistication of personnel (systems and forecasting) and systems?
8. Sales forecasting budget?
9. Accuracy needed?

Narrow or Broad Customer Base

The first question to ask is: Is your company's customer base narrow or broad? A narrow customer base simply means the sales of the company (regardless of the unit or dollar volume) go to a relatively small number of customers. An example of a broad customer base is the consumer markets served by packaged goods manufacturers, while an example of a narrow customer base is that served by a manufacturer of specialized industrial components. One company with which we have worked produces a product that is only sold directly to automobile assembly plants in North America. Thus, even though this is a company with annual dollar sales in excess of $50 million, its customer base is only 56 customers (the number of automobile assembly plants in North America).

The narrower the customer base, the more likely a company can rely on direct customer contact information to produce more qualitatively oriented sales forecasts. In the example just given, the sales forecasting function calls the production scheduling department of each of its 56 customers each month and asks for the schedule of car production (which is sent by EDI). From this information, a very accurate, qualitative sales forecast can be derived.

Contrast this example with a large manufacturer of consumer products that sells to all of the 65 million households in the United States. Such a broad customer base makes any appreciable customer contact impossible (even if we surveyed 1,000,000 homes, we would still have only contacted about 2% of our customers!) and causes more reliance on quantitative forecasting (i.e., time series and regression) techniques. Thus, the narrower the customer base, the more a company can rely on direct customer contact qualitative techniques (discussed in Chapter 5), and the broader the customer base, the more reliance will be placed upon quantitative techniques (Chapters 3 and 4), with qualitative adjustments.

Data Characteristics

The second set of questions concerns the type, availability, and quality of data:

1. What data are available to your company for use in the forecasting function? Specifically, do you have data available on shipment history, order history, and/or end consumer demand (e.g., point of sale data)?

2. How old are the data (i.e., how many weeks, months, or years are contained in the data)?

3. At what level of detail are the data?

4. What data external to your company can you obtain to facilitate sales forecasting (i.e., external factors that might impact product demand for use in a regression model)?

5. How accurate are the available data?

Sales, Shipments, and Demand. The answer to the first question determines what we will forecast. It is important to distinguish between sales, shipments, and demand. Although called sales forecasting, this function is really about forecasting demand. *Demand* is what our customers would buy from us if they could; *sales* is our ability to accept orders from our customers; and *shipments* is what our operations system can actually deliver to our customers. Suppose, for example, that demand for one of our products next month is 10,000, but our salespeople (due to uncertainty about delivery time commitments) can only confirm 9,000 units in actual sales. Suppose, further, that our production/logistics system can only produce and deliver 7,500 units of those ordered (sold). If our information system only collects and records shipments, our historical record of this month will show shipments of 7,500 units, **and nothing else**! What will be lost is the fact that we actually sold 1,500 units more, and could have sold 2,500 units more, if the capacity to produce and deliver had been available. With only this shipments history available to the forecasting function, we will continue to forecast "demand" to be 7,500 units per month, never recognize the lost sales each month, and never increase capacity to capture this extra true demand. However, if the only data we have is a history of what we have shipped in the past, this is the data we will have to use until more meaningful demand data can be gathered—but the commitment should be immediately made to begin gathering this more accurate sales and demand data.

Data Age. How much historical data are available largely defines the sales forecasting techniques that can be used. If less than one year of data are available, only the more simplistic fixed-model time series techniques (FMTS) are going to work—any time series technique that considers seasonality needs at least two years of data (so it can identify two complete seasonal patterns) to begin forecasting effectively. Open-model time series techniques (OMTS) typically need at least four years of data, while regression typically needs at least five periods of data for each variable in the regression equation (so if we had sales as one variable, and advertising, price, and trade promotions as the three independent variables, we would need at least 4 variables times 5, or 20 periods of data). Of course, many companies have such a short life cycle for their products that many of these techniques are simply never practical.

Data Level. The level of detail of the data refers to the planning detail required. If we are forecasting annual dollar sales by product line for a marketing plan, data at the same level and time horizon are fine. However, if we also need weekly unit forecasts by SKUL, annual product line data will be of little help. Because we need sales forecasts for a number of different functional plans, data at the level of detail corresponding to each of these planning needs is necessary.

This level of detail is called the **forecasting hierarchy**, and is defined as all the planning levels and time horizons/intervals at which forecasts are needed. Figure 1.7 illustrates one such forecasting hierarchy for a company with which we have worked. In this company, the logistics function needs forecasts by week, by stock keeping unit by location (SKUL); the production and purchasing functions needs forecasts bi-weekly, by stock keeping unit; the sales function needs dollar

Figure 1.7   Example of a Forecasting Hierarchy

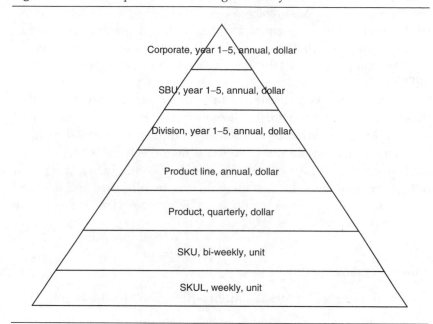

sales by product by quarter; the marketing function needs annual dollar sales for the next year by product line and for the next five years by division; and finance needs annual dollar sales for the next five years by strategic business unit (SBU) and for the overall corporation. The data detail required for developing a forecast for each of these functions must match each planning level, horizon, and interval. The figure is drawn as a triangle to represent the number of forecasts that are required at each level of the hierarchy. Many more forecasts are required at the SKUL level than at the SKU level, more at the SKU than at the product level, and so on.

External Data Availability. Finally, the availability of data on factors external to the actual sales history determines whether or not regression analysis can be used. If the only data available are concerned with sales, shipments, or demand history, there is no information on which to build a regression model. To complete the variable selection stage discussed in Chapter 4, historical data on factors such as price, advertising, trade and consumer promotions, economic activity, and competitive actions (for just a few examples) must be available.

Data Quality. Corporate records are not always as trustworthy as we would like them to be. Invoices sometimes do not get entered, when they are entered they are entered with errors, or demand is recorded in the wrong period. All these are examples of data-quality problems.

One company with which we worked was quite proud of their "EDI" system of recording their distributors' POS demand. However, when we interviewed distributors for this company, we found that these POS orders were actually taken and filled by a paper system and entered into the electronic system later. During high-demand months, distributors "simply do not have the time to keep the system up-to-date—we are too busy selling." The result was that many orders did not get entered into the system until the month after the demand occurred. Of course, this resulted in inaccurate data on monthly demand patterns.

Number of Forecasts

The third set of questions concerns how many forecasts you need, and this is a function of:

1. At what levels, time horizons, and intervals are forecasts required?

2. How many products, i.e., product lines and product items (SKUs), must be forecast?

3. In how many distribution channels are your products marketed?

4. How many product/location combinations (e.g., by sales regions, distribution centers, individual customers) must be forecast?

Levels, Horizons, and Intervals. Different functional areas require forecasts at different levels, time horizons, intervals, and forms. Examination of Table 1–1 to determine how the various functional areas in your company fill in the bottom four rows begins to answer this question of how many forecasts are required and how often they are required (i.e., defining the forecasting hierarchy).

Number of Products. To understand the impact of forecasting different numbers of products, contrast the forecasting process for a company that manufactures a group of specialized industrial components versus the forecasting process for an apparel manufacturing company that must forecast the numerous SKUs generated by multiple size, color, style, and fabric combinations. Limited product line companies can devote considerably greater attention to any one forecast than broad line companies that have literally thousands of products to forecast for each of the levels, horizons, and intervals mentioned in the previous question. For example, one telephone company we worked with in the 1980s had essentially only one product to forecast—new phone installations. With no local competition, this was the only forecast relevant to all the planning functions and, thus, a team of three people devoted their full attention to developing one forecast each month. This team could put considerably greater time into using sophisticated OMTS and regression analysis than a company like Brake Parts, Inc., which has several hundred thousand products to forecast each month (Mentzer & Schroeter, 1993).

Distribution Channels. The third question in this set considers companies that have multiple channels for the same product. For example, an automotive parts manufacturer may market a certain product directly to original equipment manufacturers, through a separate channel under its own brand name, and through a large retailer channel under the brand name of that retailer. Thus, this one product is now marketed through three separate channels, each with its own demand patterns and, therefore, forecasting needs.

Product/Location Combinations. Similarly, the difference between the number of SKUs and SKULs can dramatically change the number of forecasts that are required. The number of forecasts needed to meet the planning needs of all business functions is determined by the number of products we produce **and** the number of locations where they are shipped or sold.

New Products

Similarly, the number of new products introduced in a given planning horizon affects how we will forecast. Are these variations on existing products or truly new products? Not surprisingly, we have found that the forecasting of genuinely new products is cited by many companies as one of the most difficult forecasting problems they face. At its best, new product forecasting is a leap into the future with little or no historical information to tell us which way to leap. New product forecasting can take a great deal of sales forecasting personnel time, can hurt the credibility of the forecasting group through poor new product forecasting accuracy, and can reduce the morale of the forecasting group. It is, however, a necessary function in a competitive environment and should be augmented by procedures such as those discussed in Chapters 5, 6, and 9.

Regional Differences

Regional differences in demand for products increases the number of forecasts to be made and the analysis required. For example, manufacturers of agricultural chemicals have a very different market in the United States, as opposed to the Canadian market. The much shorter growing season in Canada creates entirely different market behaviors that must be forecast differently.

Seasonality

Similarly, the degree of seasonality of the products that we market affects the techniques used to forecast. Many FMTS techniques and regression do not consider seasonality and, thus, either should not be used in highly seasonal situations or should be used in conjunction with techniques that do consider seasonality.

Personnel and Systems Sophistication

How sophisticated are the personnel involved in the sales forecasting function? Do they have educational backgrounds in statistics or econometrics? What is their level of experience and knowledge regarding the industry in which your company does business? If the answers to these questions are on the lower side, additional training of sales forecasting personnel is probably in order (statistical/quantitative analysis training for those with business experience and business experience/qualitative analysis training for those with statistical backgrounds), and the sophistication of the techniques used should be limited until such training is obtained.

How sophisticated are the hardware and software systems available for use in forecasting? Are there electronic interfaces among the systems (hardware and software applications) in use by producers and users of the sales forecasts? Without such interconnectivity, much of the benefits that accrue from the sales forecasting systems principles discussed in Chapter 6 cannot be realized.

Budget

Similarly, without a commitment to the sales forecasting budget, these training and systems problems will probably not get fixed. Interestingly, in our studies of hundreds of companies, few felt their sales forecasting budget was adequate.

Accuracy Needed

Finally, what level of accuracy is required for the various forecasts? That is, what are the consequences of forecasting error at various levels (e.g., SKU by location), time horizons, and time intervals? We have found that forecasting accuracy is often considered to be like customer service—the more the better. However, true analysis of sales forecasting management often produces the conclusion that the benefit of improved accuracy is not worth the cost. All the dimensions of sales forecasting performance measurement discussed in Chapter 2 should be taken into consideration to conduct a return on investment analysis of any changes to sales forecasting management. The costs of training, new systems, and improved techniques should all be weighed against the improvements in supply chain costs, planning costs, and customer service levels. In most cases, the ROI on such investments is dramatic, but it should still be evaluated to determine what is an acceptable level of sales forecasting accuracy for each business function in each level, horizon, and interval.

❖ SALES FORECASTING AND PLANNING: AN ITERATIVE PROCESS

An integral part of any sales forecasting process is an implementation of the iterative process of sales forecasting and planning. Many companies use the business plan to drive the sales forecast—a naïve approach, because the forecast should be driven by the realities of the marketplace, not the financial needs of the corporation. More sophisticated companies develop the sales forecast independently of the business plan, but when the forecast and the plan diverge, the forecast is made to "fit" the plan.

In fact, companies that are effective at sales forecasting and business planning start with the sales forecasting process. Remember our definition of a sales forecast: **a projection into the future of expected demand, given a stated set of environmental conditions**. Given expected economic and competitive conditions **and** initial marketing/sales/production/logistics plans, we make a projection of future expected demand. From this base, the business plan can be developed. When the resultant business plan does not meet the financial needs/goals of the company, we iterate back to the sales forecast and examine what additional efforts in marketing and/or sales can be undertaken to increase the demand forecast and what additional efforts can be undertaken by production/logistics to increase capacity to the level necessary to meet the business plan. It is this iterative process of sales forecast to business plan back to sales forecast to business plan and so forth that ensures a business plan that is based upon the financial **and** marketplace realities facing the company.

❖ FUNCTIONAL SILOS

Much has been written in recent years about the functional silos of management and how important it is to "tear down the walls" between these silos to integrate the information, goals, and strategies of the various business functions. If we look at finance/accounting, marketing, sales, production/purchasing, and logistics as separate management functions/silos, we find that two additional business functions are actually the integrating forces in the company. Figure 1.8 illustrates this concept.

All five of the business planning functions that we discuss throughout this book can be represented by the vertical, separate "silos," while information systems and sales forecasting are functions that integrate across these traditional silos. The integrating role of information systems comes from the fact that information systems need to take in information from all five of these business functions **and** all five of these business functions need information from information systems. Finance/accounting takes in information on marketing expenditures, sales commissions, production costs, and so forth **and** reports performance metrics back to each of these functions.

Figure 1.8   Information Systems and Sales Forecasting: Integrating "Silos"

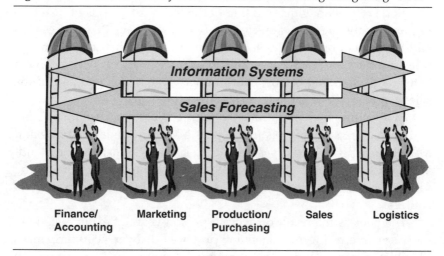

| Finance/
Accounting | Marketing | Production/
Purchasing | Sales | Logistics |

In addition, information systems provide *coordinating information*—information that crosses functional silo boundaries to coordinate the planning of each business function with the plans of the other business functions.

In like manner, sales forecasting needs information on marketing plans, sales plans, production/purchasing schedules, and logistics capacities to develop informed forecasts. In addition, each of these functions needs sales forecasts at the appropriate level and horizon and updated at the appropriate intervals to develop effective plans. Sales forecasting depends upon information systems to provide this information and to communicate the forecasts back to the other functions. In this manner, the five traditional functional silos are actually brought together by information systems and sales forecasting. In fact, to effectively manage the business, information systems and sales forecasting should be inextricably intertwined with each other and the other business functions.

❖   OVERVIEW OF THIS BOOK

This book has been designed to give sales forecasting analysts more of an understanding of the role their function plays in the organization and the supply chain **and** to give managers of the sales forecasting function more of an understanding of the technical aspects of developing and analyzing sales forecasts and of managing this process. **In addition**, users of the sales forecast (marketing, finance/accounting, sales, production/purchasing, and logistics managers) will receive a better understanding of how sales forecasts are developed and of the sales forecasting needs of all the business functions.

In addition, numerous schools teach a course in sales forecasting and/or require sales forecasting as part of certain undergraduate and MBA courses. This book is designed to serve as a text for the stand-alone forecasting course and as a required reading for the forecasting section of other marketing, logistics, and supply chain management courses.

The book is the result of over 40 person-years of experience with the sales forecasting management practices of over 400 companies. This experience includes the personal experience of the authors in advising companies on how to improve their sales forecasting management practices, and a program of research that includes two major surveys of companies' sales forecasting practices (one conducted in 1982 and the other in 1992), an in-depth study between 1994 and 1996 of the sales forecasting management practices of 20 major companies, and an ongoing study of how to apply the findings from the 1994–96 study in conducting Sales Forecasting Audits of additional companies. These studies in total are referred to as the **benchmark studies**, with the 1982 study referred to as Phase 1, the 1992 study referred to as Phase 2, the in-depth study referred to as Phase 3, and the sales forecasting audits referred to as Phase 4. Although these phases of the benchmark studies are discussed in detail later in specific chapters, where relevant, the findings from these studies and our experience are laced throughout the book.

Following Chapter 1 are thorough, yet easy-to-understand chapters on performance measurement (Chapter 2) and the technique categories of time series (Chapter 3), regression (Chapter 4), and qualitative techniques (Chapter 5). These chapters provide the reader with a fundamental understanding of how each technique works, its advantages and disadvantages, and under what circumstances each works best.

Because the communication and computer systems used by, and interacting with, the sales forecasting function can profoundly affect sales forecasting effectiveness, Chapter 6 examines our Seven Principles of Sales Forecasting Systems and presents an example system that embodies all of these principles. From this base of understanding, we move to chapters describing what a benchmark of companies is doing in managing sales forecasting. This discussion will be based upon the two surveys of over 360 companies (Chapter 7) and how they manage their sales forecasting function. Chapter 8 will draw from both the in-depth, Phase 3 of the benchmark studies, and Phase 4 of the research (ongoing series of Forecast Audits) to describe our "vision" of World Class Forecasting.

Chapter 9 discusses how the insights gained from the first three phases of the benchmark studies have been applied in Sales Forecasting Audits of more than 25 additional companies. This chapter will provide the reader with a blueprint of how a Sales Forecasting Audit can be conducted in his or her individual organization. It details the steps involved, the benefits to be gained, and ideas for how to manage the audit process so it can serve as the impetus for true process improvement.

Chapter 10 concludes our discussion by pulling together the managerial implications of what we know about sales forecasting techniques, systems, and management.

2

Sales Forecasting Performance Measurement

❖　❖　❖

When we first visited a company we work with in the grocery products industry, we spent several days interviewing everyone involved in the sales forecasting process—either those involved in developing or using the forecasts. One of the surprising results of these interviews was the response to questions about how well the present forecasting process worked.

Everyone interviewed was unanimous that the first need for the company was some allowance in the process for measuring and rewarding forecasting performance. However, no one could define what the basis for that performance measurement should be. Everyone felt accuracy of the forecast should be part of it, but there must be something more.

In fact, just the estimates of accuracy ranged from 30% error to 60% error, with no one able to explain where they got that estimate or actually define how they calculated it.

Clearly, this company has a management problem: here it has an important management function (sales forecasting) and no concept of how well it is doing in that function or on what basis to reward those performing the function.

Unfortunately, this is not an unusual situation in companies today.

❖ INTRODUCTION

The example just described is not unusual because we, as managers, often forget a basic management principle when applied to the function of sales forecasting:

What gets measured, gets rewarded

and

what gets rewarded, gets done.

So, our job in managing the sales forecasting function is to determine what it is we want to get done, then how we will measure it so we can reward those who do it. In other words, what is it we want to accomplish when we set out to forecast sales? The answer is often and immediately "accuracy," but accurate sales forecasts are only a means to a management end. What we really want to accomplish with the sales forecast is to obtain a level of accuracy that helps us plan better. "Better" in this case means lowering the marketing and operations costs to market and deliver the product in a way that creates customer satisfaction. In other words, money invested in forecasting should be viewed as a return on investment decision investment, with the returns of lower supply chain management costs and improved customer service (more on this at the end of the chapter).

Thus, we have three dimensions to sales forecasting performance:

- Accuracy
- Costs
- Customer Satisfaction

If we can develop measures that tap all three of these dimensions, we will have what we have termed "multidimensional metrics" of sales forecasting performance. These metrics will help us define for those responsible for sales forecasting what needs to be improved. This chapter's purpose is to do just this—to develop multidimensional metrics of sales forecasting performance measurement. We accomplish this by taking each of these three dimensions in turn, then by bringing the three together into one set of metrics, and we conclude with a model of the impact of sales forecasting performance on shareholder value.

❖ SALES FORECASTING ACCURACY

Accuracy in sales forecasting seems like a fairly straightforward concept, but it gets a bit more complicated when we try to implement it. The straightforward part is that we just want to know how much we missed the actual demand in a given time period with our forecast of sales for that period. The complicated part is interpreting exactly what the accuracy numbers mean after we get them.

For example, suppose we found our forecast for one product was off by 2% each month for the last year. That is a straightforward statement, but what does it mean? Did we forecast high or low? What was the actual unit amount that the forecast was off? Is that a good or bad forecast?

If we sold 100 units per month of a fairly low-value product that did not upset our customers when it was not available and we were only off by +/– 2 units each month, it is probably acceptable accuracy. (The cost of marketing it, carrying it in inventory, and the likelihood of losing the customer were all negligible.) However, suppose it was an expensive product that was vital to our customers' satisfaction with our company and we sold 1,000,000 units per month. A 2% error means our forecast was off each month by +/– 20,000 units! Clearly, there is something wrong with this rather simple performance measure, because it does not distinguish between these two situations.

Sales forecasting accuracy is further complicated by the fact that a myriad of accuracy statistics may be provided by any given forecasting system. What do all these numbers mean? To answer both questions ("How do we find an accuracy metric that works with different forecasting problems?" and "What do all of these different accuracy measures mean?"), we will review the range of forecasting accuracy statistics available, discuss the advantages and disadvantages of each, and suggest a practical solution to the sales forecasting accuracy measurement problem.

Actually, this myriad of forecasting accuracy measures falls into three categories:

- Actual measures
- Measures relative to a perfect forecast
- Measures relative to a perfect forecasting technique

We will take each of these categories in order to understand what each provides as a metric for measuring sales forecasting accuracy performance.

Before we can do this, however, we have to forecast something. Table 2.1 presents a record of monthly demand for a product manufactured by a company in the business of providing replacement parts to the aerospace industry. We forecast this demand with a technique called Mentzer's Adaptive Extended Exponential Smoothing (more on this technique in Chapter 3). For simplicity, we only tried to forecast next month's demand during each month, although later in this chapter we will have to deal with the problem of measuring forecasting performance when we are forecasting further into the future.

Actual Measures of Forecasting Accuracy

Several measures of forecasting accuracy exist that in some way describe the actual difference between actual sales for a product in a given period and what was forecast to be the sales for that period at some previous date. All are based on the simple calculation of:

$$\text{Error}_t = E_t = \text{Forecast}_t - \text{Sales}_t \tag{1}$$

where: t = the time period in which the sales occurred.

Notice that although we could have calculated error as either forecast minus sales or as sales minus forecast, the former gives us a more meaningful number. When calculated as forecast minus sales, a positive sign always tells us that we forecast high for that period, and a negative sign always tells us that we forecast low for that period. It is a minor point but one that has strong intuitive value to managers.

Mean Error. The first actual measure of forecasting accuracy is called the mean error and is simply a running average of how much the forecast has been off in the past. It is calculated as:

$$\text{Mean Error} = ME = \sum E/N \tag{2}$$

where: N = the number of periods for which we have been tracking the error.

For example, the Mean Error for May 2003 in Table 2.1 is:

$$\begin{aligned}
ME_{\text{May03}} &= (\text{Jan}_{03} + \text{Feb}_{03} + \text{Mar}_{03} + \text{Apr}_{03} + \text{May}_{03})/5 \\
&= (3 + 1 - 37 + 20 - 6)/5 = -3.8
\end{aligned}$$

Table 2.1   Aerospace Aftermarket Product Demand and Forecast: Actual Measures

Month	Sales (S)	Forecast (F)	Error (F − S)	Mean Error	Mean Absolute Error	Sum of Squared Errors	Mean Squared Error
J03	100	103	3	3	3	9	9
F03	119	120	1	2	2	10	5
M03	478	441	−37	−11	13.66667	13.79	459.6667
A03	98	118	20	−3.250000	15.25000	1,779	444.7500
M03	110	104	−6	−3.800000	13.40000	1,815	363
J03	93	103	10	−1.500000	12.83333	1,915	319.1667
J03	104	105	1	−1.142860	11.14286	1,916	273.7143
A03	96	101	5	−0.37500	10.37500	1,941	242.6250
S03	96	98	2	−0.111111	9.44444	1,945	216.1111
O03	103	109	6	0.500000	9.10000	1,981	198.1000
N03	94	99	5	0.909091	8.72727	2,006	182.3636
D03	102	105	3	1.083333	8.25000	2,015	167.9167
J04	98	101	3	1.230769	7.84615	2,024	155.6923
F04	120	119	−1	1.071429	7.35714	2,025	144.6429
M04	469	453	−16	−0.066667	7.93333	2,281	152.0667
A04	99	115	16	0.937500	8.43750	2,537	158.5625
M04	99	106	7	1.294118	8.35294	2,586	152.1176
J04		101					

which apparently tells us that we have forecast, on average, 3.8 units low (notice the negative sign) in each of the first five months. However, an important problem with this measure is that the positive and negative errors in each period cancel each other out. If you look more closely at Table 2.1, you can see that our forecasts have actually been off far more than 3.8 units, but the large −37 in March 2003 is mostly canceled in this calculation by the large +20 in the following month. So we need a similar calculation where the positive errors and the negative errors do not cancel each other out and cause us to draw misleading conclusions about forecasting accuracy.

Mean Absolute Error. The Mean Absolute Error, also sometimes called Mean Absolute Deviation (or MAD), overcomes the problem of positive and negative sign cancellation by simply looking at the absolute value of each error. For example, the error in March 2003 of −37 would be treated in the calculation as 37 (the negative sign is dropped). This is represented in the calculation as:

$$\text{Mean Absolute Error} = \text{MAE} = \sum |E|/N \qquad (3)$$

where: $|E|$ = the absolute value of the error (i.e., drop all the negative signs).

For example, the Mean Absolute Error for May 2003 in Table 2.1 is:

$$\text{MAE}_{\text{May03}} = (3 + 1 + 37 + 20 + 6)/5 = 13.4$$

which now tells us that, on average, our forecast has been off by 13.4 units in each of the first five months. This is a truer representation than the Mean Error of how much the forecast has been off each month. However, MAE does not tell us much else. Is an error of 13.4 units a good forecast or a bad forecast? For a base of around 100 units, it is probably not bad, but if we did not have this base number in a report, we would not know how much the error is, relative to overall volume. An additional problem with this measure is that now we do not know (by simply looking at the number) whether the forecasts were high or low. We need to look at the history of sales and forecasts to determine that.

A final problem for some companies is that the months where the forecasts were off a little count as heavily in the calculation of MAE as months in which forecasts were off a lot. If very large errors have a greater impact on company or supply chain operations, we probably want a measure of forecasting accuracy that puts more weight on larger errors.

Sum of Squared Errors. The simplest way to magnify larger errors and still keep the positive and negative signs from canceling each other is to square the error in each period. This calculation causes all the resultant numbers to be positive and magnifies the larger errors. For example, a ratio of an actual error of 5 in one month and an actual error of 10 in another month is ½ (or 5 to 10), but a ratio of the same two errors *squared* is ¼ (25 to 100). Thus, the larger errors are magnified.

By adding these squared errors together, we obtain an overall measure of how much the forecast has been off. The calculation for Sum of Squared Errors is:

$$\text{Sum of Squared Errors} = \text{SSE} = \sum E^2 \qquad (4)$$

For example, the Sum of Squared Errors for May 2003 in Table 2.1 is:

$$\text{SSE}_{\text{May03}} = (3^2 + 1^2 + (-37)^2 + 20^2 + (-6)^2) = 1{,}815$$

which now tells us that the sum total of our squared forecast error up to this point has been 1,815. Unfortunately, this calculation also does not tell us much else. To make matters worse, this calculation has lost all intuitive information for the manager. Is 1,815 good or bad? In fact, just what does 1,815 squared units mean? It is impossible to tell anything other than the closer SSE gets to zero, the better the forecast. For this reason, we need a more intuitive measure of absolute error than SSE.

Mean Squared Error. A small improvement in the last measure is the Mean Squared Error, a number that is often displayed in forecasting software reports. Mean Squared Error still magnifies larger errors and still keeps the positive and negative signs from canceling each other by squaring the error in each period. By taking an average of these squared errors, we obtain an overall measure of how much the forecast has been off; that is a little more intuitive than the Sum of Squared Errors. The calculation of Mean Squared Error is as follows:

$$\text{Mean Squared Error} = \text{MSE} = \sum E^2/N \qquad (5)$$

For example, the Mean Squared Error for May 2003 in Table 2.1 is:

$$\text{MSE}_{\text{May03}} = (3^2 + 1^2 + (-37)^2 + 20^2 + (-6)^2)/5 = 363$$

which now tells us that, on average, our squared forecast error has been 363 for each period. Unfortunately, this is still not a very intuitive number, but (as we will see later) can be useful when used with another, more intuitive measure of relative performance, particularly if management considers the ability to magnify larger actual errors to be important.

Accuracy Measures Relative to a Perfect Forecast

Obviously, what we would like from a sales forecast is perfection; we would like to be able to forecast in advance *exactly* what sales will be. If we could do this, the forecasting error in each period would be zero. To overcome some of the disadvantages of the actual measures of accuracy just discussed, three measures of accuracy relative to such a perfect forecast have been developed.

Percent Error. Because a perfect forecast would have a zero error in any given period, it is of some value to calculate the percent by which the forecasting technique we are using is off each period. This is accomplished by the following calculation:

$$\text{Percent Error}_t = PE_t = ((\text{Forecast}_t - \text{Sales}_t)/\text{Sales}_t) \times 100 \qquad (6)$$

where: t = the time period in which the sales occurred.

For example, the Percent Error for June 2003 in Table 2.2 is:

$$PE_{June03} = ((103 - 93)/93) \times 100 = 10.75268\%$$

which tells us that in June 2003 our forecast was high (remember that a positive sign means an overforecast) by a little more than 10.75%.

Notice that this calculation divides the actual error (Forecast$_t$ – Sales$_t$) in each period t by the *actual sales* that occurred in period t, not by the *forecast*. This is an important point. Sometimes this is calculated incorrectly as actual error divided by forecast, but this calculation gives a misleading metric. The reason it is misleading takes us back to our discussion at the beginning of this chapter, which focused on what we are trying to accomplish with sales forecasting performance measurement. We want metrics that allow us to measure how well we are doing in anticipating *actual sales*. Expressing percent error as a percent of forecast tells us the percent the *forecast* was off from *sales*, not the other way around. Take June of 2003 again. The correct way to interpret this number is that our forecast was 10.75% above what actually occurred. If we calculate it with the forecast in the denominator, it becomes:

$$\text{Incorrect } PE_{June03} = ((103 - 93)/103) \times 100 = 9.70873\%$$

which is a different answer and must be interpreted as the percent *sales* was off from the *forecast*. This may seem like a minor point, but the difference in the answers can be significant. (Try a forecast of 200 and actual sales of 100 to demonstrate this difference; PE the correct way comes out to 100% error but comes out to only 50% error the incorrect way.) In performance measurement, we are always trying to compare our performance (in forecasting, this means our forecast) to what actually happened (in forecasting, this means actual sales).

Table 2.2   Aerospace Aftermarket Product Demand and Forecast:
Relative Measures

Month	Sales (S)	Forecast (F)	Error (F − S)	Percent Error (PE) (F − S)/S	Mean Absolute Percent Error (MAPE)	Year to Date Mean Absolute Percent Error (YTD MAPE)	Sales Forecasting Technique Accuracy Benchmark (SFTAB)
J03	100	103	3	3	3.00		
F03	119	120	1	0.84034	1.92		.2405
M03	478	441	−37	−7.74059	3.86		.1272
A03	98	118	20	20.40816	8.00		.0668
M03	110	104	−6	−5.45455	7.49		.0765
J03	93	103	10	10.75268	8.03		.0948
J03	104	105	1	0.96154	7.02		.0948
A03	96	101	5	5.20833	6.80		.1032
S03	96	98	2	2.08333	6.27		.1071
O03	103	109	6	5.82524	6.22		.1165
N03	94	99	5	5.31915	6.14		.1243
D03	102	105	3	2.94118	5.88	5.88	.1280
J04	98	101	3	3.06122	5.66	5.88	.1325
F04	120	119	−1	−0.83333	5.32	5.88	.1299
M04	469	453	−16	−3.41151	5.19	5.52	.1201
A04	99	115	16	16.16162	5.88	5.16	.0921
M04	99	106	7	7.07071	5.95	5.30	.0990
J04		101					

One last point about PE: What if sales are zero? We will end up dividing the forecasting error by zero, which means PE is infinite; this is not a very good performance report! The solution is a simple decision rule. Whenever the forecast is a real number and sales are zero, set the PE for that period equal to 100%.

One of the values of the PE calculation is its ability to graphically give us insights into what we are doing wrong in our forecasts. Figure 2.1 illustrates such a simple graphical analysis of the percent error for the technique we are using in Tables 2.1 and 2.2. Regardless of whether we are satisfied with the percent errors we are receiving, an examination of Figure 2.1 indicates that most of our forecasts are high (all but four

Figure 2.1   Percent Error Plot

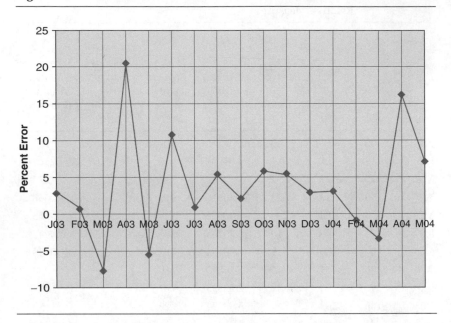

periods have a positive percent error). This could indicate that the technique we are using is over-forecasting a positive trend (we are forecasting sales going up at a faster rate than they actually are), or it is under-forecasting a negative trend (we are forecasting sales going down at a slower rate than they actually are), either of which would cause more over-forecasting than under-forecasting. It may merely indicate that we need to subjectively lower the technique forecast. Which of these is correct is not important now. What is important is to realize the value of a Percent Error Plot in measuring the performance of any sales forecasting technique.

Let's look at another example. The Percent Error Plot in Figure 2.2 (which is derived from a different set of data and a different technique than those used in Tables 2.1 and 2.2) indicates that we over-forecast during certain periods of the year and under-forecast at other periods. This is a rather classic Percent Error Plot that results when we use a forecasting technique that does not consider seasonality to forecast sales that are seasonal. In the periods during which we are experiencing positive percent errors, the technique assumes there is no seasonal

Figure 2.2   Percent Error Plot: Seasonal Sales with a Non-Seasonal
Technique

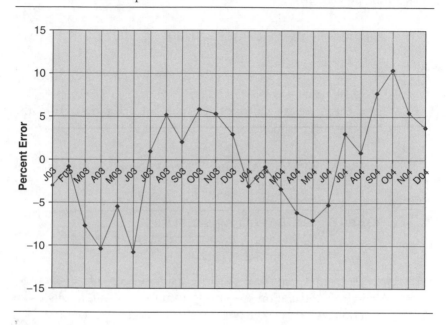

effect when, in fact, this is the season of low sales; that is, we over-forecast. The opposite logic works when we are under-forecasting. Such a plot indicates that we need to switch forecasting techniques to one that considers seasonality. Thus, the Percent Error Plot can help us make subjective adjustments to technique forecasts and/or select more appropriate techniques to use.

Finally, the Percent Error in any given month has strong intuitive appeal—it tells us by what percent the forecast was off in any given month. Although the Percent Error Plot is valuable, percent error itself does not tell us how we are performing over a number of periods. For this information, we need to turn to two other relative accuracy measures.

Mean Absolute Percent Error (MAPE). To measure how well we are doing over time in terms of percent error, we only need to take an average of the percent error calculation in Equation (6). However, to avoid the problems of positive and negative signs canceling each other out (as we had with the Mean Error), we will take an average of the *absolute value* of the percent error as follows:

$$\text{Mean Absolute Percent Error} = \text{MAPE} = \sum |PE| / N \qquad (7)$$

where: N = the number of periods for which we have been tracking the percent error

|PE| = the absolute value of the percent error (i.e., drop the negative signs)

For example, the Mean Absolute Percent Error for May 2003 in Table 2.2 is:

$$\text{MAPE}_{May03} = (3 + 0.840336 + |-7.740586| \\ + 20.40816 + |-5.454545|)/5 = 7.49\%$$

which tells us that by May 2003 our forecast had been off, on average, 7.49%. Again, this calculation has strong intuitive appeal; it tells us, at any point in time, what average percent the forecast has been off. When managers say the forecast error in the past has been 7%, they are typically referring to MAPE, whether they realize it or not.

One problem with this measure is that it continues to consider all percent errors as far back as we have been forecasting, regardless of how old those numbers may be. This may be undesirable if the errors back when we first started forecasting were very high (due to lack of data) and are no longer representative of forecasting accuracy. In other words, MAPE does not give a good measure of how well we have been forecasting *in the recent past.*

Year-to-Date Mean Absolute Percent Error. What a manager may need is a MAPE type measure that measures recent performance. This is precisely what Year-toDate (YTD) Mean Absolute Percent Error is designed to do. It is a rolling 12-month (or 52-week, or 4-quarter, and so on depending on the forecasting time intervals used) calculation of MAPE that gives recent performance. For monthly forecasting, it is calculated as follows:

$$\text{YTD Mean Absolute Percent Error} = \text{YTD MAPE} = \sum_{t}^{t-11} |PE| / 12 \quad (8)$$

For example, the YTD Mean Absolute Percent Error for May 2004 in Table 2.2 is:

$$
\begin{aligned}
\text{YTD MAPE}_{\text{May04}} = {}& (10.75269 + 0.96154 + 5.20833 + 2.08333 \\
& + 5.82524 + 5.31915 \\
& + 2.94118 + 3.06122 + |{-}0.83333| + |{-}3.41151| \\
& + 16.16162 + 7.07071)/12 \\
= {}& 5.30\%
\end{aligned}
$$

which tells us that over the 12 months ending with May 2004, our forecast was off, on average, 5.30%. This calculation still has strong intuitive appeal, with the added benefit of telling us, at any point in time, what percent the forecast has been off for the last year.

Although the measures of forecast accuracy relative to a perfect forecast give the manager much more intuitively appealing numbers, what neither they nor the absolute measures give is any indication of whether the forecast is "good" or "bad." By the way, this was part of the motivation for the benchmark studies discussed in Chapters 7, 8, and 9—to establish benchmarks of what levels of MAPE that companies were achieving in different sales forecasting situations so companies could determine whether their MAPE numbers were "good" or "bad" compared to the benchmarks. However, we can also provide a metric that addresses this question without always resorting to a comparison to other companies' performance.

Accuracy Measures Relative to a Perfect Forecasting Technique

The original attempt to overcome this lack of a standard against which to gauge whether we have a good forecast was developed by Theil (1966). The logic of Theil's U statistic was that a perfect forecasting technique is one that forecasts well and is easy to use. What could be easier, Theil reasoned, than to simply take sales from last month as our forecast for next month? (This is called a naïve forecast.) If any other technique we try cannot come up with a more accurate forecast than this relatively easy one, why bother using it?

Theil's U statistic simply calculates a ratio of the accuracy of the technique we are using to the naïve forecast's accuracy. If the U statistic is greater than 1.0, our technique is worse than the naïve forecast and should be discarded. If the U statistic is less than 1.0, our technique is better than the naïve technique and should be kept until we find another technique that gives an even lower U statistic (a technique that provides perfect forecasts will yield a U statistic of zero).

Unfortunately, the calculation of Theil's U statistic is sufficiently complicated that it is seldom used in practice. However, we can accomplish the same thing by developing a simple ratio of the MAPE of our forecast, divided by the MAPE of the naïve forecast. We can call this ratio the Sales Forecasting Technique Accuracy Benchmark (SFTAB), and the calculation for this benchmark is:

$$SFTAB = MAPE_E/MAPE_N \qquad (9)$$

where: $MAPE_E$ = the MAPE for the technique we are *evaluating*
          $MAPE_N$ = the MAPE for the *naïve* technique.

For example, the SFTAB for May 2004 is the MAPE for our technique of 5.95 divided by the MAPE that would have been achieved for the same month with the same data and using the naïve technique (60.10), or

$$SFTAB_{May03} = 5.95 / 60.10 = 0.0990$$

indicating our technique is much better than the naïve standard. If, however, we can find another technique that provides an even lower SFTAB, that is one closer to zero, it would be better than the one we are presently using.

Of course, a similar measure could be developed that compares the naïve technique to the one we are evaluating, based upon year-to-date (YTD) MAPE instead of MAPE.

Multidimensional Measures of Accuracy

Because none of these measures of forecasting accuracy seems to be perfect, perhaps what we need is a combination of several to provide the best performance measurement of forecasting accuracy—one that provides the pattern of a relative monthly measure of a Percent Error Plot, the relative overall measure of MAPE and/or YTD MAPE, an actual measure of error, and some comparison to a standard forecast.

This is precisely what is provided in Figure 2.3. The Percent Error Plot of Figure 2.1 is maintained but is augmented by several cumulative statistics. Specifically, we provide MAPE, YTD MAPE, MAE, and SFTAB. By using this combination (and also providing plots over time of MAPE, YTD MAPE, MAE, and SFTAB as well), the manager can look at the patterns of error (the Percent Error Plot), an overall measure of relative accuracy (MAPE), a current measure of relative accuracy (YTD MAPE), an overall measure of magnitude of error (MAE), and a comparison standard (SFTAB). MSE could be substituted for MAE if management feels larger forecasting errors should be emphasized, but we prefer MAE because it still offers some intuitive appeal (i.e., MSE has no real intuitive meaning).

Examining Figure 2.3 tells us that we have fairly good overall accuracy performance with this technique. On average we have been off about 8 units in our forecast, representing a 5.95% error (5.30% in the last year), and we are forecasting much more accurately than the standard (naïve) forecasting technique. There is room for improvement, however, because our forecasts are typically high. Such an analysis is

Figure 2.3   Multidimensional Metrics of Sales Forecasting Accuracy

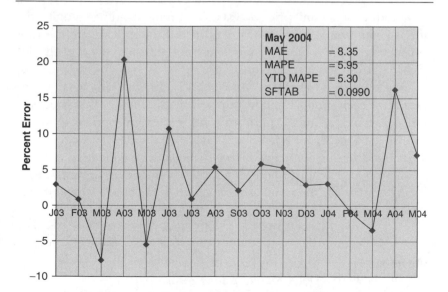

just the type of conclusions for performance improvement that should be provided by our accuracy metric.

Measuring Accuracy Across Multiple Products

All of the measures presented so far have been intended to evaluate forecasting performance with respect to one product. Suppose, however, that we have several thousand products to forecast and want a metric of how well we are doing. How do we evaluate the forecasting accuracy for a large number of products? The answer lies in a weighted MAPE or weighted YTD MAPE.

If we simply took the MAPE for each product and averaged all MAPEs, we would get considerable distortion in the result. For instance, a product for which demand was only 2 units and that we had forecast to be 1 unit would have a MAPE of 50%, but a product for which demand was 1,000 units and that we had forecast to be 1,100 units would have a MAPE of 10%. When we average them together, the average MAPE is 30%. The low unit demand product had the same weight in the metric as the high unit demand item and makes our forecasting performance look much worse than it actually is.

If we weight this calculation by unit volume (which we may want to do for a metric to measure operations performance), we get distortions from products with different prices. In the above example, if the first product had a unit price of $5,000 and the second had a unit price of $0.01, the unit volume MAPE would put too much weight on the second (high unit volume) product and not represent the contribution of each to overall dollar revenue.

The solution is to take the MAPE or YTD MAPE (whichever is preferred) for each product and multiply it by the ratio of that product's dollar demand volume (again, unit volume is appropriate if we are developing a metric for operational forecasts) divided by the total dollar demand for the company. If these calculations are added together for all products, a realistic and representative metric for aggregate forecasting accuracy is the result. This calculation for MAPE is as follows:

$$\text{Aggregate MAPE} = \sum_{p=1}^{P} \text{MAPE}_p \times (D_p/D_T) \qquad (10)$$

where: MAPE_p = MAPE for Product p
D_p = Dollar demand for Product p
D_T = Total dollar demand for all P products

In our original example, dollar demand for the first product is $10,000 (2 × $5,000) and dollar demand for the second product is $10 ($0.01 × 1,000), so the aggregate MAPE is:

$$\text{Aggregate MAPE} = (0.50 \times (10{,}000/10{,}010)) + (0.10 \times (10/10{,}010))$$
$$= 0.4996$$

which tells us that, on a revenue basis, we are not doing a very good job of forecasting on a dollar basis. This happens despite the fact that the forecast accuracy for most *units* is quite good.

Of course, this aggregate MAPE does not provide us with any insight into which products are forecast well and which are not (we need to look at individual product metrics in Figure 2.3 for that insight), but it does give us an overall metric of how well we are forecasting on a corporate or product line level.

Sales Forecasting Time Horizon

With this multidimensional metric of sales forecasting accuracy defined, we need to briefly turn our attention to the issue of sales forecasting time horizon. As we discussed in Chapter 1, the time horizon is determined by the planning purpose to which the sales forecast will be applied. If, as in the example used in this chapter, the sales forecasting time interval is monthly (one reason for this might be because we are forecasting for inventory planning), we will want to consider the production planning schedule for creating this inventory to determine the sales forecasting time horizon. If the production planning schedule cycle happens to be three months ahead, we will want all the metrics we have discussed to measure our accuracy in forecasting three periods (months) in the future. The same can be said for quarterly forecasts where our purpose is to plan promotion schedules for four quarters ahead, yearly forecasts where we are planning two years ahead, and so on. All of these combinations define the sales forecasting time intervals *and* the sales forecasting time horizon for measuring the accuracy metrics.

With the forecasting accuracy metric and its related issue of time horizon defined, we will now turn our attention to measuring the other two dimensions of sales forecasting performance: costs and customer service.

❖ SALES FORECASTING COSTS

The primary reason that accuracy is the most often measured dimension of sales forecasting performance is that it is the most straightforward. The dimensions of costs and customer service have less direct relationships with forecasting, are not as easily attributed to specific sales forecasting time intervals, and, thus, are less easily quantified. Because the ambiguity of these relationships varies by company, it is not possible to put forward such universal measures of these dimensions of sales forecasting performance as we can in the dimension of accuracy. Rather, we need to discuss the impact that sales forecasting has on both costs and customer service and leave the development of company-specific metrics to individual companies.

On the dimension of costs related to sales forecasting, we can break down the discussion into a return on investment (ROI) decision, where management costs are the investment and reductions in operations costs and marketing costs are the return.

Management Costs

The costs of managing the sales forecasting function involve the fixed and variable expenses associated with staffing the function, training the personnel involved in developing and using the sales forecasts, and providing the computer systems necessary for maintaining the relevant data, analyzing that data, and communicating the resultant information.

The size of the sales forecasting staff varies depending upon the number of forecasts to be made in a given period, the accuracy required, and the degree of automatic (as opposed to qualitative) forecasting conducted. Brake Parts, Inc., a company in the automobile aftermarket, made more than 250,000 forecasts each month and accomplished this with a staff of 12 (Mentzer & Schroeter, 1993). This phenomenal ratio of assigning more than 20,000 forecasts per month to each forecaster can only be accomplished by the fact that most of the forecasts are developed automatically by the computer, with the forecasters only examining the forecasts for those products for which the system has not automatically achieved what management considers to be acceptable accuracy levels (based on an ROI analysis of management costs, operations costs, marketing costs, and desired customer service levels).

Another company with which we have worked is a multibillion-dollar chemical manufacturer with global operations but with a forecasting staff of only one person. This company is able to have only one forecasting person on staff because the sales force adjusts quantitative forecasts for the company's products and customers. This "decentralization" of the forecasting function allows acceptable levels of forecasting accuracy while keeping the staffing costs lower.

One of the common factors for sales forecasting effectiveness we have found across a multitude of companies is the need for a forecasting champion—someone who is the central focus of the sales forecasting function. The personnel costs associated with this individual are the salary and training of someone who has the experience and training necessary to make informed decisions on all aspects of managing the sales forecasting function (more on the specific qualifications needed for this champion will be discussed later in this book).

Training costs should be an ongoing investment to keep various personnel trained in those areas of sales forecasting that are most appropriate to their responsibilities. Those involved in maintaining quantitative forecasts should be trained in the correct use of time series and regression forecasting techniques, where they do and do not work best, and how to qualitatively adjust their use. Those involved in making qualitative adjustments to these quantitative forecasts should be trained in how to take their experience and outside input to systematically make judgment forecasts and to document their thought processes, thereby developing a logical process that others involved in the forecasting process can understand and use. Those who use the sales forecasts need continued training in how the forecasts were developed, what are the limitations of the forecasts, and how all users of the forecasts apply them to their various planning processes.

Finally, computer system costs have changed dramatically over the last decade. In the 1970s and 1980s, when we talked about measuring the computer costs of sales forecasting, we had to discuss the cost of mainframe time, terminals, printing costs, and so on, which were usually a substantial part of the sales forecasting budget. In many cases today, the forecasting software is more expensive than the hardware on which it will run, and even the software can be comparatively inexpensive. As we will see later in this chapter, relatively minimal investment can result in dramatic operational savings and customer satisfaction improvements.

Operations Costs

Considerable production and logistics costs can be incurred through sales forecasting inaccuracy. Although the production system may work perfectly, we may produce the wrong product based upon the sales forecasts. This will cause inventory levels, and our cost of storing that inventory, to increase. Even if we realize our mistake and change the production schedule, changing the production schedule also causes higher production costs. Many companies try to schedule production several months in advance based on the sales forecast but can adjust that forecast as the actual production date gets closer. However, the more often the production schedule is changed, the higher the costs of production personnel changes, equipment changes, and expediting raw materials.

Inaccurate forecasts also create higher inbound materials costs. Often the raw material ordering cycle (especially for companies with global suppliers) can run into months. By forecasting inaccurately, the cost of expediting raw materials that are not ordered on time and the cost of storing raw materials that are not immediately needed can be substantial.

Sales forecasts that cause us to ship the product to the wrong location cause extra logistics costs in storing the inventory in the wrong location, transshipping the product from one location to another, and discounting the price of the product to get it sold, and they cause us to lose customers who are dissatisfied with not being able to obtain the product. There is more on this aspect in the later section on customer satisfaction.

To give you an idea of how significant the operations costs of forecasting inaccuracy can be, in one company with which we have worked, the costs incurred by production planning as a result of the inaccuracy of the forecasts generated by marketing caused the production planners to totally reject marketing's forecasts. Instead, production planning began developing its own forecasts.

Additional examples could be provided for specific companies, but the important point is that any metric of sales forecasting performance should address the production and logistics costs of inaccurate forecasts. A first step in doing this is to match monthly or quarterly production overrun costs, raw material and finished goods excess inventory costs, and finished goods transshipment costs with forecasting error in the same periods. By correlating these costs with forecasting error, a clearer picture is provided of the impact of forecasting accuracy on operations costs. When this aspect of sales forecasting performance is measured, the savings from a minor expenditure on the sales forecasting function are often dramatic.

Marketing Costs

The cost savings from improved sales forecasting accuracy can also be dramatic for marketing. One manufacturer of consumer products with which we work originally spent more than $100 million each year on trade promotions on the belief that these promotions stimulated demand and took market share away from the company's three major competitors. In the process of analyzing the company's sales forecasting needs, we conducted a series of regression-based forecasts and discovered something interesting: There seemed to be no relationship between dollars spent on trade promotions and company sales, industry sales, or market share! From a forecasting accuracy perspective, we could have simply concluded that these were not good variables for developing a forecast and moved on. However, the metric of marketing costs led us to suggest a strategy of everyday low prices (EDLP), and guess what happened? The competitors were also only too happy to get rid of this drain on their balance sheets and also quickly went to EDLP as well. In the aftermath of this change, industry size did not change, market share did not change (so, of course, company sales did not change), but the unnecessary marketing expense of excessive trade promotions went away.

Marketing costs of inaccurate forecasting include not only trade promotions but also include the costs of:

- Ineffective advertising
- Product development of new products without adequate demand
- Pricing at a level that does not maximize profit contribution
- Inappropriate sales quotas

The last point bears elaboration. Sales people often have conflicting goals when they are a part of the sales forecasting process. It is in the nature of sales people to be optimistic and set goals for themselves that they will strive to achieve. This is fine for motivation but can be detrimental to the sales forecasting process. High sales forecasts may lead to unrealistic sales quotas, which may lead to lower sales force morale.

Conversely, sales people are often rewarded for exceeding their quotas. When such is the case, a strong motivation exists to forecast low so that quotas will be set at a low level that can be easily exceeded. This makes life easier for the sales force but may result in lost sales opportunities because the "bar has been set too low."

We actually worked with one company that explained to us their unique "quarterly seasonal pattern." This pattern clearly showed that sales were always high in the first two months of each quarter and low in the third month. This pattern repeated each quarter, and the company wanted to know what would cause their customers to buy in such a way. Upon investigation, we found that sales quotas (that were based upon sales forecasts) were actually set too low, and the sales force received a lower commission for any sales in excess of the quota in any month (an interesting concept in itself, because it reduces motivation to beat the goal). Thus, the sales force (being intelligent people) simply sold at normal levels until their quota was met (this usually only took two of the three months in each quarter) and would not call on customers during the third month. Literally, customers could not buy from the company for four months each year! Of course, this caused considerable production and logistics costs to address this "seasonal" pattern and was all a marketing cost associated with an inaccurate forecast.

The Costs Are Not Always Justified

As these examples illustrate, the management, operations, and marketing costs associated with sales forecasting performance measurement vary by company. What is important to realize here is that it is not just accuracy that counts; the cost implications of that accuracy should be measured as well.

Another example on this point may help. We were asked by one company to develop a sales forecasting system to improve their accuracy. Sales forecasting errors at the time ranged from 20% to 30%, and management set the goal of reducing errors to below 15%. This all seems like a reasonable goal when only accuracy is examined. However, when we looked at the cost aspect, several factors became important. First, the company's product line was fairly low value, with few special storage needs. Thus, it was inexpensive to keep in inventory. Second, the production process was very flexible and allowed for daily changes in production schedules with little added cost. Finally, the low cost of the product and the fact that it represented a small cost component of the final product produced by the company's customers led to the fact that customers tended to carry sufficient quantities in inventory to cause little customer service problems from late deliveries. These factors led to a conclusion that the operations and marketing cost savings from improved forecasting accuracy would be minimal. In fact, the total savings from these areas would result in only an estimated savings of $50,000 per year.

However, the management costs of reducing forecasting errors to 15% would include hiring a director of forecasting to champion the new process; new forecasting software and the hardware on which to operate it; and training for numerous personnel involved in making qualitative adjustments to the forecasts. The estimated annual costs of these activities totaled over $65,000, so literally improving accuracy would have cost the company money! Although this is an extreme example (though a true one), it illustrates the importance of examining not just sales forecasting accuracy, but its cost implications as well.

❖ CUSTOMER SATISFACTION

The customer satisfaction implications of inaccurate sales forecasting involve:

- Dissatisfying customers by designing and producing products that customers do not want
- Dissatisfying customers by not designing and producing products that customers do want
- Dissatisfying customers by not having products desired by customers in the locations and in the quantities demanded

The metrics of all three of these implications involve surveys of customers to determine their satisfaction with all the marketing activities of the company and, as such, vary from company to company. For example, one company selling its products through grocery stores found that when loyal customers came into the store to buy their brand and the store did not have it in stock (through either operations errors or forecasting errors), the customers typically bought the major competitor's brand and *permanently switched brands*. Thus, in this example, the customer satisfaction implications of inaccurate forecasts were considerable (a lost customer).

Regardless of the specifics, use of this dimension of sales forecasting performance metrics involves some form of research to determine the customer satisfaction implications of inaccurate forecasts. As such, the metrics are more suited to the particular company's customer mix and the intricacies of the specific situation. The latter intricacies can involve not only market characteristics, but also investigation of operational characteristics. For instance, loss of customer sales due to the product not being available on the retail shelves may lead to research on what caused this customer a dissatisfying incident. We may find that forecasts of point of sale (POS) demand were, in fact, accurate, but lack of communication with production and logistics failed to alert marketing that the forecast demand for that time interval exceeded the capacity of the operations system to produce and deliver the product. Thus, the customer dissatisfaction resulting from not having the product available was caused by a problem in the forecasting information system.

Although the specific metrics used to measure customer satisfaction with the company's delivery system should reflect the context of that specific company, research has shown that efforts to assess delivery system customer satisfaction should evaluate customers' perceptions of the timeliness, availability, and condition of the distribution service they receive (Bienstock, Mentzer, & Bird, 1997), and the overall customer satisfaction process (Mentzer, Flint, & Hult, 2001). Timeliness addresses whether or not customers receive products when they are required. Availability addresses whether products are available in inventory when customers order them. Condition taps the concepts of whether or not orders are picked accurately, as well as the degree of damage to products that occurs during distribution.

❖ PUTTING IT ALL TOGETHER—A FORECASTING ROI DECISION

No company was ever successful simply from more accurate sales forecasting (Mentzer, 1999). Unless these more accurate forecasts can be translated into higher levels of customer service and lower supply chain costs, the impact of improved forecasting accuracy is lost on corporate profitability. By the same token, "C-level" executives (CEO, COO, CFO, and so on) are not interested in investing corporate dollars to improve forecasting performance unless it can be translated into higher returns for the shareholders. After all, return on shareholder value is the primary concern of upper management. Although improved forecasting accuracy often has a profound impact upon corporate profit and shareholder value, it is seldom presented as such to upper management.

Given this reality of business management, what is the most effective way to demonstrate the impact of improved sales forecasting performance? The answer lies in the translation of forecasting accuracy into improved operational plans and execution and improved service to customers. The former results in lower costs per dollar of sales, and the latter results in increased sales.

A Model of Return on Shareholder Value

The improvement in shareholder value resulting from improvement in forecasting accuracy can be visualized with the help of the "duPont Model" of financial performance. The duPont Model is a framework for viewing the impact of changes in sales, capital, and operating expenses on return on net assets. A slight revision in this model gives us a return on shareholder value model (see Figure 2.4). In this model, we start with sales revenue and subtract from it all the costs of doing business. Notice this is not a gross margin calculation, where only the costs of goods sold are subtracted from sales revenue, but rather all costs (fixed and variable) are subtracted to give us the profitability of the business unit.

In the lower-right part of the model, we examine the total investment by shareholders in capital, both working (primarily accounts receivable and inventory) and fixed. Ordinarily, retained earnings of the company are added to this to arrive at shareholder value. However, retained earnings are a financial decision by the board of directors and the shareholders regarding whether to leave money not invested in capital in the company or take it out. Further, because we are solely concerned here with the impact of operations decisions on shareholder value, retained earnings are irrelevant and, thus, left out of the decision model in Figure 2.4.

Dividing profit by shareholder value (capital investment) gives us return on shareholder value, or the percent of capital invested that is returned in the form of profits each year. This is a primary factor for any decision made by chief executive officers, chief operating officers, chief financial officers, and, in fact, any executive in the business unit.

Figure 2.4   Impact of Forecasting Improvements on Shareholder Value

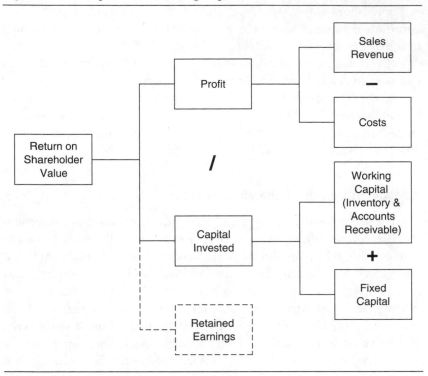

An Actual Example

Figure 2.5 illustrates an actual example of how improved forecasting performance impacts shareholder value. Although the numbers have been slightly altered to protect the identity of the example company, this company originally had sales revenue of $2,000,000,000 and total costs of $1,900,000,000 (annual profit of $100,000,000), on a working capital base of $200,000,000. The fixed capital base (consisting primarily of plant and equipment and three distribution centers) was $500,000,000. This resulted in a return on shareholder value (RSV) each year of 14.29%.

Based on a sales forecasting audit (discussed in detail later in this book), many areas for potential improvement were discovered. As a result, management authorized a series of actions to implement recommended improvements to these processes—actions that included a new sales forecasting package to provide a more accurate base forecast;

Figure 2.5   An Example of Forecasting Improvement Impact on
Shareholder Value

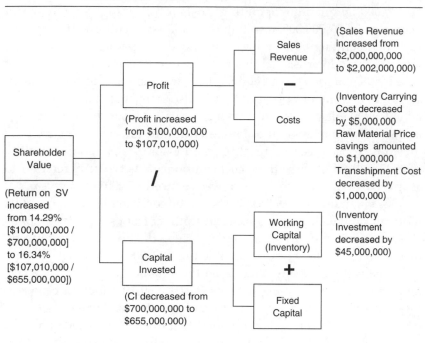

a revised process that included greater input from marketing, sales, and operations to the base forecast to arrive at a final revised forecast; a computer and communications system to augment this process; and a new performance evaluation system to measure and reward everyone involved in the forecasting process who improved forecasting accuracy or who used those improved forecasts to lower supply chain costs and/or improve customer service.

From the start of this effort, upper management insisted upon dollar measures of the impact of these more accurate forecasts upon lower operations costs and increased sales from improved customer service. It was quickly realized that the latter of these two could not be fully and accurately measured, so the company settled for documenting only when the more accurate forecasts led to improvements in inventory available to meet customer demand—in other words, when sales were made because the inventory was available, as opposed to a lost sale due to stockouts.

The results of this documentation are illustrated in Figure 2.5. Increased sales as a result of improved in-stock situations were $2,000,000, while the operating costs of meeting total demand decreased by $7,000,000, resulting in increased profit of $7,010,000.

The operating cost savings fell into three main categories. First, more accurate forecasts led to a reduction in the amount of inventory held by the company to meet uncertain demand variations (i.e., safety stock) in the amount of $45,000,000 (also note that the reduction in inventory resulted in lower working capital). This resulted in savings in the cost of money on those invested funds, lower risk costs on the inventory (obsolescence, shrinkage, and insurance), and lower facility costs. The total of these three cost components is typically referred to as inventory carrying cost, which was reduced $5,000,000 per year.

Second, more accurate forecasts led the company to buy more of its required raw materials on long-term contract from supply chain partners, rather than on the spot market. The reduction in price between these two methods of procurement led to a $1,000,000 annual savings.

Finally, the company often faced the situation of producing a certain product and shipping it to its East Coast distribution center to meet anticipated demand, only to find the demand was lower than forecast on the East Coast and higher than forecast on the West Coast. As a result, some of the inventory of that product that had already been shipped from the production facility (located in the Midwest) to the East Coast distribution center would have to be moved (transshipped) to the West Coast distribution center. Improved forecasting accuracy by product and by distribution center lowered the incidence of this scenario and its accompanying costs in the amount of $1,000,000 a year.

Although fixed capital was negligibly affected by these changes, working capital (money invested in inventory) decreased by $45,000,000. This resulted in a decrease in capital invested in the company by the shareholders of $45,000,000. As we mentioned, whether this $45,000,000 is paid out to the shareholders as a dividend or kept in retained earnings for future investments is irrelevant to the financial impact being evaluated here.

The result of all these changes in forecasting performance was improvement in profit by $7,010,000 each year, the capital investment base went down by $45,000,000, and return on shareholder value increased from 14.29% to 16.34%. The total cost of all the improvements in sales forecasting management was approximately $1,650,000, for a return on investment result of 7,010,000/1,650,000, or 425%! All of this clearly shows that improvement in forecasting accuracy can have a dramatic effect on corporate profitability and shareholder value.

Lessons Learned

The most important lesson learned from this example is that we should estimate the potential impact on return on shareholder value (RSV) *prior to* making investments in sales forecasting and demand planning improvements. We make a serious mistake in sales forecasting and demand management when we go to upper management with a proposal to spend money to improve forecasting accuracy, without indicating what "impact" it will have on revenues, supply chain costs and, subsequently, on shareholders.

To properly document the impact of improved sales forecasting performance, forecasting managers must answer the following questions:

1. What will be the total investment in all improvements to the sales forecasting and demand planning processes (packages, systems, staffing, training, performance rewards)?

2. What will be the estimated improvement in sales forecasting accuracy?

3. To what degree will this improved accuracy reduce the incidence of stockouts? In which products? By how much?

4. To what degree will this improved accuracy reduce inventory levels? What is the total dollar investment in this inventory that will be reduced? What is the cost of money for this investment? How much are the risk costs pertaining to obsolescence, shrinkage, and insurance reduced because of reductions in inventory? How much are facility costs related to receiving, handling, and shipping reduced because of reductions in inventory?

5. How much savings in production (overtime, expedited operations, and so on) will result from more accurate forecasts?

6. How much procurement savings will result from more accurate forecasts?

7. How much saving in transshipments will result from more accurate forecasts?

Answering these questions provides the information needed to prepare a proposal similar to Figure 2.5—a proposal that touches the heart of C-level decision makers.

It is important to remember that there is nothing wrong with projecting improvements in accuracy, but without carrying this to the final step—the ultimate impact on shareholder value—we are not providing upper management with the information necessary to make informed business decisions about improvements in sales forecasting and demand management.

❖ CONCLUSIONS

In this chapter, we have discussed the three dimensions of sales forecasting performance measurement: accuracy, costs, and customer satisfaction. For accuracy, we provided specific recommendations for multidimensional metrics of this aspect of sales forecasting performance. For the other two dimensions, we discussed what constitutes each dimension and made recommendations on the directions management should take in measuring each. A truly multidimensional metric of sales forecasting performance must include all three aspects. Without such multidimensional metrics, management cannot make decisions on the cost efficiency or customer satisfaction effectiveness of improving the accuracy of the sales forecasts they develop.

3

Time Series
Forecasting Techniques

❖ ❖ ❖

Back in the 1970s, we were working with a company in the major home appliance industry. In an interview, the person in charge of quantitative forecasting for refrigerators explained that their forecast was based on one time series technique. (It turned out to be the exponential smoothing with trend and seasonality technique that is discussed later in this chapter.) This technique requires the user to specify three "smoothing constants" called α, β, and γ (we will explain what these are later in the chapter). The selection of these values, which must be somewhere between 0 and 1 for each constant, can have a profound effect upon the accuracy of the forecast.

As we talked with this forecast analyst, he explained that he had chosen the values of 0.1 for α, 0.2 for β, and 0.3 for γ. Being fairly new to the world of sales forecasting, we envisioned some sophisticated sensitivity analysis that this analyst had gone through to find the right combination of the values for the three smoothing constants to accurately forecast refrigerator demand.

However, he explained to us that in every article he read about this technique, the three smoothing constants were always referred to as α, β, and γ, in that order. He finally realized that this was because they are the 1st, 2nd, and 3rd letters in the Greek alphabet. Once he realized that, he "simply

took 1, 2, and 3, put a decimal point in front of each, and there were my
smoothing constants."

After thinking about it for a minute, he rather sheepishly said, "You know,
it doesn't work worth a darn, though."

❖ INTRODUCTION

We hope that over the years we have come a long way from this type
of time series forecasting. First, it is not realistic to expect that each
product in a line like refrigerators would be accurately forecast by the
same time series technique—we probably need to select a different
time series technique for each product. Second, there are better ways
to select smoothing constants than our friend used in the previous
example. To understand how to better accomplish both of these, the
purpose of this chapter is to provide an overview of the many techniques that are available in the general category of time series analysis. This overview should provide the reader with an understanding
of how each technique works and where it should and should not
be used.

Time series techniques all have the common characteristic that
they are endogenous techniques. This means a time series technique
looks at only the patterns of the history of actual sales (or the series of
sales through time—thus, the term time series). If these patterns can
be identified and projected into the future, then we have our forecast.
Therefore, this rather esoteric term of endogenous means time series
techniques look inside (that is, endo) the actual series of demand
through time to find the underlying patterns of sales. This is in contrast to regression analysis, which is an exogenous technique that we
will discuss in Chapter 4. Exogenous means that regression analysis
examines factors external (or exo) to the actual sales pattern to look for
a relationship between these external factors (like price changes) and
sales patterns.

If time series techniques only look at the patterns that are part
of the actual history of sales (that is, are endogenous to the sales
history), then what are these patterns? The answer is that no matter
what time series technique we are talking about, they all examine one
or more of only four basic time series patterns: level, trend, seasonality, and noise. Figure 3.1 illustrates these four patterns broken out of a
monthly time series of sales for a particular refrigerator model. The

level is a horizontal sales history, or what the sales pattern would be if there were no trend, seasonality, or noise. For a product that is sold to a manufacturing concern as a component in another product whose demand is stable, the sales pattern for this product would be essentially level, with no trend, seasonality, or noise. In our example in Figure 3.1, however, the level is simply the starting point for the time series (the horizontal line), with the trend, seasonality, and noise added to it.

Trend is a continuing pattern of a sales increase or decrease, and that pattern can be a straight line or a curve.

Of course, any business person wants a positive trend that is increasing at an increasing rate, but this is not always the case. If sales are decreasing (either at a constant rate, an increasing rate, or a decreasing rate), we need to know this for forecasting purposes. In our example in Figure 3.1, trend is expressed as a straight line going up from the level.

Seasonality is a repeating pattern of sales increases and decreases that occurs within a one-year period or less ("seasonal patterns" of longer than one year are typically referred to as "cycles," but can be forecast using the same time series techniques). Examples of seasonality

Figure 3.1   Time Series Components

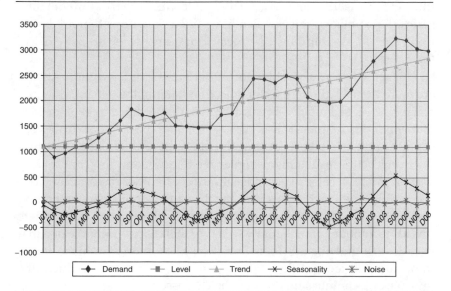

are high sales every summer for air conditioners, high sales of agricultural chemicals in the spring, and high sales of toys in the fall. The point is that the pattern of high sales in certain periods of the year and low sales in other periods repeats itself every year. When broken out of the time series in Figure 3.1, the seasonality line can be seen as a regular pattern of sales increases and decreases around the zero line at the bottom of the graph.

Noise is random fluctuation—that part of the sales history that time series techniques cannot explain. This does not mean the fluctuation could not be explained by regression analysis or some qualitative technique; it means the pattern has not happened consistently in the past, so the time series technique cannot pick it up and forecast it. In fact, one test of how well we are doing at forecasting with time series is whether the noise pattern looks random. If it does not have a random pattern like the one in Figure 3.1, it means there are still trend and/or seasonal patterns in the time series that we have not yet identified.

We can group all time series techniques into two broad categories—*open-model time series techniques* and *fixed model time series techniques*—based on how the technique tries to identify and project these four patterns. Open-model time series (OMTS) techniques analyze the time series to determine which patterns exist and then build a unique model of that time series to project the patterns into the future and, thus, to forecast the time series. This is in contrast to fixed-model time series (FMTS) techniques, which have fixed equations that are based upon *a priori* assumptions that certain patterns do or do not exist in the data.

In fact, when you consider both OMTS and FMTS techniques, there are more than 60 different techniques that fall into the general category of time series techniques. Fortunately, we do not have to explain each of them in this chapter. This is because some of the techniques are very sophisticated and take a considerable amount of data but do not produce any better results than simpler techniques, and they are seldom used in practical sales forecasting situations. In other cases, several different time series techniques may use the same approach to forecasting and have the same level of effectiveness. In these latter cases where several techniques work equally well, we will discuss only the one that is easiest to understand (following the philosophy, why make something complicated if it does not have to be). This greatly reduces the number of techniques that need to be discussed.

Because they are generally easier to understand and use, we will start with FMTS techniques and return to OMTS later in the chapter.

❖ FIXED-MODEL TIME SERIES TECHNIQUES

FMTS techniques are often simple and inexpensive to use and require little data storage. Many of the techniques (because they require little data) also adjust very quickly to changes in sales conditions and, thus, are appropriate for short-term forecasting. We can fully understand the range of FMTS techniques by starting with the concept of an average as a forecast (which is the basis on which all FMTS techniques are founded) and move through the levels of moving average, exponential smoothing, adaptive smoothing, and incorporating trend and seasonality.

The Average as a Forecast

All FMTS techniques are essentially a form of average. The simplest form of an average as a forecast can be represented by the following formula:

$$\text{Forecast}_{t+1} = \text{Average Sales}_{1 \text{ to } t} = \sum_{t=1}^{N} S_t / N \qquad (1)$$

where: S = Sales
        N = Number of Periods of Sales Data (t)

In other words, our forecast for next month (or any month in the future, for that matter) is the average of all sales that have occurred in the past.

The advantage to the average as a forecast is that the average is designed to "dampen" out any fluctuations. Thus, the average takes the noise (which time series techniques assume cannot be forecast anyway) out of the forecast. However, the average also dampens out of the forecast **any** fluctuations, including such important fluctuations as trend and seasonality. This principle can be demonstrated with a couple of examples.

Figure 3.2 provides a history of sales that has only the time series components of level and noise. The forecast (an average) does a fairly good job of ignoring the noise and forecasting only the level. However, Figure 3.3 illustrates a history of sales that has the time series components of level and noise, *plus trend*. As will always happen when

Figure 3.2   Average as a Forecast: Level and Noise

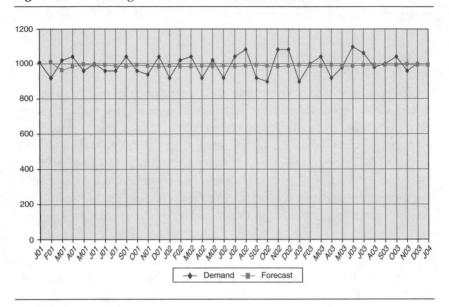

the average is used to forecast data with a trend, the forecast always lags behind the actual data. Because the average becomes more "sluggish" as more data are added, the lagging of the forecast behind the actual sales gets worse over time. If our example in Figure 3.3 had been a negative trend, lagging behind would have meant the average would have always forecast high.

As a final example, Figure 3.4 illustrates a history of sales that has the time series components of level and noise, *plus seasonality*. Notice that the average has the unfortunate effect of losing (dampening out) the seasonal pattern. Thus, we would lose this important component of any possible forecast.

The conclusion from these three illustrations is that the average should only be used to forecast sales patterns that contain only the time series components of level and noise. Remember that FMTS techniques assume certain patterns exist in the data. In the case of the average, we are assuming there is no trend or seasonality in the data. This is why we stated earlier that the forecast for the next period is also the forecast for all future periods. Because the data are supposed to be level, there should be no pattern of sales increasing (trend) or increasing and

Figure 3.3   Average as a Forecast: Level, Trend, and Noise

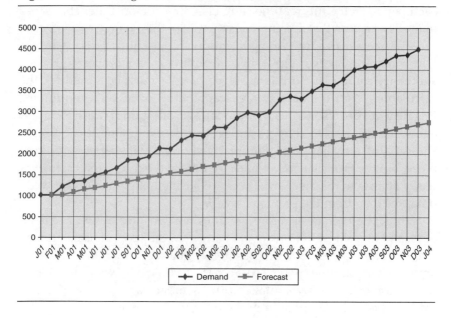

Figure 3.4   Average as a Forecast: Level, Seasonality, and Noise

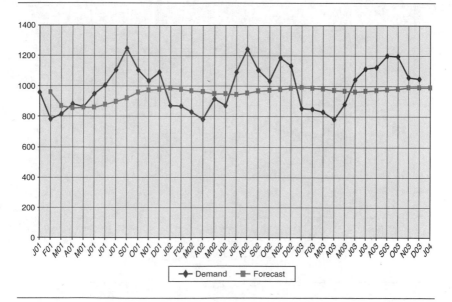

decreasing (seasonality). Therefore, sales should be the same (level) for each period in the future. If nothing else, this demonstrates the rather naïve assumption that accompanies the use of the average as a forecast.

The average as a forecasting technique has the added disadvantage that it requires an ever-increasing amount of data storage. With each successive month, an additional piece of data must be stored for the calculation. With the data storage capabilities of today's computers, this may not be too onerous a disadvantage, but it does cause the average to be sluggish to changes in level of demand. One last example should illustrate this point. Figure 3.5 shows a data series with little noise, but the level changes. Notice that the average as a forecast never really adjusts to this new level because we cannot get rid of the "old" data (the data from the previous level).

Thus, the average as a forecast does not consider trend or seasonality, and it is sluggish to react to changes in the level of sales. In fact, it does little for us as a forecasting technique, other than give us an excellent starting point. All FMTS techniques were developed to overcome some disadvantage of the average as a forecast. We next explore the first attempt at improvement, a moving average.

Figure 3.5   Average as a Forecast: Level Change

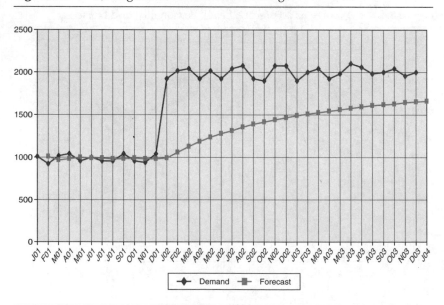

Moving Average

Rather than use all the previous data in the calculation of an average as the forecast, why not just use some of the more recent data? This is precisely what a moving average does, with the following formula.

$$F_{t+1} = (S_t + S_{t-1} + S_{t-2} + \cdots + S_{t-N-1})/N \qquad (2)$$

where: F_{t+1} = Forecast for Period t + 1
S_{t-1} = Sales for Period t − 1
N = Number of Periods in the Moving Average

So a three-period moving average would be:

$$F_{t+1} = (S_t + S_{t-1} + S_{t-2})/3$$

a four-period moving average would be:

$$F_{t+1} = (S_t + S_{t-1} + S_{t-2} + S_{t-3})/4$$

a five-period moving average would be:

$$F_{t+1} = (S_t + S_{t-1} + S_{t-2} + S_{t-3} + S_{t-4})/5$$

and so on, for as many periods in the moving average as you would like.

The problem with a moving average is deciding how many periods of sales to use in the forecast. The more periods used, the more it starts to look like an average. The fewer periods used, the more reactive the forecast becomes, but the more it starts to look like our naïve technique from Chapter 2 (the forecast for the next period equals the sales from the last period). Applying 3-period, 6-period, and 12-period moving averages to each of the demand patterns in Figures 3.2, through 3.5 (now Figures 3.6 through 3.9, respectively) should illustrate some of these points.

For a time series that has only level and noise (Figure 3.6), our three moving averages work equally well. This is because all dampen out the relatively small amount of noise, and there is no change in level to which to react. Because it uses the least data, the three-period moving average is superior in this case.

However, for the time series with trend added (Figure 3.7), very different results are obtained. The longer the moving average, the less reactive the forecast, and the more the forecast lags behind the trend (because it is more like the average). Again, this is because moving averages were not really designed to deal with a trend, but the shorter moving averages adjust better (are more reactive) than the longer in this case.

An interesting phenomenon occurs when we look at the use of moving averages to forecast time series with seasonality (Figure 3.8). Notice that both the three-period and the six-period moving averages lag behind the seasonal pattern (forecast low when sales are rising and forecast high when sales are falling) and miss the turning points in the time series. Notice also that the more reactive moving average (three-period) does a better job of both of these. This is because in the short run (defined here as between turning points), the seasonal pattern simply looks like trend to a moving average.

However, the 12-period moving average simply ignores the seasonal pattern. This is due to the fact that any average dampens out

Figure 3.6   Moving Average as a Forecast: Level and Noise

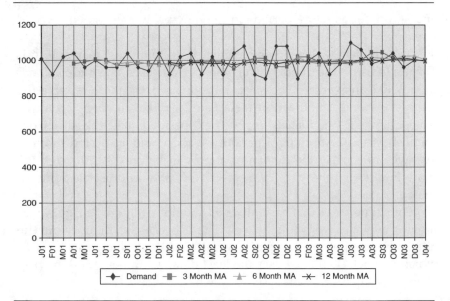

Figure 3.7   Moving Average as a Forecast: Level, Trend, and Noise

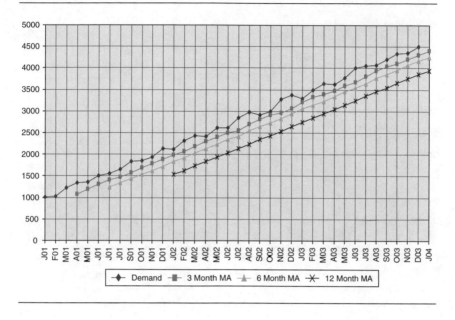

Figure 3.8   Moving Average as a Forecast: Level, Seasonality, and Noise

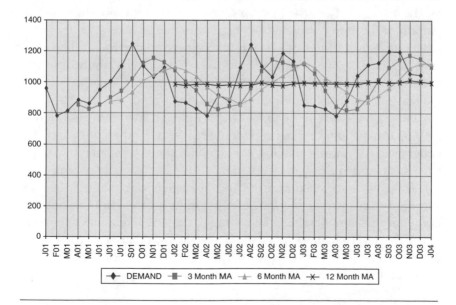

Figure 3.9   Moving Average as a Forecast: Level Changes

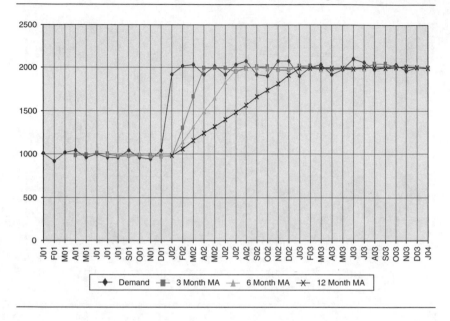

random fluctuations (noise) *and* any patterns that are the same length as the average. Because this time series has a 12-month seasonal pattern, a 12-month moving average completely loses the seasonal component in its forecast. This is particularly dangerous when you consider how many sales managers use a simple 12-month moving average to generate a forecast—they are inadvertently dampening out the seasonal fluctuations from their forecasts.

Finally, let's look at the time series where the level changes (Figure 3.9). Again, the longer moving average tends to dampen out the noise better than the shorter moving average, but the shorter moving average reacts more quickly to the change in level.

Thus, what we need in a moving average is one that acts like an average when there is only noise in the time series (dampens out the noise but uses less data than an average), but acts like a naïve forecast when the level changes (puts more weight on what happened very recently). The problem with this is how to recognize the difference in a change that is noise, as opposed to a change in level, a trend, or a seasonal pattern.

A final problem with the moving average is that the same weight is put on all past periods of data in determining the forecast. It is more reasonable to put greater weight on the more recent periods than the older periods (especially when a longer moving average is used). Therefore, the question when using a moving average becomes how many periods of data to use and how much weight to put on each of those periods. To answer this question about moving averages, a technique called exponential smoothing was developed.

Exponential Smoothing

Exponential smoothing is the basis for almost all FMTS techniques in use today. It is easier to understand this technique if we acknowledge that it was originally called an "exponentially weighted moving average." Obviously, the original name was too much of a mouthful for everyday use, but it helps us to explain how this deceptively complex technique works. We are going to develop a moving average, but we will weight the more recent periods of sales more heavily in the forecast, and the weights for the older periods will decrease at an exponential rate (which is where the "exponential smoothing" term came from).

Regardless of that rather scary statement, we are going to accomplish this with a very simple calculation (Brown & Meyer, 1961).

$$F_{t+1} = \alpha\, S_t + (1 - \alpha)\, F_t \qquad\qquad (3)$$

where: F_t = Forecast for Period t
S_t = Sales for Period t
$0 < \alpha < 1$

In other words, our forecast for next period (or, again, any period in the future) is a function of last period's sales and last period's forecast, with this α thing thrown in to confuse us.

What we are actually doing with this exponential smoothing formula is merely a weighted average. Because α is a positive fraction (that is, between 0 and 1), $1 - \alpha$ is also a positive fraction, and the two of them add up to 1. Any time we take one number and multiply it by a positive fraction, take a second number and multiply it by the reciprocal of the positive fraction (another way of saying 1 – the first fraction), and add the two results together, we have merely performed a weighted average. Several examples should help:

1. When we want to average two periods' sales (Period 1 was 50 and Period 2 was 100, for example) and not put more weight on one than the other, we are actually calculating it as $((0.5 \times 50) + (0.5 \times 100)) = 75$. We simply placed the same weight on each period. Notice that this gives us the same result as if we had done the simpler equal-weight average calculation of $(50 + 100)/2$.

2. When we want the same two periods of sales but want to put three times as much weight on Period 2 (for reasons we will explain later), the calculation would now be $((0.25 \times 50) + (0.75 \times 100)) = 87.5$. Notice that in this case α would be 0.25 and $1 - \alpha$ would be 0.75.

3. Finally, if we want nine times as much weight on Period 2, the resultant calculation would be $((0.1 \times 50) + (0.9 \times 100)) = 95$. Again, notice that in this case α would be 0.1 and $1 - \alpha$ would be 0.9.

Therefore, we can control how much emphasis in our forecast is placed on what sales actually were last period. But what is the purpose of using last period's forecast as part of next period's forecast? This is where exponential smoothing is "deceptively complex" and requires some illustration.

For the purpose of this illustration, let's assume that on the evening of the last day of each month, we make a forecast for the next month. Let's also assume that we have decided to use exponential smoothing and to put 10% of the weight of our forecast on what happened last month. Further, let's assume this is the evening of the last day of June. Thus, our value for α would be 0.1 and our forecast for July would be:

$$F_{JULY} = .1\ S_{JUNE} + .9\ F_{JUNE}$$

But where did we get the forecast for June? In fact, a month ago on the evening of the last day of May, we made this forecast:

$$F_{JUNE} = .1\ S_{MAY} + .9\ F_{MAY}$$

Again, where did we get the forecast for May? And again, a month ago on the evening of the last day of April, we made this forecast:

$$F_{MAY} = .1\, S_{APRIL} + .9\, F_{APRIL}$$

We could keep this up forever, but suffice it to say that each month the forecast from the previous month has in it the forecasts (and the sales) from all previous months. Thus, 10% of the forecast for July is made up of sales from June, but the other 90% is made up of the forecast for June. However, the forecast for June was made up of 10% of the sales from May. Thus, 90% times 10% (or 9%) of the July forecast is made up of the sales from May. The rest of the forecast for June was made up of 90% of the forecast for May, which in turn was made up of 10% of the sales from April (so April sales comprises 90% times 90% times 10%, or 8.1%, of the July forecast) and 90% of the forecast from April, and so on back to where we made our first forecast. This leads us to the fact that the forecast for July is actually made up of the following rather complicated formula:

$$F_{JULY} = .1\, S_{JUNE} + (.9)\,(.1)\, S_{MAY} + (.9)^2\,(.1)\, S_{APRIL} \\ + (.9)^3\,(.1)\, S_{MARCH} + \cdots + (.9)^N\,(.1)\, S_{JULY-(N+1)}$$

If we take a second to study this formula, we see that sales from June make up 10% of our forecast, sales from May make up 9% $(.9 \times .1)$ of our forecast, sales from April make up 8.1% $(.9 \times .9 \times .1)$ of our forecast, sales from March make up 7.2% $(.9 \times .9 \times .9 \times .1)$ of our forecast, and so on back to the first month we used this technique.

What is happening with the rather simple-looking exponential smoothing formula is that we are putting α weight on last period's sales, α times $(1 - \alpha)$ weight on the previous period's sales, and changing the weight for each previous period's sales by multiplying the weight by $(1 - \alpha)$ for each successive period we go into the past.

For $\alpha = 0.1$, this causes the weights for the previous period's sales to decrease at the following exponential rate: 0.1, 0.09, 0.081, 0.072, 0.063, . . . and for $\alpha = 0.2$, the weights for the previous period's sales to decrease at the following exponential rate: 0.2, 0.16, 0.128, 0.1024, 0.08192, . . .

We could try to develop a similar series for every value of α (by the way, the possible values of α between 0 and 1 are infinite, so our attempt might take a while), but it is not necessary—the simple exponential smoothing formula does it for us. We do need to remember, however, that the higher the value of α, the more weight we are putting on last period's sales and the less weight we are putting on all the previous periods combined. In fact, as α approaches one, exponential smoothing puts so much weight on the past period's sales and so little on the previous periods combined, that it starts to look like our naïve technique ($F_{t+1} = S_t$) from Chapter 2. Conversely, as α approaches zero, exponential smoothing puts more equal weight on all periods and starts to look much like the average as a forecast.

This leads us to some conclusions about what the value of α should be:

1. The more the level changes, the larger α should be, so that exponential smoothing can quickly adjust.

2. The more random the data, the smaller α should be, so that exponential smoothing can dampen out the noise.

Several examples should help illustrate these conclusions. For our first illustration, we can use the data pattern from Figure 3.9 for the moving average, now Figure 3.10 for exponential smoothing.

Figure 3.10   Exponential Smoothing as a Forecast: Level Change

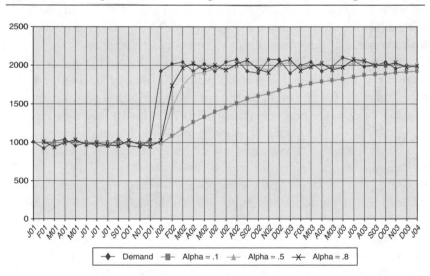

In Figure 3.10, we can see three exponential smoothing forecasts of the time series. All three do a fairly good job when the level is stable, but the higher the value of α in the forecast, the quicker it reacts to the change in level. Because a low value of α is much like an average, the forecast for the low α never quite reaches the new level.

However, a very different result is found when we observe the forecasts of the time series in Figures 3.11 and 3.12. Figure 3.11 is a reproduction of the data series used in Figures 3.2 and 3.6 and represents a time series with no trend and a low amount of noise. In this series, the exponential smoothing forecasts with various levels of α all perform fairly well. However, in the time series of Figure 3.12, which has a stable level but a high amount of noise, the forecasts with the higher values of α overreact to the noise and, as a result, jump around quite a bit. The forecast with the lower level of α does a better job of dampening out the noise.

Given these illustrations of our conclusions about the value of α that should be used, we have in exponential smoothing a technique that overcomes many of the problems with the average and the moving average as forecasting techniques. Exponential smoothing is less

Figure 3.11   Exponential Smoothing as a Forecast: Low Noise

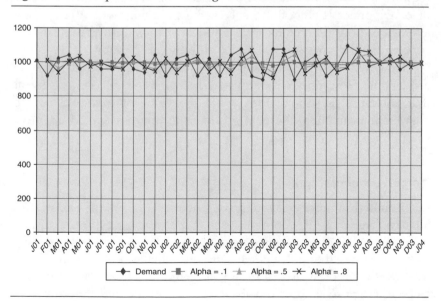

Figure 3.12   Exponential Smoothing Average as a Forecast: High Noise

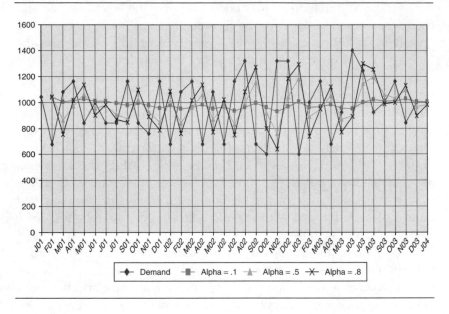

cumbersome than the average because exponential smoothing only requires the values of last period's sales and forecast and the value of α. Exponential smoothing solves the problems with the moving average of how much data to use and how to weight it by using an exponentially decreasing weight for all previous periods.

However, with exponential smoothing we are still faced with a dilemma: How do we determine whether the level is changing or if it is simply noise and, thus, what the value of α should be? To answer this dilemma, the next group of techniques (called adaptive smoothing) was developed.

Adaptive Smoothing

Although a number of adaptive smoothing techniques exist, they all have one thing in common: each is an attempt to automatically select the value of α. Because there are so many adaptive smoothing techniques and they all work essentially equally well, we will only discuss the simplest of this group of techniques here. This adaptive smoothing approach uses the absolute value of the percent error from the previous period's forecast to adjust the value of α for the next period's forecast (Trigg & Leach, 1967). Thus, the original exponential smoothing formula is still used:

$$F_{t+1} = \alpha S_t + (1 - \alpha) F_t \qquad (4)$$

but after each period's sales are recorded, the value of α is adjusted for the next period by the following formula:

$$\alpha_{t+2} = |\ (F_{t+1} - S_{t+1})/S_{t+1}\ | = |PE_{t+1}| \qquad (5)$$

Because Equation (5) can produce values outside the range of α, this calculation is adjusted by the following rules:

If $|PE_{t+1}|$ is equal to or greater than 1.0, then $\alpha_{t+2} = 0.99999$

If $|PE_{t+1}|$ is equal to 0.0, then $\alpha_{t+2} = 0.00001$

We can illustrate the adaptability of this technique by forecasting the times series with level change in Figure 3.10, now Figure 3.13 for

Figure 3.13   Adaptive Smoothing as a Forecast: Level Change

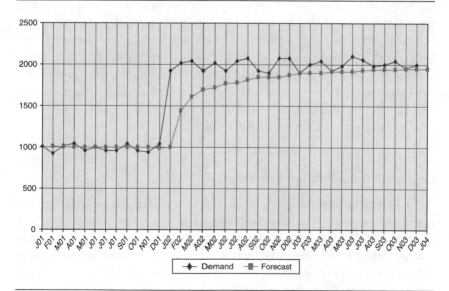

adaptive smoothing. To illustrate the changes in α that result in this technique, the calculations are also reproduced in Table 3.1.

To get the process started, we used the usual convention of setting the initial value of α at 0.1, although any value can be chosen without changing the resultant forecasts. The reason for this is that we also assume that the initial forecast was equal to the first period demand, so the first forecast becomes:

$$F_2 = \alpha\, S_1 + (1 - \alpha)\, S_1$$

So regardless of the initial value of α that is chosen, the forecast for period two is always equal to sales from period one. The true calculation of a forecast and the adapted values of α begin at that point.

Notice that the value of α stays low (well below 0.1) while the time series is level (a low value of α dampens out the noise), but as soon as the level changes, the value of α jumps dramatically to adjust. Once the time series levels off, the value of α again returns to a low level.

This adaptive smoothing technique overcomes one of the major problems with exponential smoothing: what should be the value chosen for α? However, all the techniques we have discussed so far have a common problem: none of them considers trend or seasonality. Since this technique assumes there is no trend or seasonality, our forecast of January 2004 is 1950 and is also our forecast for *every month* in 2004—we assume there will be no general increase or decrease in sales (trend), nor will there be any pattern of fluctuation in sales (seasonality). Because this is unrealistic for many business demand situations, we need some way to incorporate trend and seasonality into our FMTS forecasts. To do so, we temporarily set aside the concept of smoothing constant adaptability and introduce first trend and then seasonality into our exponential smoothing calculations.

Exponential Smoothing With Trend

Although we tend to think of trend as a straight or curving line going up or down, for the purposes of exponential smoothing, it is helpful to think of trend as a series of changes in the level. In other words, with each successive period, the level either "steps up" or "steps down." This "step function," or changing level pattern, of trend is conceptually illustrated in Figure 3.14. Although demand is going up

Table 3.1   Adaptive Smoothing Forecast Calculations

Month	Demand	Forecast	Percent Error	Absolute PE or α_{t+1}
J01	1010			
F01	920	1010	0.098	0.098
M01	1020	1002	−0.018	0.018
A01	1040	1002	−0.037	0.037
M01	960	1003	0.045	0.045
J01	1000	1001	0.001	0.001
J01	960	1001	0.043	0.043
A01	960	999	0.041	0.041
S01	1040	998	−0.041	0.041
O01	960	999	0.041	0.041
N01	940	998	0.061	0.061
D01	1040	994	−0.044	0.044
J02	1920	996	−0.481	0.481
F02	2020	1441	−0.287	0.287
M02	1920	1607	−0.163	0.163
A02	2040	1658	−0.187	0.187
M02	2080	1729	−0.169	0.169
J02	1920	1789	−0.068	0.068
J02	2040	1798	−0.119	0.119
A02	2080	1826	−0.122	0.122
S02	1920	1857	−0.033	0.033
O02	1900	1859	−0.021	0.021
N02	2080	1860	−0.106	0.106
D02	2080	1883	−0.095	0.095
J03	1900	1902	−0.001	0.001
F03	2000	1902	−0.049	0.049
M03	2040	1907	−0.065	0.065
A03	1920	1916	−0.002	0.002
M03	1980	1916	−0.033	0.033
J03	2100	1918	−0.087	0.087
J03	2060	1933	−0.061	0.061
A03	1980	1941	−0.020	0.020
S03	2000	1942	−0.029	0.029
O03	2040	1944	−0.047	0.047
N03	1960	1948	−0.006	0.006
D03	2000	1948	−0.026	0.026
J04		1950		

Figure 3.14   Trend in a Time Series

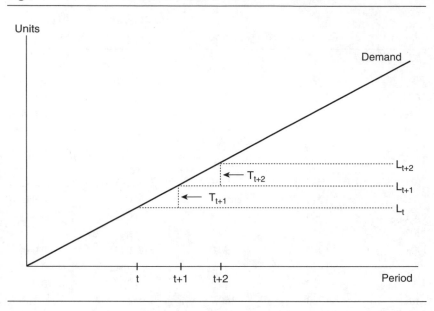

in a straight line, we can conceive of it as a series of increases in the level (the dashed horizontal lines). This is much like climbing a set of stairs. Although we make steady progress up the stairs, we are actually stepping up one step each period (the amount we step up, or the height of each step, on a set of stairs is called the riser). The height of each step (the riser) is what we call "trend" in exponential smoothing, and that trend is designated in Figure 3.14 as T. For period $t + 1$, the trend is the amount the level changed from period t to period $t + 1$ ($L_{t+1} - L_t$), or T_{t+1}. Similarly for period $t + 2$, the trend is the amount the level changed from period $t + 1$ to period $t + 2$ ($L_{t+2} - L_{t-1}$), or T_{t+2}.

To understand the calculation of trend in exponential smoothing, we must also understand that an exponential smoothing calculation is just a weighted average of two measures of the same thing. Our original exponential smoothing formula (Equation 4) was:

$$F_{t+1} = \alpha S_t + (1 - \alpha) F_t$$

In this calculation, S_t is one measure of past sales (last period's sales) and F_t is another measure of past sales (a weighted average of sales in all periods prior to t). Thus, we were taking a weighted average of two measures of the same thing. We are now going to do the same thing for level and trend with the following formulae (Holt et al., 1960):

$$L_t = \alpha \, S_t + (1 - \alpha) \, (L_{t-1} + T_{t-1}) \qquad (6)$$

$$T_t = \beta \, (L_t - L_{t-1}) + (1 - \beta) \, T_{t-1} \qquad (7)$$

where: L = Level
        T = Trend
        $0 < \alpha < 1$
        $0 < \beta < 1$

Notice that Equation (6) looks very similar to our earlier exponential smoothing forecast calculation—we still use α in the same way and we still use last period's sales. This difference is the addition of trend into the second part of Equation (6) and the fact that it is not a forecast for next period (F_{t+1}) but rather a measure of level for this period (L_t). In fact, in our original exponential smoothing formula (Equation [4]), we did not include trend because we assumed it did not exist. Because trend was assumed not to exist, our estimate of level this period *was* our forecast of next period.

What we need are two estimates of level for this period so we can exponentially smooth them. The first estimate is simply sales for this period. Since we assume there is no seasonality in the time series (an assumption we will discard in the next section), then this sales value has no seasonality in it. Because the trend is a change in level from one period to the next, any given value of sales does not have trend in it (that is, trend is in the *change* in sales from one period to the next, not any single sales value). Finally, when we perform the weighted averaging of the exponential smoothing calculation in Equation (6), we get rid of the noise. (Remember that averaging removes noise.) Since this logic says there is no trend or seasonality in the sales value and we will get rid of this noise when we do our exponential smoothing calculation, we are only left with one time series component in the sales value, and that component is level.

The second estimate of level is our estimate of level from last period, plus the estimate of how much level should have changed from last period to this period (that is, the trend). This gives us two measures of level to exponentially smooth with α.

Our two estimates of trend in Equation (7) are how much the level changed from last period to this period and our estimate of trend from last period. These two measures of trend are exponentially smoothed with our new smoothing constant, β. β is just like α in that it is a positive fraction (that is, between zero and one). It is designated by a different Greek symbol to indicate that α and β can have different values.

Once we have our new estimates of level (L) and trend (T), we can forecast as far into the future as we want by taking the level and adding to it the trend per period times as many periods into the future as we want the forecast. This can be represented by the following formula:

$$F_{t+m} = L_t + (T_t \times m) \tag{8}$$

where: m = the number of periods into the future to forecast.

To illustrate this technique, consider the time series with trend introduced in Figure 3.3, now Figure 3.15 for exponential smoothing with trend. To illustrate the calculations involved in this technique, Table 3.2 provides the calculations of level and trend and a forecast forward for one period throughout the time series (also provided in Figure 3.15). For the purposes of illustration, we arbitrarily chose the value of 0.1 for α and the value of 0.2 for β. Notice that to get the process started, we used the usual convention of assuming the level for the first period equaled first period demand, and the trend for the first period equaled the change in demand from the first to the second period.

To provide a forecast for any period more than one in the future (April 2004, for example), it is merely a task of taking the most recent value of level that has been calculated (in this case, December 2003) and adding to it the most recent value of trend that has been calculated (also in this case, December 2003) times the number of months into the future that we wish to forecast (because April is four months past December, it would be times four). For April 2004, the calculations are:

$$F_{A04} = L_{D03} + (T_{D03} \times m)$$

$$F_{A04} = 4614 + (106 \times 4)$$

$$F_{A04} = 5038$$

Figure 3.15   Exponential Smoothing With Trend as a Forecast

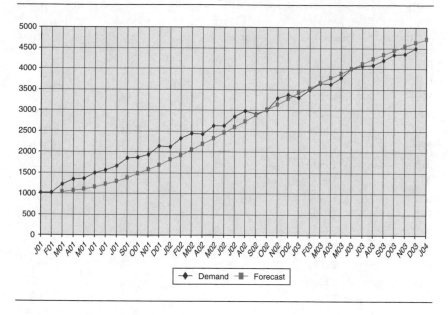

Now that we have the logic for introducing trend into the exponential smoothing calculations, it is fairly easy to also bring in seasonality.

Exponential Smoothing With Trend and Seasonality

To introduce seasonality, let's first think of a simple demand example where we sell 12,000 units of a product every year. If there is no trend, no noise, and no seasonality, we would expect to sell 1,000 units every month (that is, the level). If, however, we noticed that every January we sold, on average, 1,150 units, there is clearly a pattern here of selling more than the level in January. In fact, we are selling 1,150/1,000, or 1.15, times the level.

This value of 1.15 is called a *multiplicative seasonal adjustment* and means that sales in that month are 15% higher than they would be without a seasonal pattern. Similarly, a seasonal adjustment of 1.00 means that sales are right at the non-seasonal level, and a seasonal adjustment of 0.87 means that sales are 13% below what we would expect if there was no seasonal pattern.

Table 3.2   Exponential Smoothing With Trend Forecast Calculations

Month	Demand	Level ($\alpha = 0.1$)	Trend ($\beta = 0.2$)	Forecast
J01	1010	1010	10	
F01	1020	1020	10	
M01	1220	1049	14	1030
A01	1340	1091	19	1063
M01	1360	1135	24	1110
J01	1500	1193	31	1159
J01	1560	1258	38	1224
A01	1660	1332	45	1296
S01	1840	1424	54	1377
O01	1860	1516	62	1478
N01	1940	1615	69	1578
D01	2140	1729	78	1684
J02	2120	1839	85	1808
F02	2320	1963	93	1924
M02	2440	2094	100	2056
A02	2420	2217	105	2195
M02	2620	2352	111	2322
J02	2620	2478	114	2462
J02	2840	2617	119	2592
A02	2980	2760	124	2736
S02	2920	2887	124	2884
O02	3000	3011	124	3012
N02	3280	3149	127	3135
D02	3380	3287	129	3277
J03	3300	3404	127	3416
F03	3500	3528	126	3531
M03	3640	3653	126	3654
A03	3620	3763	123	3779
M03	3780	3875	121	3886
J03	4000	3996	121	3996
J03	4060	4111	120	4117
A03	4080	4216	117	4231
S03	4200	4319	114	4332
O03	4340	4424	112	4433
N03	4360	4518	109	4536
D03	4500	4614	106	4627
J04				4720

We are now going to use this concept of a multiplicative seasonal adjustment to introduce seasonality into the exponential smoothing calculations. Again, we will develop two different measures of each seasonal adjustment and take a weighted average of them (through exponential smoothing) to come up with our new estimate. To do this, however, we also need to update our formulae for Exponential Smoothing with Trend (Equations [6] and [7]) to take into account the fact that seasonality is now assumed to exist. This leads us to the following formulae (Winters, 1960):

$$L_t = \alpha \, (S_t / SA_{t-C}) + (1 - \alpha) \, (L_{t-1} + T_{t-1}) \tag{9}$$

$$T_t = \beta \, (L_t - L_{t-1}) + (1 - \beta) \, T_{t-1} \tag{10}$$

$$SA_t = \gamma \, (S_t / L_t) + (1 - \gamma) \, (SA_{t-C}) \tag{11}$$

where: L = Level
    T = Trend
  SA_t = Seasonal Adjustment for Period t
   C = The Cycle Length of the Seasonal Pattern (that is, the cycle length for a 12-month pattern is C = 12)
    $0 < \alpha < 1$
    $0 < \beta < 1$
    $0 < \gamma < 1$

We have revised our calculation for level to take seasonality into account in our first estimate of level. Recalling our previous example of annual sales of 12,000, how would we take the seasonality out of January sales? If sales were 1,150 and our previous estimates of the seasonality adjustment for January were 1.15, we can de-seasonalize January sales simply by dividing the sales value of 1,150 by the seasonal adjustment of 1.15. This gives us a de-seasonalized value of 1,000—precisely the value we said was the expected level if there were no seasonality.

Thus, by dividing sales for any period by the seasonal adjustment for the same period last year (that is, divide sales for January 2004 by the seasonal adjustment for January 2003), we have an estimate in the first formula of level with the seasonality taken out (recall that the original formula already took out the trend and the noise). Because the second part of this formula contains the level from the last period, which was de-seasonalized at that time, we now have two estimates of level to exponentially smooth.

Thankfully, the formula for trend (Equation [10]) does not change. Therefore, we do not have to revisit it here.

However, we now have added a formula to calculate the seasonal adjustments (Equation [11]). Again, we need two estimates of the seasonal adjustment for each period, so we can exponentially smooth each. This means we have 12 of these calculations per year if we are forecasting monthly sales, 52 if we are forecasting weekly, and 4 if we are forecasting quarterly.

The first part of Equation (11) is, again, a throwback to our initial example. If we take the sales value for this period and divide it by the most recently calculated level (which was just done two formulas before and is L_t), we have one estimate of the seasonal adjustment for this period. In our initial example, we did the same thing when we divided 1,150 by 1,000 to obtain 1.15 as our estimate of the seasonal adjustment for January.

For our second estimate of the seasonal adjustment for this period, we need to look back one year to the same period last year. We can now exponentially smooth these two estimates of the seasonal adjustment for this period using the smoothing constant, γ. Again, γ is just like α and β in that it is a positive fraction (that is, between zero and one). It is designated by a different Greek symbol to indicate that α, β, and γ can all have different values.

Once we have our new estimates of level (L), trend (T), and seasonal adjustments (SA), we can forecast as far into the future as we want by taking the level, adding to it the trend per period times as many periods into the future as we want the forecast, and multiplying that result by the most recent seasonal adjustment for that period. This can be represented by the following formula:

$$F_{t+m} = (L_t + (T_t \times m)) \times SA_{t-C+m} \qquad (12)$$

where: m = the number of periods into the future to forecast.

The last component of Equation (12) probably needs a little illustration. If we have just received sales for December 2003 and want to forecast April 2004, we will use the values of L and T calculated in December 2003 (in this case, December 2003 is "t") for the first part of the forecast. However, our most recent estimate of the seasonal adjustment for April was calculated back in

April 2003. The symbol to represent using this value is to take "t" (December 2003); subtract C, or 12, months from it (placing us in December 2002); and add to it m, or 4, months to bring us to the seasonal adjustment for April 2003.

To illustrate this technique, we will go all the way back to our original time series with trend and seasonality introduced in Figure 3.1, now Figure 3.16, for exponential smoothing with trend and seasonality. To illustrate the calculations involved in this technique, Table 3.3 provides the calculation of level, trend, seasonality, and a forecast forward for one period throughout the time series (also provided in Figure 3.16). For the purposes of illustration, we arbitrarily chose the value of 0.1 for α, the value of 0.2 for β, and the value of 0.15 for γ. Notice that to get the process started, we used the usual convention of assuming the level for the first period equaled first period demand, the trend for the first period equaled the change in demand from the first to the second period, and the initial 12 seasonal adjustment values were equal to 1.00. Notice, also, that this technique does a pretty terrible job

Figure 3.16   Exponential Smoothing With Trend and Seasonality as a Forecast

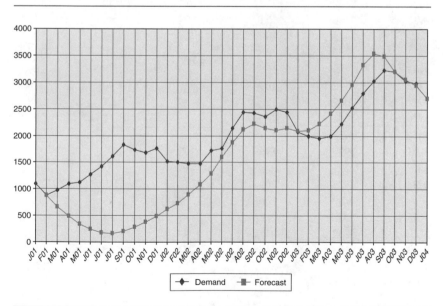

Table 3.3   Exponential Smoothing With Trend and Seasonality Forecast
Calculations

Month	Demand	Level ($\alpha = 0.1$)	Trend ($\beta = 0.2$)	Seasonality ($\gamma = 0.15$)	Forecast
J01	1104	1104	−219	1.00	
F01	885	885	−219	1.00	885
M01	976	697	−213	1.06	666
A01	1101	546	−200	1.15	484
M01	1120	423	−185	1.25	345
J01	1276	342	−164	1.41	238
J01	1419	302	−139	1.56	178
A01	1615	308	−110	1.64	162
S01	1836	361	−78	1.61	197
O01	1730	428	−49	1.46	284
N01	1686	510	−22	1.35	380
D01	1769	616	3	1.28	488
J02	1521	709	21	1.17	619
F02	1504	808	37	1.13	730
M02	1478	899	48	1.15	895
A02	1480	981	54	1.21	1091
M02	1726	1070	61	1.30	1291
J02	1759	1143	64	1.43	1595
J02	2137	1223	67	1.58	1877
A02	2436	1310	71	1.67	2113
S02	2425	1393	73	1.63	2227
O02	2355	1482	76	1.48	2136
N02	2499	1588	82	1.38	2097
D02	2442	1694	87	1.30	2140
J03	2069	1780	87	1.17	2087
F03	1992	1856	85	1.12	2108
M03	1958	1918	80	1.13	2227
A03	1990	1963	73	1.18	2409
M03	2222	2003	67	1.27	2651
J03	2525	2039	60	1.40	2958
J03	2789	2066	54	1.55	3327
A03	3017	2088	47	1.64	3542
S03	3232	2120	44	1.62	3485
O03	3198	2165	44	1.48	3195
N03	3028	2207	44	1.38	3048
D03	2985	2255	45	1.31	2938
J04					2692

of forecasting until at least one year of the seasonal pattern is available. Thus, exponential smoothing with trend and seasonality needs at least one complete year of data before it is "warmed up" and can start to forecast fairly effectively.

To provide a forecast for any period more than one in the future (April 2004, for example), it is merely a task of taking the most recent value of level that has been calculated (in this case, December 2003), adding to it the most recent value of trend that has been calculated (also in this case, December 2003), times the number of months into the future we wish to forecast (because April is four months past December, it would be times four), and multiplying this value by the seasonal adjustment for April of last year (2003). For April 2004, the calculations are:

$$F_{A04} = (L_{D03} + (T_{D03} \times m)) \times SA_{A03}$$

$$F_{A04} = (2255 + (45 \times 4)) \times 1.18$$

$$F_{A04} = 2874$$

Now that we have introduced the components of trend and seasonality into our basic exponential smoothing formula, we can return to the idea of how to set the value of the smoothing constants. However, now it is not simply a matter of choosing a value for α, but one of choosing values for β and γ, as well. In fact, the accuracy of exponential smoothing with trend and seasonality is very sensitive to the values chosen for the smoothing constants, so this is no small matter.

Adaptive Exponential Smoothing With Trend and Seasonality

As with regular adaptive smoothing, there are several techniques that are adaptive and consider trend and seasonality. One of the most complex computationally is called the Self Adaptive Forecasting Technique (SAFT) and was developed more than 35 years ago (Roberts & Reed, 1969). SAFT is a heuristic technique that examines different combinations of α, β, and γ to arrive at the most accurate forecast. For each forecast each period, SAFT tries each combination of α, β, and γ starting with a value of 0.05 for each and incrementally increasing the values by 0.05 until a value of 0.95 for each is reached. For each of these

6,859 ($19 \times 19 \times 19$, where the 19 is the number of values between 0 and 1, incrementing by 0.05 at a time) combinations, SAFT starts at the beginning of the time series and forecasts using exponential smoothing with trend and seasonality, and it records the resultant value of MAPE. Once the lowest MAPE value combination of α, β, and γ is determined, a local search for a lower MAPE is implemented by examining the values of α, β, and γ above and below each value (including the original three values) at a rate of change of 0.01.

For example, if the first search found the lowest value of MAPE to come from the combination of $\alpha = 0.15$, $\beta = 0.20$, and $\gamma = 0.30$, SAFT would then try all the combinations of $\alpha = 0.11$, 0.12, 0.13, 0.14, 0.15, 0.16, 0.17, 0.18, 0.19; $\beta = 0.16$, 0.17, 0.18, 0.19, 0.20, 0.21, 0.22, 0.23, 0.24; and $\gamma = 0.26$, 0.27, 0.28, 0.29, 0.30, 0.31, 0.32, 0.33, 0.34. These 729 ($9 \times 9 \times 9$) combinations are compared to the original best MAPE combination and, again, the lowest combination is chosen.

It should be clear by now that SAFT is a very computationally cumbersome technique (after all, it requires 7,588 trial forecasts for each product each period before it actually makes a forecast) and, as a result, is in little use today. More computationally efficient versions of SAFT try to calculate values of α, β, or γ and use a heuristic similar to SAFT for the smoothing constants that are not directly calculated.

As with adaptive smoothing, because these adaptive exponential smoothing techniques with trend and seasonality essentially all work equally well, we will only discuss the simplest of this group of techniques here. This adaptive smoothing approach, called Adaptive Extended Exponential Smoothing (AEES), uses the absolute value of the percent error from the previous period's forecast to adjust the value of α for the next period's forecast and uses the SAFT heuristic to adjust the values of β and γ (Mentzer, 1988). Thus, the exponential smoothing with trend and seasonality formulae (Equations [9], [10], [11], and [12]) are still used,

$$L_t = \alpha \, (S_t/SA_{t-C}) + (1 - \alpha) \, (L_{t-1} + T_{t-1})$$

$$T_t = \beta \, (L_t - L_{t-1}) + (1 - \beta) \, T_{t-1}$$

$$SA_t = \gamma \, (S_t/L_t) + (1 - \gamma) \, (SA_{t-C})$$

$$F_{t+m} = (L_t + (T_t \times m)) \times SA_{t-C+m}$$

but after each period's sales are recorded, the value of α is adjusted for the next period by Equation (5), repeated here as:

$$\alpha_{t+2} = |\ (F_{t+1} - S_{t+1})/S_{t+1}\ | = |PE_{t+1}|$$

Because this calculation can still produce values outside the range of α, this calculation is again adjusted by the following rules:

If $|PE_{t+1}|$ is equal to or greater than 1.0, then $\alpha_{t+2} = 0.99999$

If $|PE_{t+1}|$ is equal to 0.0, then $\alpha_{t+2} = 0.00001$

Once the new value of α has been calculated, AEES tries each combination of β and γ starting with a value of 0.05 for each and incrementally increasing the values by 0.05 until a value of 0.95 for each is reached. For each of these 361 (19 × 19, where the 19 is the number of values between 0 and 1, incrementing by 0.05 at a time) combinations, AEES starts at the beginning of the time series and forecasts using exponential smoothing with trend and seasonality and records the resultant value of MAPE. Once the lowest MAPE value combination of the calculated value of α and the heuristic values of β and γ is determined, a local search for a lower MAPE is implemented by examining the values of β and γ above and below each value (including the original two values) at a rate of change of 0.01.

For example, if the first search found the lowest value of MAPE to come from the calculated value of $\alpha = 0.15$, and combination of $\beta = 0.20$, and $\gamma = 0.30$, AEES would then try all the combinations of $\beta = 0.16, 0.17$, 0.18, 0.19, 0.20, 0.21, 0.22, 0.23, 0.24; and $\gamma = 0.26, 0.27, 0.28, 0.29, 0.30$, 0.31, 0.32, 0.33, 0.34. These 81 (9 × 9) combinations are compared to the original best MAPE combination and, again, the lowest combination is chosen.

It should be clear by now that AEES is a much less computationally cumbersome technique than SAFT. AEES requires 442 trial forecasts for each product each period before it actually makes a forecast, rather than the 7,588 trial forecasts of SAFT. Further, the exact value of α is calculated rather than the approximation obtained from the SAFT heuristic.

We can illustrate the adaptability of AEES by forecasting the times series with trend and seasonality used in the last section. (See Figure 3.17.) Notice that the forecast in Figure 3.17 "tracks" the demand better

Figure 3.17   AEES With Trend and Seasonality as a Forecast

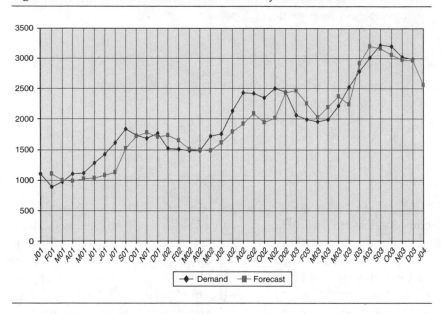

than the forecast in Figure 3.16. This is due to the adaptability of α, β, and γ. Also, the year-to-date MAPE for exponential smoothing with trend and seasonality (Figure 3.16) at the end is 9.73%, while the same calculation for AEES (Figure 3.17) is 7.00%.

❖ FIXED-MODEL TIMES SERIES TECHNIQUES SUMMARY

Considerable effort has been devoted over time to testing the various FMTS techniques discussed here (and variations on these techniques as well) over a wide variety of time series and forecasting horizons and intervals. (For a summary of these efforts, see Mentzer & Gomes, 1994.) To date, no FMTS technique has shown itself to be clearly superior to any of the other FMTS techniques across a wide variety of forecasting levels and time horizons. For this reason, it is recommended that FMTS users keep in mind where the general category of techniques works well and the time series scenario for which each technique was designed.

In general, FMTS techniques should be used when a limited amount of data is available on anything other than an actual history

Table 3.4   FMTS Technique Selection Guidelines

Time Series Component Characteristics	FMTS Technique
Stable Level, with No Trend or Seasonality	Exponential Smoothing
Changing Level, with No Trend or Seasonality	Adaptive Smoothing
Level and Trend	Exponential Smoothing with Trend
Level, Trend, and Seasonality	Exponential Smoothing with Trend and Seasonality
Changing Level, Trend, and Seasonal Patterns	AEES

of sales (that is, little data on outside factors such as price changes, economic activity, promotional programs, and so on). This lack of outside (exogenous) data precludes the use of regression (discussed in the next chapter). Further, FMTS techniques are useful when the time series components change fairly regularly. That is, the trend rate changes, the seasonal pattern changes, or the overall level of demand changes. FMTS is much more effective at adjusting to these changes in time series components than are the OMTS techniques to be discussed next, which require more data with stable time series components over a long period of time.

In terms of which FMTS to use in which situations, a general guideline is provided in Table 3.4. However, remember that these are only general guidelines, and it is best to incorporate these techniques into a system (such as the one discussed in Chapter 6) that allows the system to try each FMTS technique on each forecast to be made and select the one that works best in terms of accuracy.

With these general guidelines established, we will now move on to a discussion of the open-model time series (OMTS) techniques.

❖ OPEN-MODEL TIMES SERIES TECHNIQUES

Open-model time series (OMTS) techniques assume that the same components exist in any time series—level, trend, seasonality, and noise—but take a different approach to forecasting these components. Where FMTS techniques assume that certain components exist in the time series and use one set of formulae to forecast this series (that is, the formulae are "fixed"), OMTS techniques first analyze the components in the time series to see which exist and what is their nature. From this information, a set of forecasting formulae unique to that time series is built (that is, the formulae are "open" until the time series components are analyzed).

Various forms of OMTS exist, including decomposition analysis (Shiskin 1961a, 1961b), spectral analysis (Nelson, 1973), fourier analysis (Bloomfield, 1976), and auto-regressive moving average (ARMA) or Box-Jenkins analysis (Box & Jenkins, 1970). All of these OMTS techniques have in common the fact that they first try to analyze the time series to determine the components and, as a result, require a considerable amount of history before any forecasts can be made. For instance, many OMTS techniques recommend no less than 48 periods of data prior to using the technique. Obviously, this is a disadvantage for situations where a limited amount of history is available.

OMTS techniques also have in common the need for considerable understanding of quantitative methods to properly use the techniques. The analysis with OMTS can become quite complex and require considerable input from the forecaster. For these reasons (large data requirements and considerable user experience), OMTS techniques have seen limited use in practice (Mentzer & Kahn, 1995; Mentzer & Cox, 1984a). Improvements in systems technology have made OMTS techniques easier to use (as we will see in Chapter 6), but the data requirements still limit their use.

As with FMTS techniques, there is no evidence that the performance of one of these OMTS techniques is clearly superior to any of the others. Thus, we will again only discuss the simplest of the OMTS techniques here. This technique is called decomposition analysis. To demonstrate decomposition analysis, we will use the time series presented at the beginning of the chapter in Figure 3.1.

Like all OMTS techniques, the purpose of decomposition analysis is to decompose the data into its time series components. The first step in doing this is to remove noise and seasonality from the original time series. As we discussed earlier in the chapter, one of the characteristics of a moving average is that it dampens out any noise and dampens out any regular pattern of fluctuation that has a pattern length that is equal to the number of periods in the moving average. Thus, one of the first things we have to do in decomposition analysis is make a judgment about how long the seasonal pattern is.

Visual examination of Figure 3.1 will, we hope, lead us to conclude that the seasonal pattern takes 12 months. Therefore, a 12-month moving average should remove noise and seasonality from the time series. As in the discussion earlier in the chapter, the value of the moving average in any given period is our estimate of level, and how much that level estimate changes from one period to the next is our estimate of trend. However, because our purpose here is not to forecast, but to decompose the data, we will perform this moving average calculation in a slightly different way than previously discussed. This calculation is as follows:

$$MA_t = (S_{t-5} + S_{t-4} + S_{t-3} + S_{t-2} + S_{t-1} + S_t + S_{t+1} + \\ S_{t+2} + S_{t+3} + S_{t+4} + S_{t+5} + S_{t+6}) / 12$$

Notice that this is a *centered moving average*, which means that we take an average of 12 months and assign that value to the month in the center. The purpose of this is to find a more accurate estimate of the level. If we placed the moving average value at the end of the 12 months used in the calculation, it would have too much old data (lower trend) to accurately represent the level for that period. Conversely, if we place the moving average value at the beginning of the 12 months used in the calculation, it would have too much new data (higher trend) to actually represent the level at that period. Thus, the best place to position this estimate of level is in the center of the periods used in its calculation.

Because this moving average contains the level and the trend, we can simply take the difference between each period to determine the trend. Similarly, since the moving average contains the level and the trend, if we subtract it from the original time series (which contained level, trend, seasonality, and noise), the result is a series of data that contains only the seasonality and the noise. These calculations are demonstrated in Table 3.5.

We now have decomposed the original time series into the level and the trend. All that is left is to remove the noise from the data series containing seasonality and noise, and we will have our final component, seasonality. Again, to remove noise we use an average. However, because each month of the year represents a different season, we want to perform this average calculation within each season. Thus, we take all the January values and average them, then take an average of all the February values, and so on for all 12 months. This calculation is shown

Table 3.5   Decomposition Analysis

Month	Demand	Level and Trend	Trend	Seasonality and Noise	Seasonality	Forecast
J01	1104					
F01	885					
M01	976					
A01	1101					
M01	1120					
J01	1276	1376		−100	−140	
J01	1419	1411	35	8	60	
A01	1615	1463	52	152	261	
S01	1836	1505	42	331	325	
O01	1730	1536	32	194	200	
N01	1686	1587	51	99	204	
D01	1769	1627	40	142	165	
J02	1521	1687	60	−166	−203	
F02	1504	1755	68	−251	−308	
M02	1478	1804	49	−326	−396	
A02	1480	1856	52	−376	−440	
M02	1726	1924	68	−198	−258	
J02	1759	1980	56	−221	−140	
J02	2137	2026	46	111	60	
A02	2436	2067	41	370	261	
S02	2425	2107	40	319	325	
O02	2355	2149	43	206	200	
N02	2499	2190	41	309	204	
D02	2442	2254	64	188	165	
J03	2069	2309	54	−240	−203	
F03	1992	2357	48	−365	−308	
M03	1958	2424	67	−466	−396	
A03	1990	2494	70	−504	−440	
M03	2222	2539	44	−317	−258	
J03	2525	2584	45	−59	−140	
J03	2789		45		60	
A03	3017		90		261	
S03	3232		135		325	
O03	3198		180		200	
N03	3028		225		204	
D03	2985		270		165	
J04			315		−203	2696

Table 3.6   Decomposition of Seasonality

Month	2001	2002	2003	Average
January		−166	−240	−203
February		−251	−365	−308
March		−326	−466	−396
April		−376	−504	−440
May		−198	−317	−258
June	−100	−221	−59	−140
July	8	111		60
August	152	370		261
September	331	319		325
October	194	206		200
November	99	309		204
December	142	188		165

in Table 3.6, and the resultant values are added to Table 3.5 in the Seasonality column. Notice that this is not a *multiplicative seasonal adjustment* like we used in FMTS. Rather, it is an *additive seasonal adjustment;* to determine the seasonal adjustment, we add it to (not multiply it by) the level plus trend.

We now have our most recent estimate of level (2,584 in June 2003), our most recent estimate of trend (45 units per month from June 2003), and our most recent estimates of the additive seasonal adjustments for the last 12 months. To forecast a future period (such as January 2004), we take the last estimate of level and add to it the trend times the number of periods into the future. To this value, we add the seasonal adjustment. For January 2004, the calculation is:

$$\text{Forecast}_{\text{Jan04}} = \text{Level}_{\text{June03}} + (7 \times \text{Trend}_{\text{June03}}) + \text{Seasonality}_{\text{Jan03}}$$
$$= 2584 + (7 \times 45) - 203 = 2696$$

This example illustrates just how much data are required to complete OMTS analysis. Although we have 3 years of monthly data in this example, for all but June, only two values were available to estimate the seasonality adjustment for each season (month). With another year's data, three values would be available for each season, which should improve the seasonality adjustment estimates. However, one of the primary drawbacks to OMTS is this dependency on a large amount of data.

❖ SUMMARY

In this chapter, we have covered a number of time series techniques. All have in common a recognition of the time series components—level, trend, seasonality, noise. FMTS techniques deal with these components by assuming certain components are (and are not) in the data, while OMTS techniques analyze the data to determine which components exist. This greater level of sophistication in OMTS is somewhat ameliorated by the considerable data requirements for analysis.

Another characteristic of all the techniques included in this chapter is the fact that they ignore other factors that might have influenced demand, such as price changes, advertising, trade promotions, sales programs, competitive actions, economic activity, and so on. In many cases, much of what time series techniques classify as noise can be explained by looking at these "exogenous" factors. In the next chapter, we turn our attention to regression analysis, a technique that considers these exogenous factors.

4

Regression Analysis

❖ ❖ ❖

During a visit to one company, we asked a sales forecasting analyst what modeling techniques were used to generate their forecasts. His reply was that he used regression analysis. When we asked what predictor variables were in the model, however, he said he did not know. He was equally uninformed about how the predictor variables were selected, if they ever changed, or how the forecast model was calculated. In fact, after a number of questions about the specifics of the model, his reply was, "It's just—you know—regression analysis." It probably comes as no surprise that both he and management were not very pleased with the forecasting results obtained from this rather uninformed approach to forecasting.

When used properly, regression analysis can provide considerable insight into the various factors that affect demand and, as a result, can be very useful in forecasting demand. However, regression models must be created and evaluated in an informed way to make certain they accomplish what they were intended to do—to accurately forecast product demand. Once evaluated, they must be assessed for generalizability, that is, their ability to continue to accurately forecast demand in the future.

❖ INTRODUCTION

As we discussed in the last chapter, what regression analysis provides that time series does not is an assessment of how outside factors are related to fluctuations in demand. This assessment is called a *correlation*, meaning how demand (which is called the dependent variable, since it is dependent on the values of the other factors) and these outside factors (called the independent, or predictor, variables) are correlated (or co-related). If we can find factors that are highly correlated to demand, then we can use the future values of those factors to forecast future demand.

Regression analysis accomplishes this assessment by building a regression model, which represents the relationship between the dependent variable (y) and a set of independent variables (x_i). This model is a mathematical equation of the general form:

$$y = \beta_0 + \beta_1 x_1 + \beta_2 x_2 + \cdots + \beta_k x_k \qquad (1)$$

The values of the β_i, the model parameters, are assumed to describe the "true" relationship (that is, the correlation) between the dependent variable (y) and each of the independent variables (x_i). Since we do not have perfect information, it is assumed that we cannot find the true values in equation (1). Rather, we will come up with an estimated model of the "true" model, using the data that are available to us. Using past data on the values of y and x_i, regression analysis generates estimates of the "true" model parameters. These estimates are designated as b_i:

$$\hat{y} = b_0 + b_1 x_1 + b_2 x_2 + \cdots + b_k x_k \qquad (2)$$

Regression analysis has a number of applications. Regression models may be used:

1. To explain the behavior of a system (understanding which factors are related to demand helps explain why demand fluctuates);

2. To discover the importance of certain factors within a system (of all the marketing inputs on which we can spend our money, which has the most effect on demand?); or

3. For forecasting (Myers, 1990).

When used in sales forecasting, the primary purpose of a regression model is prediction, not explanation.

Using regression analysis for forecasting demand requires an understanding of the process of creating and evaluating regression models. Using regression analysis without an understanding of these concepts is frustrating for the analyst and can lead to some costly mistakes. The forecaster in the example described at the beginning of this chapter was certainly frustrated with his inability to answer our questions about his regression model, but more importantly, he was frustrated with trying to employ a technique blindly. He also knew the model was leading to some decisions that were flawed.

The purpose of this chapter is to discuss how to create and evaluate regression models used for forecasting demand. Our objective is to provide a general understanding of the technique and to recommend guidelines and criteria for the evaluation of regression models that are meant for use in sales forecasting. To accomplish this, we first start with a straightforward discussion of how regression analysis works and the concept of R^2 as a measure of correlation. This is followed by a three-step procedure to develop regression analysis forecasting models. We conclude with a description of how regression analysis can be used to place a "confidence interval" around the forecast.

❖ HOW REGRESSION ANALYSIS WORKS

Conceptually, regression analysis is simply trying to find the best line to draw through a set of data. For instance, if we take the data in Figure 4.1a, we see that for each month's expenditures on promotions, we have also noted the sales that resulted. Figure 4.1a represents a set of what are called "matched pairs" data. That is, we have matched the promotional expenditures in a given month with the sales that resulted from those expenditures. Which months we match is a function of how long it takes the promotional expenditures to have an effect. If, for example, we think promotional expenditures this month affect sales next month, we will "lag" the data by one month, meaning we match promotional expenditures in each month with sales from the next month (one-month lag).

What regression analysis does mathematically is represented graphically in Figure 4.1b; regression analysis tries to find the one line that most closely "fits" the data. In the case of regression analysis, fit is defined as finding the one line through the data that minimizes the mean squared error, or minimizes the sum total of the distance of each data point from the line.

Figure 4.1   How Regression Analysis Works

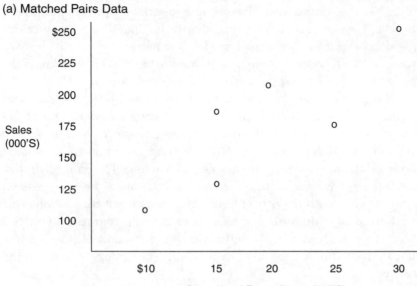

(a) Matched Pairs Data

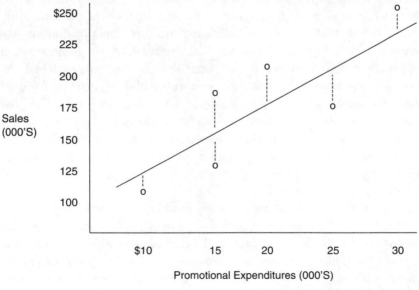

(b) Regression Line

But how does this tell us anything about the correlation between sales and promotional expenditures? The answer to this is in a statistic called the coefficient of determination, or R^2. If we knew nothing about the relationship between sales and promotional expenditures (and no other information, for that matter), the best forecast of any future value of sales would be the average (just like it was our starting point in the last chapter). This best forecast of sales, regardless of the level of promotional expenditures (since we start off believing that sales and promotional expenditures are not related), is the average and is represented graphically by the horizontal line in Figure 4.2.

However, once we have conducted regression analysis and found the line that was illustrated in Figure 4.1b (now shown graphically as the line $\hat{y} = b_0 + b_1x_1$ in Figure 4.2), we see that increases in promotional expenditures lead to increases in sales. Notice also that the regression line goes through the point that is the average of both sales (y) and promotional expenditures (x). Mathematically, this has to happen since regression analysis is designed to determine whether y is above or below its average when x is above or below its average. In other words, regression analysis tells you whether the relationship between x and y is positive (when x is above its average, y is above its average, and when x is below its average, y is below its average) or negative (when x is above its average, y is below its average, and when x is below its average, y is above its average).

For any given observation (Point P), we can observe what sales were given the matched value of promotional expenditures. The difference between this point and the average value of y is called the *total variation*, or the total amount that the actual value varies from the simple average as the forecast. The distance from the average to the regression model forecast value of y ($\hat{y}$) is called the *explained variation*, or the amount of the variation of the actual sales value from the average that is explained by the relationship between sales and promotional expenditures (the regression model). If we take the average of the explained variation divided by the total variation for each sales value, we have a good estimate of the mathematical value of R^2.

The mathematical value of R^2 is between zero and one and tells us the percent of fluctuation in the dependent variable (sales) that is explained by the predictor variable (promotional expenditures). Incidentally, the sign of R (the square root of R^2) tells us whether the correlation between x and y is positive (as x goes up, y goes up) or negative (as x goes up, y goes down).

Figure 4.2   The Concept of R^2

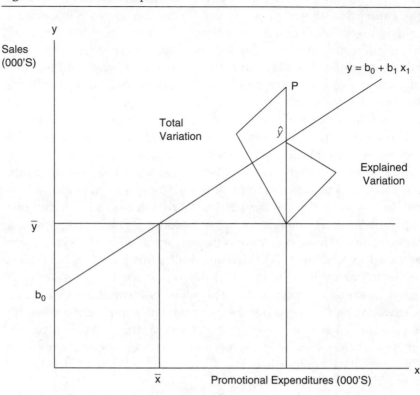

We will discuss later how to test whether the value of R^2 is significant enough to use promotional expenditures to forecast sales. Conceptually, however, this significance means how different the regression equation in Figure 4.2 is from the horizontal line. If the line, $\hat{y} = b_0 + b_1 x_1$, is not significantly different than a horizontal line, there is no reason to conclude that the best estimate of y is not still its average, regardless of the value of x. This means there is no co-relation between x and y, and x should not be used to forecast y.

Before we go on, we must introduce the concept of *multiple regression*. The illustrations in Figures 4.1 and 4.2 are *simple regression*, meaning that only one independent variable is used to forecast the dependent variable. In multiple regression, we use two or more independent variables to forecast the dependent variable (as in equation 2). The concepts just discussed are the same for multiple regression as they are for simple regression, but it gets a bit difficult to provide an illustration.

The only additional concept that needs to be introduced for multiple regression is *multicollinearity*. This rather daunting term simply means that not only are the independent variables correlated to the dependent variable, but they are also correlated to each other. Since the purpose of regression analysis is to explain the variation in the dependent variable with the independent variables, we do not want independent variables that are correlated to each other. If this multi-collinearity exists, then the independent variables may all be explaining the same part of the fluctuation in sales, and each independent variable adds little to the overall accuracy of the regression model after the first independent variable. If each new independent variable is not correlated with the other independent variable, then whatever part of the fluctuation in sales it explains is new to the forecast model and should improve forecasting accuracy. Thus, we want to minimize multicollinearity. As with the significance of R^2, how to test for multi-collinearity is discussed later in the recommended process for using regression analysis for forecasting.

❖ THE PROCESS OF REGRESSION ANALYSIS FOR FORECASTING

Creation and evaluation of regression models for use in sales forecasting involves three steps: generating a set of potential predictor variables (variable selection); constructing a regression model by assessing subsets of the selected predictor variables (model construction); and validating the final model by evaluating the generalizibility of its predictive ability (model validation).

During variable selection, factors (predictor variables) are chosen for their presumed usefulness in forecasting demand. Model construction consists of evaluating subsets of potential predictor variables and selecting the subset we believe comprises the "best" regression model. Model validation involves evaluating a model for its generalizability (Myers, 1990; Stevens, 1992). In a forecasting context, a generalizable or valid model will accurately forecast demand when new data on the predictor variables are used in the model (that is, data other than those used to formulate the model). Figure 4.3 contains a flowchart summarizing these three steps.

Figure 4.3   The Process of Regression Analysis

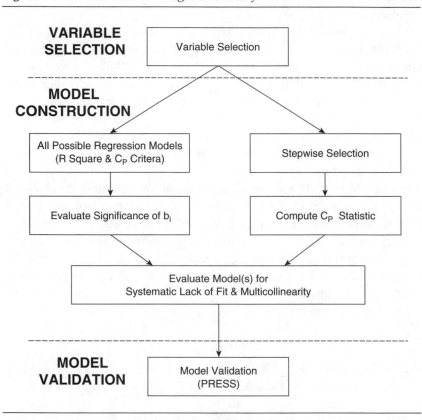

Although this discussion on predictor variable selection, model construction, and model validation may give the impression that these three procedures are conducted in a sequential fashion, this is not necessarily the case. In the first place, the problems that variable selection, model construction, and model validation procedures are meant to detect do not always fit neatly into these three categories. For example, we may learn something about the forecasting environment during model validation that highlights requirements for additional predictor variables that are different from those we first chose.

In addition, the various criteria used for predictor variable selection, model construction, and model validation will not always agree on what constitutes the "best" model. Because of the relationships among the criteria used for these three procedures, the process of creating and evaluating a regression model may not always proceed sequentially. For instance, a set of potential predictor variables may be generated and a model constructed consisting of a subset of those predictors. However, the model may encounter difficulties during model validation procedures (that is, the model construction went well, but the model does not work well with new data), causing the predictor variable selection procedure or the model construction procedure to be reexamined.

Variable Selection

If we wanted to use regression analysis to generate a demand forecast, how would we come up with the factors for the model to use to forecast (predict) demand, that is, the predictor variables?

Although criteria for model construction and model validation are largely quantitative, guidelines for generating a set of potential predictor variables for forecasting demand are, of necessity, qualitative. That is because the single most important tool available to us as we begin the process of creating a regression model is our own expertise (Stevens, 1992); that is, our knowledge of the factors that we believe influence the demand for our products. Statistical techniques used during model construction and model validation cannot replace this understanding, for the simple reason that it is up to you to initially produce a set of variables from which to select a subset that will comprise your model. Quantitative techniques cannot generate these initial variables; they can only evaluate the subsets and combinations of them.

As you begin to think about which variables should be in your regression model, you should constantly ask yourself, "Given what I know about the demand for this product line or brand, what factors are likely to affect that demand?" The primary source of information on variables that should be included in your model is the experience of people familiar with the nature of the demand for the product(s). Other possible sources include models that have been constructed previously for the product(s), models constructed to predict demand for similar products, and information on predictor variables used by other firms or trade groups in your industry.

When attempting to predict product demand, do not ignore the possibility of using "dummy variables." These are predictor variables that are qualitative or categorical, rather than quantitative, in nature. Dummy variables, such as the presence (denoted by a value of 1) or absence (denoted by a value of 0) of a sales promotion, can be effective when combined with quantitative variables to model product demand.

Finally, after you have selected the predictor variables you want to use in constructing your model, you must determine whether data on this variable is actually available. Without complete data on a predictor variable, it is unlikely to survive the next step, model construction.

Model Construction

Once you have generated a set of potential predictors for your proposed regression model, you must determine which subset of those predictors yields the "best" model. An important point to remember, however, is that there are likely to be a number of models that will do an adequate job (Myers, 1990; Stevens, 1992). Our job is to pick the best of these adequate models. An effective strategy to do this during model construction is the following two-step procedure:

- Use a computer routine to generate a candidate model or a set of candidate models.
- Evaluate the candidate model(s) through the use of additional regression diagnostics to yield a preliminary model (Stevens, 1992).

Once these two steps are completed, the preliminary model can be subjected to model validation procedures to ascertain the generalizability of its predictive ability.

Generating Candidate Models

There are two procedures recommended for generating a set of candidate models: *All Possible Regression Models* and *Stepwise selection*. Since each works equally well, we present both here so the reader can pick the most comfortable procedure.

All Possible Regression Models. This procedure consists of examining all the possible models for a set of predictor variables. For example, if we identified variables A, B, C, and D as possible predictor variables, we would test the following variable combinations as potential regression models:

1. A

2. B

3. C

4. D

5. AB

6. AC

7. AD

8. BC

9. BD

10. CD

11. ABC

12. ABD

13. ACD

14. BCD

15. ABCD

When using a computer routine, the output obtained generally presents models sorted from best to worst on the specified criteria.[1] Usually, there will be a small number of models that appear near the top of each set of sorted models (Stevens, 1992). Although there are a number of criteria that can be used to examine (and sort) all of the possible models that can be formed from a given set of predictors, the criteria discussed below are good choices because they enable a range of model attributes to be evaluated.

The first criterion that is useful for model evaluation is R^2, the *Coefficient of Determination*, which (as we discussed earlier) indicates the proportion of variation in the dependent variable that is explained by the regression model. For example, if you are trying to predict product demand:

$$R^2 = \frac{\text{Variation in Product Demand Explained by the Model}}{\text{Total Variation in Product Demand Around the Average}} \quad (3)$$

The value of R^2 varies between 0 and 1; but the closer the value is to 1, the greater the proportion of the variation in product demand the regression model explains. Obviously, the more variation in product

124   SALES FORECASTING MANAGEMENT

demand you are able to explain with your model, the better. However, one problem with using only R^2 to select which predictor variables belong in your model is that adding predictor variables to a model always increases the R^2, even if the additional predictor variables do not add significantly to the ability of the model to forecast demand.

An additional consideration regarding R^2 is that this statistic tends to overestimate the proportion of variation in product demand explained by a regression model. The reason for this overestimation is that the proportion of variance explained (R^2) is computed using the model that has been fitted to a specific data set, that is, the data set that was used to construct the regression model (Pedhazur, 1982; Stevens, 1992). However, once you have constructed a regression model, you want to forecast demand using new, perhaps more accurate or timely data. The Adjusted R^2 (which is calculated and printed by most computer programs) attempts to correct the overly optimistic estimation of the proportion of variance explained by R^2. That is, the Adjusted R^2 is an attempt to more closely represent the proportion of variation product demand that would be explained if data other than that used to construct the model were used to forecast demand.

Although both R^2 and Adjusted R^2 are useful criteria for evaluating regression models, they need to be combined with additional criteria for model evaluation, since the proportion of variance in product demand is not the only consideration when constructing a model to forecast the dependent variable (Myers, 1990; Ott, 1988). Two additional model evaluation issues are: whether or not the model is generating unbiased forecasts; and the stability of the forecasts generated by the model.

Mallow's C_p (also known as Mallow's C and Mallow's C_k) makes it possible to evaluate both these aspects of the model's ability to accurately forecast demand: *model bias* and *model stability* (Myers, 1990; Stevens, 1992). The value of C_p indicates the degree to which the model tends to overforecast or underforecast demand, that is, the extent of *model bias*. An important source of bias in regression models is underfitting the model, that is, not including a sufficient number of predictor variables in the model. If a regression model is biased, it lacks accuracy, which limits its usefulness in forecasting demand.

The C_p statistic also gives an indication of *model stability*. Model stability addresses the consistency or precision of the model's forecasts. Including too many predictor variables in a regression model causes the model's forecasts to be unstable or imprecise. Like model bias, lack of model stability can limit the value of a regression model that is used for forecasting. The C_p statistic increases as the amount of bias and/or variability in the regression model increases. Models that have C_p values approximately equal to the number of predictor variables (k) in the model ($C_p \approx k$) are preferred over models having C_p values greater than the number of predictor variables in the model ($C_p > k$) (Stevens, 1992). For example, consider the following two regression models:

(a) $\hat{y} = 153.39 + 5.29x_1 + 0.98x_2 - 3.25x_3$ $\qquad\qquad$ $C_p = 2.92$

(b) $\hat{y} = 293.31 + 1.30x_1 + 2.84x_2 - 5.88x_3 + 37.53x_4$ $\qquad$ $C_p = 8.16$

Model (a) would be preferred over Model (b) because Model (a)'s C_p (2.92) is closer to the number of predictor variables (k) in the model. For Model (a), k = 3 and C_p = 2.92, consequently, $C_p \approx k$. However, for Model (b), k = 4 and C_p = 8.16, making $C_p > k$, and Model (b) less useful as a forecasting model.[2]

The third criterion used to evaluate candidate models generated using the All Possible Regression Models procedure is *statistical significance* of the regression estimates. Statistical significance of the regression estimates (b_i in equation [2]) for each candidate model can be evaluated by testing how much the values of b_i differ from zero. Referring back to Figure 4.2, we can see that the value of b_i (the slope) in the horizontal line is zero. The value of b_1 only takes on a value other than zero when there is a relationship between x_1 and y. We can test whether each b_i is sufficiently different from zero to believe there is a relationship between x_i and y. We do this by entering the predictor variables for each model into a regression procedure and checking the "t-value" for the estimate of the regression coefficient of that predictor variable.[3] The t-value for each variable will be zero if the value of b_i is zero and the t-value gets larger as b_i gets larger. Thus, the t-value for each variable tells us whether or not that predictor variable is sufficiently important for the prediction of the dependent variable in the model. As a general rule, any variable whose t-value is not greater than 1.65 should be deleted as a predictor variable (Ott, 1988).

Stepwise Selection. Stepwise selection is one of a group of sequential procedures for automatically selecting the best model for forecasting a dependent variable (demand). These sequential procedures were designed to explore sets of possible predictor variables using the most efficient computation techniques (Myers, 1990). Although there are several sequential selection procedures available, Stepwise selection is the only one of these procedures that considers the effects of multi-collinearity in selecting which predictor variables to include in the regression model (Myers, 1990; Stevens, 1992), so it is the one discussed here.[4]

Stepwise selection sequentially enters predictor variables into the regression model based on each variable's ability to contribute to the prediction of the dependent variable (e.g., demand).[5] At each stage in the analysis—that is, as each new predictor variable enters the model—variables currently in the model are re-evaluated for their contribution to the prediction of the dependent variable. Due to this re-evaluation at each stage of the analysis, the possibility exists for variables in the model to be deleted. The ability of variables to enter and leave the model is an important advantage of the Stepwise technique. Different combinations of predictor variables behave differently in their ability to predict the dependent variable. Therefore, it is important to be able to delete variables that lose their effectiveness in the model (Cohen & Cohen, 1983; Ott, 1988; Stevens, 1992).

Although it is widely available in computer programs, the limitations of Stepwise selection are threefold:

1. Stepwise selection proposes a "best" candidate model, when in fact there is likely to be a set of good models, instead of just one "best" model;

2. Stepwise selection does not consider predictor variables on criteria other than their ability to explain variance in the dependent variable (that is, their contribution to R^2);

3. Stepwise selection tends to result in a model that is data specific; that is, a model that will work well with the data set that is used to estimate the model's parameters (Myers, 1990; Ott, 1988; Stevens, 1992), but not necessarily a model that will work well in the future.

The last limitation is especially problematic if the regression model is to be used with different data sets for forecasting demand. For this reason, it is particularly important to validate Stepwise regression models to assure that these models can predict accurately and consistently using data other than the data used to estimate the model.

As a step toward this assurance, if a Stepwise selection technique is used to generate a candidate model, the C_p statistic for the model should still be computed and compared to the value for k (the number of predictor variables in the model) to verify that $C_p \approx k$ before proceeding with further evaluation of the model.

Once a "best" model is selected using a Stepwise selection technique or a set of candidate models is selected using All Possible Regression Models, additional evaluation is required to investigate the model formulation and the relationships among the predictor variables.

❖ FURTHER EVALUATION OF CANDIDATE MODELS

Regardless of whether the All Possible Regression Models or the Stepwise approach was taken to this point in model construction, there are two additional issues that, due to their potential impact on the predictive ability of the regression model, should be investigated prior to validating the candidate model(s). This section discusses how to evaluate candidate models for:

- The presence of systematic lack of "fit" between the model and the data; and
- The presence of large and/or multiple intercorrelations among the predictor variables.

Systematic Lack of Fit. The first issue, a systematic lack of fit between the model and the data, is important to investigate because this suggests that the model may not be formulated correctly. Problems with model formulation are caused by:

- Assuming an incorrect model formulation for the relationship between the dependent variable and the predictor variables.
- The presence of non-constant variance.

The first source of systematic lack of fit arises as a result of the form of the equation assumed to represent the relationship between the dependent variable (what is being predicted) and the predictor variables. The general form of a multiple regression model assumes that the relationship between what is being predicted (the dependent variable, y) and the predictor variables (the independent variables, the x_i) can be represented by a "first order" (or linear) equation (Equation [1]), described below and graphically represented in Figure 4.4a.

$$y = \beta_0 + \beta_1 x_1 + \beta_2 x_2 + \cdots + \beta_k x_k$$

Figure 4.5   Plots of Standardized Residuals Versus Predicted Values of y

(a) Residual Plot of Valid Model Formulation

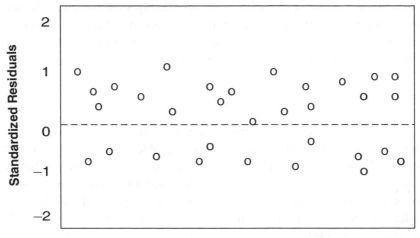

(b) Residual Plot of Invalid Model Formulation

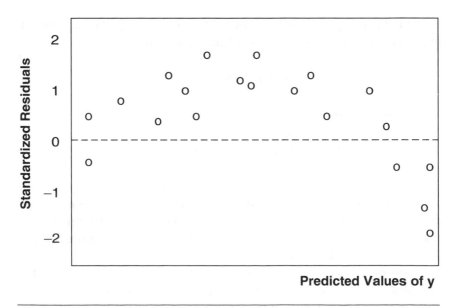

depicts a residual plot for a regression model with no model formulation problems. The standardized residuals are scattered randomly around the line passing though 0 (that is, there is no pattern related to the value of y), and all values are between −2 and +2. Figure 4.5b depicts a residual plot for a regression model that portrays a systematic pattern, suggesting that the model is doing a poor job of forecasting the dependent variable. This suggests that the model should be reformulated, perhaps using a curvilinear (that is, second order) model.

If an examination of the residual plots of any candidate model or models reveals such systematic patterns, suggesting that forecasting demand with this model may be very inaccurate for certain values, then an exploration of a curvilinear model formulation may be worth considering (Pedhazur & Schmelkin, 1991; Ott, 1988),[7] which puts us back at the beginning of the model construction stage for this new, curvilinear model.

The second source of systematic lack of fit for a regression model is the presence of non-constant variance in the data used to estimate the regression coefficients. This means that the degree of variability in the residuals changes, depending on the value of the dependent variable (y). The degree of variability in the residuals should be the same, no matter what the value of y (Myers, 1990; Stevens, 1992). The rather intimidating term for this constant variability is homoscedasticity.

The way to detect the presence of non-constant variance (heteroscedasticity) is, again, by examining the residual plots discussed above. Figure 4.6a shows a residual plot with constant variance, that is, the residual terms are spread out equally around the 0 line. Figure 4.6b shows a residual plot with non-constant variance. In this case, the variance increases as the value of the predicted dependent variable increases.

If non-constant variance is present, the consequences are similar to the consequences of incorrect model formulation. At certain values of the dependent variable (e.g., for high or low levels of demand), the model will not accurately forecast the dependent variable. If the residual plot of the candidate model shows a pattern of non-constant variance, transforming the data (such as converting data values to their logarithm or square root) could be a solution to the problem, facilitating the model's predictive ability.[8] Alternately, we may simply want to turn to a different candidate model that does not exhibit heteroscedasticity.

Figure 4.6   Plots of Standardized Residuals Versus Predicted Values of y

(a) Residual Plot of Constant Variances

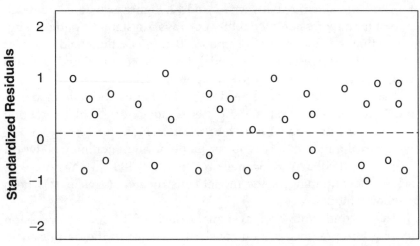

(b) Residual Plot of Non-Constant Variance

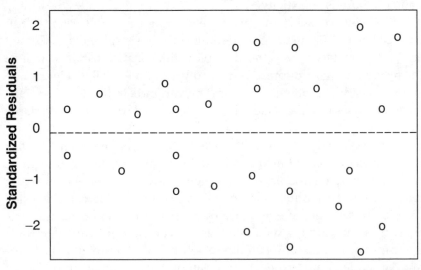

Inter-Correlations Among Predictor Variables. The second issue for which candidate models should be evaluated is the presence of inter-correlations among the predictor variables. As we introduced earlier, the presence of moderate to high correlations among the predictor variables is known as multicollinearity. In a regression model used to make forecasts, multicollinearity can: 1) increase the variance for the estimates of the regression parameters (the b_i), causing the forecasts made by the model to be unstable or inconsistent; and/or 2) limit the accuracy of R^2 (Stevens, 1992).

To evaluate whether multicollinearity is a problem in candidate models, we need to compute a Variance Inflation Factor (VIF) for each regression estimate (i.e., for each b_i).[9] In the absence of multi-collinearity, each VIF is equal to 1. However, since some multi-collinearity always exists, this is an unrealistic benchmark for sales forecasting. VIFs increase as multicollinearity increases. As a rule of thumb, a VIF of 10 or greater indicates that an unacceptable level of multicollinearity exists among the predictor variables (Myers, 1990).

If the VIF indicates that there is too much correlation among the predictor variables, remedies include:

- Deleting predictor variables with high VIFs.
- Combining sets of correlated predictor variables into a single measure (an index) (Stevens, 1992).

As an example of the first remedy, suppose we found that among our model's predictor variables, x_1 has a VIF of 25, while all other VIFs are below 10. We could merely delete x_1 from the model. The second remedy requires that we ascertain which predictor variables are mod-erately to highly correlated.[10] An analysis of the VIFs, along with a determination of which predictor variables have correlations that are significant, guides the decision of which predictor variables to replace with an index. An index is a predictor variable that is equal to the combination (that is, the sum or the average) of a group of predictor variables that are highly intercorrelated (Stevens, 1992).

At this point, we have selected a group of predictor variables (**Variable Selection**), investigated which combination(s) of predictor variables to use in our regression model, and examined those models for the presence of model formulation errors and multicollinearity to yield a preliminary model or models (**Model Construction**). The final step is validation of the preliminary model(s).

❖ MODEL VALIDATION

If a regression model used for forecasting is valid, we should have some assurance that it will forecast demand, using data other than that which were used to create the original model. For example, assume a model has been created using 2003 data on household size and home loan interest rates to forecast demand for a line of residential lighting fixtures. When 2004 data on household size and interest rates become available, will the model be able to accurately forecast demand for that product line, or is the model only accurate using the original data, that is, the data that were used to create the model?

Model validation can be assessed by computing the PRESS (Predicted REsidual Sum of Squares) statistic for each model under consideration. PRESS is calculated by removing each period in the data and re-computing the regression estimates (b_i) for the model. Using these regression estimates, the squared residual for that period (the squared difference between the forecast dependent variable for that period ($\hat{y}_i^*$) and the actual value of the dependent variable in the data set (y_i)) is calculated.[11]

$$\text{Squared PRESS residual for case}_i = (y_i - (\hat{y}_i^*))^2 \qquad (7)$$

This is done successively for each period (i) in the data set ($i = 1 \ldots n$) and the squared residuals are added together to find the PRESS statistic.

$$\text{PRESS} = \sum_{i=1}^{n} (y_i - (\hat{y}_i^*))^2 \qquad (8)$$

The PRESS statistic provides an estimate of how well the model fits when forecasts are obtained for data that were not used to compute the original regression estimates. There is no rule of thumb for the appropriate value of the PRESS statistic when evaluating only one model. The most valid way to apply this statistic is to compare PRESS statistics for more than one model, choosing the model with the smallest PRESS statistic (Myers, 1990; Stevens, 1992).

To clarify this overall process, the next section provides an example of regression model construction and validation, using both the All Possible Regression Models and the Stepwise approaches.

❖ AN EXAMPLE

Suppose we are trying to forecast the demand for residential lighting fixtures. Based on experience with this product, the factors we believe will be significant in forecasting demand include: average number of days of sunshine per year, housing starts for custom homes, the interest rates on home loans, and average household size.

Using data on the dependent variable (y = sales of residential lighting fixtures) and the predictor variables (x_1 = SUN; x_2 = CUSTOM; x_3 = INTEREST; and x_4 = SIZE), all possible regression models are computed. Models are sorted by R^2, and the C_p is computed for each model. Although all possible combinations of SUN, CUSTOM, INTEREST, and SIZE were tested, Table 4.1 contains only the three models that rated highly on both the R^2 and the C_p criteria. These three models have among the highest R^2 values of all the possible models and for all three models, $C_p \approx k$ (Model (1): $C_p = 3.02$ and $k = 4$; Model (2): $C_p = 2.14$, and $k = 3$; Model (3): $C_p = 0.94$ and $k = 2$).

The next step is to evaluate the significance of the predictor variables in the three candidate models. Each set of predictor variables is entered into a regression analysis procedure. Tables 4.2a, 4.2b, and 4.2c contain the results of the significance testing on the three candidate models. Tables 4.2a and 4.2b indicate that neither x_1 (SUN) nor x_3 (INTEREST) contributes significantly to the prediction of y (demand for lighting fixtures); that is, the t-values for each of these variables are less than 1.65. However, both predictor variables (x_2, CUSTOM, and x_4,

Table 4.1   Three Regression Models

Model	r-square	C_p	press
(1) $y = 9.136 - 0.027x_1 - 0.269x_2 - 0.108x_3 + 0.505x_4$	0.478	3.02	579.70
(2) $y = 8.144 - 0.289x_2 - 0.079x_3 + 0.504x_4$	0.472	2.14	571.74
(3) $y = 6.575 - 0.252x_2 + 0.505x_4$	0.467	0.94	567.48

Table 4.2   Models (1), (2), & (3)

Variable	Regression Estimate (b_i)	T (significance)
SUN (x_1)	−0.027	−1.07*
CUSTOM (x_2)	−0.269	−2.72
INTEREST (x_3)	−0.108	−1.18*
SIZE (x_4)	0.505	8.47

TABLE 4.2a: Model (1)

CUSTOM (x_2)	−0.289	−2.98
INTEREST (x_3)	−0.079	−0.90*
SIZE (x_4)	0.504	8.45

TABLE 4.2b: Model (2)

CUSTOM (x_2)	−0.252	−2.89
SIZE (x_4)	0.505	8.48

TABLE 4.2c: Model (3)

---

*t-value < 1.65; variable does not contribute significantly to prediction

SIZE) in Model (3) (Table 4.2c) have t-values greater than 1.65, indicating that both variables contribute significantly to predicting the demand for lighting fixtures. Thus, Model (3) will be further evaluated for systematic lack of fit and multicollinearity.

A residual plot for Model (3) produced in Figure 4.7 indicates no evidence of systematic lack of fit, since the data points are randomly distributed around the horizontal line passing through 0. The VIF values for the predictor variables CUSTOM and SIZE appear in Table 4.3. Both VIF are less than 10, indicating that multicollinearity is not substantially affecting model estimation for Model (3).

For the sake of comparison, PRESS statistics for Models (1), (2), and (3) were computed (Table 4.1). Although all three of the Models

Figure 4.7   Residual Plot for Lighting Fixture Model

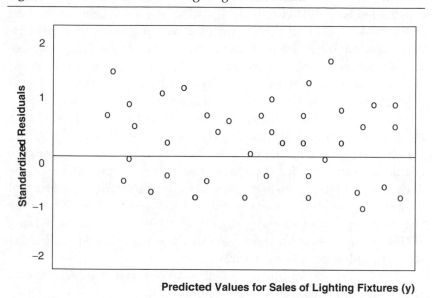

Predicted Values for Sales of Lighting Fixtures (y)

Table 4.3   VIF For Model (3)

Variable	VIF
custom (x_2)	1.024
size (x_4)	1.024

had similar PRESS statistics, PRESS for Model (3), at 567.48 was the smallest of the three. In fact the PRESS statistic for Model (3) was the smallest PRESS for any of the regression models tested. This comparatively small PRESS statistic for Model (3) indicates that it is the best of the models tested in terms of model validity, or most likely to forecast accurately with new data.

Based on the data analyses portrayed in this example, the best model to forecast demand for household lighting fixtures is Model (3):

$$\text{Residential Lighting Fixture Sales} = 6.057 - (0.252 \times \text{CUSTOM}) + (0.505 \times \text{SIZE})$$

This, of course, does not mean that a better model might not be constructed with different predictor variables, but Model (3) is the best of the models that could be constructed with the four variables originally selected. If the resultant model from this process is not satisfactory (in terms of ongoing accuracy evaluation with MAPE or other measures of accuracy discussed in Chapter 2), data on additional variables can be gathered and new models constructed.

For the purposes of illustration, the same data are used to develop a regression model using the Stepwise approach. The four predictor variables (x_1 = SUN; x_2 = CUSTOM; x_3 = INTEREST; and x_4 = SIZE) are evaluated, stepwise, for their contribution to the prediction of the dependent variable (sales of residential lighting fixtures). The results of the Stepwise analysis appear in Table 4.4. The model chosen by the Stepwise approach uses the predictor variables of CUSTOM (x_2) and SIZE (x_4)—the same two chosen in our previous example—to predict sales of residential lighting fixtures.

The C_p statistic for this model is calculated as 0.94 (see Table 4.4). Since the number of predictor variables in this model is equal to 2 ($k = 2$) and the model's $C_p \approx k$, this model is neither biased nor unstable. Further evaluation of the model chosen by the Stepwise approach reveals no evidence of a systematic lack of fit, since the data points are randomly distributed around the horizontal line passing through 0 in the residual plot (see Figure 4.7). In addition, the VIF values for the predictor variables CUSTOM and SIZE (see Table 4.4) reveal that both VIF are less than 10, indicating that significant multicollinearity is not present in the predictor variables of the model.

Finally, the PRESS statistic for the model chosen using the Stepwise approach is calculated as 567.48 (see Table 4.4). As the discussion of the PRESS statistic above indicated, the PRESS statistic is best evaluated by comparing the PRESS statistics for multiple models. This ability to compare multiple models is an advantage of the All Possible Regression Models approach. If the Stepwise approach is followed for model construction, the PRESS statistics should be recalculated as new data become available for the predictor and dependent variables. Increases in the PRESS statistic could indicate potential problems with model validity (generalizability).

The model generated using the Stepwise approach appears below:

$$\text{Residential Lighting Fixture Sales} = 6.057 - 0.252\text{CUSTOM}$$
$$+ 0.505\text{SIZE}$$

Table 4.4   Results of Stepwise Regression Approach

Variable	Regression Estimate (b_i)	T (significance)	VIF	MODEL C_p	MODEL PRESS	MODEL R-SQUARE
CONSTANT	6.575	5.31		0.94	567.48	0.467
CUSTOM (x_2)	−0.252	−2.86	1.024			
SIZE (x_4)	0.505	8.47	1.024			

Although not always the case, in this example both the All Possible Regression Models and the Stepwise approaches yield the same model. As the discussion earlier in the chapter indicated, an advantage of the All Possible Regression Models approach is the ability to view and examine a number of candidate models.

❖ CONCLUSION

In this chapter, we discussed how to create and evaluate regression models used for forecasting demand. To facilitate discussion and understanding, the process of model creation and evaluation was divided into three steps: variable generation, model construction, and model validation. For each step, we provided criteria that are important to consider for regression models used in sales forecasting. Finally, example analyses illustrated both model creation and evaluation processes.

In concluding this chapter, two limitations and one warning about regression analysis should be mentioned. Although regression analysis is a powerful statistical approach that can be brought to bear on a forecasting problem, regression analysis requires a large amount of data to produce a reliable model. A good rule of thumb is that at least five observations should be available for every variable in a regression model. Since the dependent variable also counts as a variable, this means for model construction with the variables we had in our example (SALES OF RESIDENTIAL LIGHTING FIXTURES, CUSTOM, SIZE, SUN, INTEREST) we should have at least 25 periods of data (5 variables times 5) before starting our analysis (before we leave the variable selection stage in Figure 4.3). This assumes that over the last two years, the relationships between the dependent and independent variables have remained stable. This is often a restrictive assumption for the use of regression analysis.

The second limitation is the fact that regression analysis does not consider seasonality as a cause of fluctuations in demand unless a seasonal predictor variable is entered in the variable selection stage. Since sales can vary from season to season, the effect of other predictor variables on sales may vary (thus violating our first limitation). For these reasons, it is often important to either include a seasonality variable in the selection process or "deseasonalize" the dependent variable before starting the entire process.

The warning that should always accompany any discussion of regression analysis is that regression analysis tells us the *correlation* between the dependent variable and the predictor variables, but it **does not** tell us whether *causality* exists. In fact, regression analysis is often incorrectly referred to as "causal forecasting" or "causal analysis." It is neither.

When two variables vary in a similar pattern over time, regression analysis will reveal that they are correlated, even when there is no true cause and effect relationship between them. The only way to tell whether there is true cause and effect is through the application of logic:

1. First, is there correlation? If there is no correlation, then there cannot be causation.

2. Second, does the predictor variable always change before the dependent variable? If the answer is No, then the predictor variable is not *causing* the dependent variable.

3. Does it make logical sense that the dependent variable is caused by the predictor variable?

In fact, when the answer to the first question is "Yes" and the answer to either the second or the third question is "No," we have what is called *spurious correlation,* or a correlation between two variables that is accidental (they are correlated, but not causally linked). It is important in the first stage of Figure 4.3 to only select variables that we believe have a cause and effect relationship with sales. Otherwise, we may end up constructing a regression model for forecasting that has a high R^2, but is only a coincidence. When this accidental correlation changes in the future (and it will eventually change if there is no cause and effect relationship), our forecasting model will suddenly, and without warning, give us very inaccurate results.

With this warning and the limitations about data requirements and seasonality considerations kept in mind, regression analysis can be a very useful tool in our quest to forecast sales.

We have now examined:

1. Time series analysis, which tends to adapt quickly to changing level, trend, and seasonality, but does not consider external factors; and

2. Regression analysis, which considers external factors, but requires a considerable amount of data to perform the analyses discussed in this chapter.

What we have not considered to this point is how to incorporate experience into the forecasting process. Techniques that allow for experiential forecasting are called *qualitative techniques* and are the subjects of the next chapter.

❖ NOTES

1. The PROC RSQUARE procedure in SAS can be used to generate All Possible Regression Models, ranked according to R^2. Both SAS and SPSS compute R^2 and Adjusted R^2.

2. Mallow's C_p is available in both SAS and SPSS.

3. SPSS refers to the t-value as "T"; SAS refers to the t-value as "T for H0."

4. Multicollinearity is the presence of inter-correlations among the predictor variables, which make it difficult to determine the unique contribution that each predictor variable provides to the prediction of the dependent variable. Methods for determining the presence of multicollinearity among a set of predictor variables are discussed under **FURTHER EVALUATION OF CANDIDATE MODELS**.

5. Stepwise selection techniques are available in SAS (a trademark of SAS Institute, Inc.) and SPSS (a trademark of SPSS, Inc.).

6. Residual plots are available in SAS and SPSS.

7. SAS and SPSS allow higher order and/or linear regression model formulations to be specified.

8. A discussion of alternative model formulations and suggestions for data transformations can be found in Weisberg, S. *Applied Linear Regression.* New York: Wiley, 1985.

9. Variance Inflation Factors (VIF) are available in SAS and SPSS.

10. Inter-correlations for the predictor variables can be determined by examining the correlation matrix that is provided by regression analysis procedures.

11. PRESS (PREDICTED RESID SS) is available in SAS.

5

Qualitative Sales
Forecasting

❖   ❖   ❖

*During a visit with one manufacturer, we interviewed an analyst who was
responsible for generating the sales forecasts used by logistics and production. As we began discussing the sales forecasting process used by his
department, he explained that at the beginning of each month, he generated
a quantitative forecast for the coming month for each product (SKU) and
then examined the forecast to see if it needed to be adjusted. He explained
that he made adjustments to each SKU forecast based on his knowledge of
each item's behavior, information he obtained from marketing regarding
upcoming promotions, and information he obtained from the employees
responsible for handling orders from the company's distribution centers. In
all, this single employee inspected and qualitatively adjusted between **200
and 300 SKUs each month**! His insights into the business environment
surrounding each product dramatically improved the forecasting accuracy
for each, but involved an incredible amount of information gathering on
his part. Equally important, no one else in the organization seemed to
realize the incredible resource to be found in this individual's knowledge, nor
what would happen to forecasting accuracy (and production and logistics
planning) if he left the company.*

❖ INTRODUCTION

This employee that we interviewed had a wealth of knowledge about the products he was forecasting. He had developed effective cross-functional lines of communication within the organization, enabling him to integrate the knowledge and expertise of other functional areas into his forecasts. However, when you consider the time required, along with the potential for bias inherent in generating forecasts for *several hundred SKUs each month,* you have to wonder if there is not a better way to accomplish this task. The issue is not the fact that subjectivity or judgment is being used in this company's sales forecasting process. The issue is whether or not this judgment is being used efficiently and effectively.

Even when a company employs quantitative analysis techniques in its sales forecasting process, judgment always plays an important role. In fact, decisions as fundamental as how the forecasting process is managed are inherently subjective and judgmental. Because it is important to recognize the role and significance of subjective assessments in the management of the forecasting process, we devoted considerable attention in Chapter 1 to these managerial decisions.

Furthermore, although Chapters 3 and 4 contain detailed discussions of time series and regression forecasting techniques, respectively, judgment is required when deciding which of these quantitative forecasting techniques are to be used. When using a quantitative forecasting technique, judgment is also exercised when deciding what data are to be processed during the quantitative analyses, as well as whether any modifications should be made to the data before the analyses are performed (Hanke & Reitsch, 1995). Likewise, when making a decision about how to measure forecasting accuracy and what to do about forecast error (discussed in Chapter 2), judgment is essential.

However, the discussion in this chapter focuses specifically on the efficient and effective use of qualitative (also called subjective or judgmental) forecasting techniques as procedures that turn the opinions, knowledge, and intuition of experienced people (e.g., salespeople, marketing people, corporate executives, and outside experts) into formal forecasts. When qualitative forecasting techniques are used, these people become the information processors, either supplementing or replacing mathematical models that process the data when quantitative forecasting techniques are used (Makridakis, Wheelwright, & McGee, 1983).

Qualitative forecasting analyses can be used to formulate forecasts for new products for which there are no historical data; to devise or adjust mid- or long-range forecasts for corporate planning; to adjust quantitatively generated product-line forecasts; and/or to adjust patterns (trends) generated by endogenous quantitative techniques (such as time series). When a forecaster uses an endogenous quantitative forecasting technique, there is an implicit assumption that there will be no systematic changes or departures from previously occurring patterns. If there is reason to believe this assumption is no longer valid, qualitative techniques provide the means to adjust the forecasts by tapping the experience and judgment of people knowledgeable about the product(s) being forecast and the environment affecting the forecast. In other words, one could say that qualitative forecasting emphasizes predicting the future, rather than explaining the past (Makridakis & Wheelwright, 1989).

Prior to our discussion of specific qualitative techniques, we provide an overview of the advantages and problems inherent in qualitative forecasting analyses. Following this is a discussion of specific techniques and tools used to accomplish qualitative forecasting.

❖ QUALITATIVE FORECASTING: ADVANTAGES AND PROBLEMS

The discussion in this section examines the advantages to qualitative forecasting, as well as its problems. This discussion is summarized in Table 5.1.

Advantages of Qualitative Forecasting Techniques

The principal, and very significant, advantage of qualitative forecasting techniques is their potential for predicting changes that can occur in sales patterns. Time series quantitative techniques cannot predict changes in sales or demand patterns. Regression cannot predict changes in the relationships between sales and the predictor variables. Predicting the occurrence and nature of these changes can be accomplished by qualitative analyses based on the knowledge and experience of people internal and/or external to the company. This is valuable by itself or as additional information to be utilized to adjust the quantitative forecasts.

Table 5.1   Qualitative Forecasting Technique Advantages and Problems

Advantages	*Problems*
Qualitative forecasting techniques have the ability to predict changes in sales patterns.	The ability to forecast accurately can be reduced when forecasters only consider readily available and/or recently perceived information.
Qualitative forecasting techniques allow decision makers to incorporate rich data sources consisting of their intuition, experience, and expert judgment.	The ability to forecast accurately can be reduced by the forecasters' inability to process large amounts of complex information.
	Accurate forecasts can be difficult to produce when forecasters are overconfident in their ability to forecast accurately.
	The ability to accurately forecast may be significantly reduced by political factors within organizations, as well as political factors between organizations.
	The ability to forecast accurately may be reduced because of the forecasters' tendency to infer relationships or patterns in data when there are no patterns.
	The ability to forecast accurately can be affected by anchoring; that is, forecasters may be influenced by initial forecasts (e.g., those generated by quantitative methods) when making qualitative forecasts.
	Future ability to forecast accurately may be reduced when a forecaster tries to justify, rather than understand, a forecast that proves to be inaccurate.
	Qualitative forecasting techniques encourage inconsistencies in judgment due to moods and/or emotions, as well as the repetitive decision making inherent in generating multiple individual product forecasts.
	Qualitative forecasting techniques are expensive and time intensive.

Adapted from Hogarth and Makridakis (1981).

A second advantage of qualitative forecasting techniques is that they make use of the extremely rich data sources represented by the intuition and judgment of experienced executives, sales employees, marketing people, channel members, and/or outside experts. The more experienced these members of the organization, the more prominently qualitative forecasting should be incorporated into the forecasting process. Quantitative forecasting techniques rarely make use of all of the information contained within the databases used to generate the forecasts. Moreover, there are inherent limitations in the depth of information that can be conveyed by a quantitative data format.

Problems With Qualitative Forecasting Techniques

The problems inherent in qualitative forecasting stem from two sources: the tendency for bias to be introduced into the forecasts, and the fact that qualitative forecasting is relatively expensive. Biased qualitative forecasts occur because of limitations on the forecasters' abilities to acquire and process complex information without being influenced by factors other than those pertinent to their decision. Qualitative forecasting techniques are expensive because they require a lot of managerial and analyst time to complete.

The primary sources of qualitative forecast bias are the forecasters' limited ability to process complex information, as well as a limited ability and/or lack of willingness to acquire information. It is difficult for people to integrate numerous, complex bits of information. People also have a tendency to make use of information that is already available to them, or to which they have been most recently exposed. Consequently, qualitative forecasts are frequently generated without considering all relevant information and/or using only that information that is readily available or has been most recently learned. Providing relevant information and structuring complex information are important steps for reducing this source of bias in qualitatively generated forecasts.

Effective qualitative forecasting can also be difficult when forecasters are overconfident in their ability to produce accurate forecasts. Research has shown that confidence in the forecast and the accuracy of that forecast are not always related (Makridakis & Wheelwright, 1989). This result has disturbing implications for the application of qualitative forecasting techniques—just because a forecaster is confident in his/her forecast should not necessarily lend credence to the forecast, unless the forecaster can produce evidence to support it.

Requiring explanations and/or justifications for qualitatively generated or qualitatively adjusted forecasts can help to reduce overconfidence, as can requiring regular comparisons (i.e., accuracy measures) between actual demand and the forecasts.

In our research on forecasting, we have found that political elements within a company, as well as between companies, can significantly affect the ability of forecasters to produce accurate qualitative forecasts. Biased forecasts caused by political elements within organizations are due, in large part, to the tendency for the participants in group decision-making situations to influence each other's thinking, a phenomenon known as "groupthink." Research has shown that the assessments by groups are frequently biased because of a desire on the part of group members to support each other's positions, the influence of strong leaders within groups, and/or a superficial search for information relevant to decision making (Janis & Mann, 1982).

In many companies, there is considerable pressure to make sales forecasts agree with the business plan. Frequently this pressure is manifested by the influence of a strong leader within a consensus forecasting committee. The influence of this leader, along with the tendency of members of the group to support each other's decisions and only a token effort to make objective evaluations of additional information during the decision-making process, all cause qualitative forecasts to be biased in the direction of revenue projections in the company's business plan.

Another political factor within organizations that affects forecasting accuracy concerns the sales forecasts generated by salespeople. When salespeople are required to generate forecasts, the tendency of many organizations to confuse forecasting with setting sales quotas introduces biases into the forecasts. Forecasts generated by salespeople may be biased downward because they view the forecasting activity as an opportunity to make themselves appear effective by setting low sales quotas. Conversely, forecasts generated by salespeople may be biased upward because of their propensity toward optimism (brought on by considering only readily available and/or recent information, as well as overconfidence in their ability to forecast). Salespeople's forecasts will also have an upward bias if they believe, either correctly or incorrectly, that the goods or services that they sell are capacity constrained. The thought process will then be something like "I'm only going to get 80% of what I forecast, so if I forecast 125% of what I think my customers will want, then I'll get all I need." Either form of bias adversely affects the accuracy of the resultant sales forecasts.

Finally, political factors between organizations frequently introduce bias into sales forecasts. These political pressures oftentimes occur between manufacturers and independent distributors within a supply chain. Rather than providing realistic forecasts of future product sales, distributors frequently view forecasting as an opportunity to engage in inventory management at the expense of the manufacturer. When distributors are allowed to provide input to the manufacturer's sales forecasts, distributors will often forecast high, following the logic that if demand is unexpectedly high, the manufacturer will be carrying sufficient inventory (because of the higher forecasts) to cover the distributor's needs. Similar behavior can occur in response to trade promotions offered by manufacturers, when distributors "stock up" on relatively inexpensive inventory, regardless of realistic sales projections. Finally, when manufacturers introduce a new product and distributors are unwilling to take on significant inventory of the new product until they are sure of significant sales demand, the distributor will provide an unrealistically low forecast.

When adjusting forecasts produced by quantitative techniques or when engaging in qualitative analyses of a limited number of data points, forecasters are prone to infer patterns in the data where no patterns really exist. These "false correlations" often result from a tendency to try to find patterns in complex situations, even when none exist. Tracking error that results from applying this supposed pattern is the best way to determine false correlations and discontinue their use.

A significant source of bias when forecasters are qualitatively adjusting quantitatively generated forecasts occurs as a result of a phenomenon known as anchoring. Research by Kahneman and Tversky (1973) suggests that starting values (anchors) significantly affect subsequent predictions. In a forecasting context, quantitatively generated forecasts can act as anchors. The lower the value of the quantitative forecast, the more the forecast will be biased downward; the higher the value of the quantitative forecast, the more the forecast will be biased upward. Overcoming these biases requires forecasters to be aware of and guard against the influence of the anchors by objectively considering all information available to them when qualitatively adjusting quantitatively generated forecasts.

When a forecaster makes a prediction and that prediction proves to be wrong, the forecaster, being human, frequently tries to explain and/or justify the prediction. This reaction often has the unfortunate effect of obscuring the reason for the mistaken prediction, thereby interfering with attempts to understand and learn from mistakes that were made. Instead of spending time trying to justify inaccurate forecasts, it is better to admit that a mistake was made and try to discover the reason for the mistake so that the inaccurate forecasts will not be repeated. Discovering the reasons that inaccurate forecasts occurred is easier if, at the time a forecast is made, the rationale (i.e., the justification or explanation for the forecast) is recorded. Note that this is an activity that was also suggested in the discussion above on how to counteract overconfidence in qualitative forecasts.

Biased forecasts can be caused by inconsistencies in judgment that occur when large numbers of forecasts are produced or adjusted using qualitative techniques. The repetition inherent in these multiple forecasts encourages boredom, which leads to inconsistent and inaccurate forecasts. In addition, because forecasters are human, their moods and emotions can cause bias when multiple forecasts are generated using qualitative techniques (Makridakis & Wheelwright, 1989). The forecaster in the vignette at the beginning of this chapter risked inaccuracies because of the repetitive nature of his forecasting task. When large numbers of forecasts must be generated frequently (e.g., weekly or monthly forecasts for hundreds of SKUs), quantitative forecasting techniques are more appropriate. Instead of trying to qualitatively adjust for factors, such as promotions and seasonality, for example, the forecasts should be modeled quantitatively.

The final problem with qualitative forecasting techniques is that they are expensive. In general, they require large amounts of time on the part of the participants in the qualitative forecasting process, whether they are internal to the company (e.g., executives, forecasters, salespeople) or external to the company. The expensive, time-intensive nature of qualitative forecasting is another reason (in addition to the bias caused by inconsistencies in judgment that occur in repetitive decision making, discussed above) that qualitative forecasting techniques are unsuitable for generating large numbers of forecasts, such as forecasting products by SKU and by location (SKUL).

❖ SUMMARY: QUALITATIVE TECHNIQUE
    ADVANTAGES AND PROBLEMS

Despite this rather long discussion of the problems associated with qualitative techniques, keep in mind that qualitative techniques are a valuable resource for any forecaster. The value of experience and the ability to analyze complex situations as input to sales forecasts should never be discounted. Indeed, every sales forecast involves some degree of qualitative input. The discussion of the problems associated with qualitative techniques was presented here solely for the purpose of helping you make better qualitative forecasts by avoiding some of the common "traps" associated with these techniques. With these traps in mind, we can now move to a discussion of the qualitative techniques available.

❖ QUALITATIVE TECHNIQUES AND TOOLS

In this section, we discuss several qualitative forecasting techniques using the judgment, knowledge, and intuition of experienced people to produce sales forecasts. The techniques discussed solicit expert evaluations via the jury of executive opinion; the Delphi method; and sales force composites. In addition, the information in this section includes a number of tools that enhance qualitative forecasting decisions by reducing the effects of the biases discussed in the last section that can affect the accuracy of qualitative forecasts. The tools discussed are market research (using both primary and secondary data) and decision analysis.

Expert Evaluation Techniques

Expert evaluations use the experience of people, such as executives, salespeople, marketing people, distributors, or outside experts, who are familiar with a product line or a group of products, to generate sales forecasts. The techniques in this section generally involve combining inputs from multiple sources, that is, groups of executives, salespeople, marketing people, distributors, or other outside experts. The advantage of soliciting contributions from more than one person, of course, is that it can offset biases introduced into a forecast when the forecast is produced by one person.

Jury of Executive Opinion. When executives from various corporate functions involved in forecasting sales (e.g., finance, marketing, sales, production, and logistics) meet to generate forecasts, is the meeting is termed a jury of executive opinion. The jury of executive opinion is one of the most familiar and frequently used of all forecasting techniques

(Mentzer & Kahn, 1995). It is a relatively simple forecasting technique to implement, and it is quite valuable when changes in existing demand patterns are anticipated or when there is no historical demand data available for quantitative forecasting analyses (e.g., new product forecasts). It also has the advantage of making use of the rich data represented by the intuition and judgment of experienced executives.

For example, a retailer with which we have worked makes extensive and very successful use of a jury of executive opinion for some of the long-term forecasts required for corporate planning. By using this technique, the company is able to tap the expertise of a number of its top-level managers who have had extensive experience in the industry.

Another example illustrating the use of a jury of executive opinion is a company whose personnel we interviewed in the benchmark studies. In this company, a jury of executive opinion meets monthly to produce and update the product-line level, quarterly sales forecasts. In addition to the jury's regular members, the group periodically solicits input from an economist employed by the company, who functions as a consultant to the sales forecasting process.

In our research on sales forecasting, we have found that one of the most widespread uses of a jury of executive opinion is in a consensus forecasting process. In fact, this technique forms the backbone of a consensus process, consisting as it does of representatives from multiple functional areas (e.g., marketing, finance, sales, production, and logistics). In many cases, quantitative sales forecasts are generated, and the consensus forecasting committee meets to decide whether and how much to adjust the quantitative forecasts. Frequently these consensus forecasting committees are also responsible for generating qualitative forecasts for new products. The effective use of the jury of executive opinion technique depends on the degree to which the organization is able to overcome the sources of bias inherent in individual and, particularly, group decision making. To the extent that these pressures constrain the decision-making process, biased forecasts will result.

The most frequent source of bias in a consensus forecasting context is political pressures within the company, usually in the form of influence exerted by the member of the jury whose department is the most powerful within the culture of the company (Hanke & Reitsch, 1995). Because of this influence, the contributions from other members of the jury carry relatively less weight in the final forecasts. In many companies, the most powerful member of the jury is from finance, and the influence of this member tends to constrain the forecasts so that they are biased in the direction of the revenue projections of the business plan. Qualitative forecasts that originate from these committees (e.g., new product forecasts) can also be influenced by these same pressures so that they are significantly biased in the direction of agreement with revenue projections.

In one manufacturer whose personnel we interviewed during phase three of the benchmark studies, the consensus forecasting committee meetings, although ostensibly for the purpose of arriving at a consensus forecast among marketing, finance, and operations, were, in reality, merely a formality. The forecast had been qualitatively adjusted and arrived at by marketing and finance prior to the consensus forecasting meeting. Furthermore, because of significant influence by the finance member of the forecasting committee, and a desire on the part of the rest of the committee to support the forecast presented by finance, the committee did not conduct an objective search for information to facilitate its decisions; rather, the committee simply accepted the sales forecast presented by finance.

In order to mitigate this source of bias, it is important for a company to understand the interaction between the business plan and the sales forecasts. Sales forecasting and business planning are separate but interdependent processes. Properly administered, sales forecasting can be used to facilitate business planning, but this outcome cannot occur if sales forecasts are forced to agree with independently generated revenue targets in the business plan (for more information on the interaction between sales forecasting and business planning, see the discussion in Chapter 1 under "Forecasting Versus Planning"and in Chapter 8 under "Approach").

Another way to decrease the bias that group decision making introduces into the jury of executive opinion is by making selected, relevant background information available to the executives that comprise the jury. This information may consist of, for example, relevant economic data (e.g., leading and/or simultaneous indicators); information on industry trends; information on production and/or distribution constraints within the company; the results of market research, such as focus groups; or information on forecast accuracy. Making this information accessible reduces the tendency of individuals in the group to depend entirely on their own available and/or recently experienced information sources, and it makes it less likely that the group decision-making process proceeds with only a token effort to objectively evaluate additional information that is important to the decision-making process.

An important caveat to the use of the jury of executive opinion is that the technique is not appropriate for short-term (i.e., daily, weekly, or monthly) forecasts of individual product items or product item-location combinations (i.e., SKUs or SKULs). A jury of executive opinion, by its very nature, requires valuable executive time; therefore, the most efficient use of this technique is to forecast monthly, quarterly, and/or yearly sales predictions for groups of products, that is, product lines. Using a jury of executive opinion for low-level, short-term forecasts encourages bias because of the repetitive nature of these forecasts and is a waste of costly executive time.

Companies using a jury of executive opinion in their forecasting process should also be aware that this technique tends to disperse responsibility for forecasting accuracy. We have found that unless companies using a jury of executive opinion are relatively sophisticated in managing their forecasting process, members of the jury are neither evaluated, nor rewarded, for forecasting accuracy. When no one has responsibility for forecast accuracy, inaccurate forecasts inevitably result. Companies that use a jury of executive opinion successfully do so, in part, because they both evaluate and reward members of their consensus forecasting committee for forecasting accuracy.

Another procedure that can be used to assign responsibility for accurate forecasts when using a jury of executive opinion is to require written justification for qualitative adjustments to quantitative forecasts. When this documentation is required, it not only has the effect of assigning responsibility for accurate forecasting, but it also makes it easier to perform post hoc analyses, that is, if forecasts prove to be inaccurate, the documentation makes it easier to determine the reasons for the inaccuracies. One company with which we have worked has detailed notes taken at every jury meeting, thus documenting the logic behind each adjustment to the sales forecasts.

Delphi Method. When the Delphi method is used for forecasting, the input of experts, either internal or external to a company, is solicited and proceeds as follows:

1. Each member of the panel of experts who is chosen to participate writes an answer to the question being investigated (e.g., a
   forecast for product or industry sales) and all the reasoning
   behind this forecast.

2. The answers of the panel are summarized and returned to the members of the panel, but without the identification of which expert came up with each forecast.

3. After reading the summary of replies, each member of the panel either maintains his or her forecast or reevaluates the initial forecast and submits the new forecast (and the reasoning behind changing his or her forecast) in writing.

The answers are summarized and returned to panel members as many times as necessary to narrow the range of forecast.

An appropriate use of the Delphi method is for the prediction of mid- to long-term company sales levels or long-term industry sales levels. When this technique is used within a company, it can be thought of as a kind of "virtual" jury of executive opinion, because the executives do not meet face to face. The purpose of this distance is to allow each member to use his or her reasoning to develop a forecast, without the influence of strong personalities or the fact that the "boss" has a pet forecast.

The Delphi method also reduces the effects of groupthink on the decision-making process. Since the participants do not meet face to face, the bias that occurs because of a desire on the part of group members to support each other's positions or the influence of a strong leader within the group is minimized. Removing this source of bias enables conflicting ideas to survive long enough to be examined, thus allowing a range of scenarios to emerge from the process and an outcome that is more legitimate, particularly when long-term sales forecasts are being made.

Problems with this method of qualitative forecasting focus on its tendency to be unreliable, that is, the outcomes can be highly dependent on the composition and expertise of panel members. To some extent this source of bias is the result of group members not being willing/able to seek out information other than what is readily available and/or recently perceived. Supplying panel members with relevant information (e.g., economic or industry indicators) can reduce this source of bias. In addition to this bias, the Delphi method is very time consuming and thus expensive. Such a technique is most appropriate for long-term, strategic-level forecasts rather than short-term, operational ones.

Sales Force Composite. The sales force composite is a qualitative forecasting method that uses the knowledge and experience of a company's salespeople, its sales management, and/or channel members to produce sales forecasts. The grass roots approach to a sales force composite accumulates sales forecasts for the regions, products, and/or customers of individual salespeople. The sales management approach seeks sales forecasts from sales executives and is essentially a jury of executive opinion, albeit consisting of a narrower range of executives (i.e., only sales executives or only sales and marketing executives). The distributor approach to the sales force composite solicits the sales predictions of independent distributors of a company's products.

To give a sense of how salespeople actually forecast in business organizations, the Appendix at the end of this chapter provides a summary of a recent survey of forecasting practices by salespeople. Key findings from this reported survey include:

- Almost 82% of salespeople surveyed participate in forecasting.
- At the same time, only 14% of salespeople receive training in forecasting.
- Almost half (more than 47%) of salespeople report that they have either no, little, or some knowledge of what happens to their forecasts after they are submitted.
- Only 16% of salespeople have access to forecasting software to assist them in their forecasting tasks.
- Less than half of the salespeople believe that the quality of their forecasts affects their performance evaluations.

The picture painted from this survey is that while an overwhelming majority of salespeople are responsible for forecasting, there is a considerable gap between the expectations that companies have for them and the resources that companies provide them to excel at this critical task.

Despite this gap, there are important advantages to the sales force composite forecasting technique. It has the potential for incorporating the expertise of people who are closest to the customer. In addition, the technique places forecasting responsibility on those who have both the ability to directly affect product sales and the potential to experience the impact (in the form of their customers' displeasure, for example) of forecasting errors.

There are two general situations that call for the salespeople to participate in a company's forecasting efforts. The first is when salespeople manage ongoing streams of product flow to their customers, be they end-use customers or channel partner customers. In these situations, salespeople are the most natural sources of information regarding changes to patterns of demand. For example, a candy company may have a sales team assigned to a large mass-merchandiser customer. This company may have been given prime end-of-aisle display space during the week before Halloween over the previous several years. Forecasters for this candy company will need to know if they will again have this prime end-of-aisle display space next Halloween, because if they do not, the forecast will need significant adjustment. This information has to come from the sales team.

The second situation is when salespeople work with large project or proposal-based sales. In this case, accurate forecasts require the intelligence that salespeople have concerning the likelihood of securing large orders. For example, a computer company that sells large mainframes needs a prediction of the likelihood of winning a large contract from a major customer. If such a win is likely, then the computer company needs to adequately plan for the increased demand. The salespeople are in the best position to assess that likelihood.

Although salespeople provide critical input to many forecasting processes, companies are frequently frustrated by the quality of the input that salespeople provide. There are, however, a number of things that companies can do to improve the quality of salesforce input to the forecasting process (Moon & Mentzer, 1999). The first, and perhaps most important, change that companies can make to enhance salesforce forecasting is to **make it part of their jobs**. At many companies with whom we have worked, salespeople make comments like, "Why should I spend my time forecasting? I've been hired to sell, not to forecast!" However, salespeople are responsible for three main activities: to sell products and services, to build and maintain relationships with their customers, and to provide market intelligence back to their companies. One of the most important forms of market intelligence is intelligence concerning future demand—in other words, forecasts. While most sales executives would agree that these are the critical tasks they expect salespeople to perform, in many cases, salespeople are measured and rewarded for only one of those tasks: selling and generating revenue. As we emphasized in Chapter 2, **what gets measured gets rewarded, and what gets rewarded gets done**. Thus, if salespeople are not measured and rewarded for forecasting performance, they will not perceive it as part of their jobs.

How can companies make forecasting a recognized part of a salesperson's job? A first step should be to explicitly emphasize forecasting responsibilities in a salesperson's formal job description. But beyond that, forecasting must be included in the performance evaluation process and compensation strategy for the salesforce. Companies should adopt some of the performance measurement strategies discussed in Chapter 2, and these measures should be applied to salesforce forecasts. We are by no means suggesting that forecast accuracy should be the primary measure for salesperson success or failure. However, it should be a part of a "balanced scorecard" for members of the salesforce, and forecasting performance should receive enough weight on that scorecard that it gets the attention and effort needed to do a good job.

In addition, salespeople must receive training to enhance their forecasting skills. Training is a normal part of most salespeople's jobs, yet that training seldom includes forecasting training. Topics for salesforce training should include the role of quantitative forecasting, how forecasts are used by other functions in the company, and how to work with customers to convince them that accurate forecasts are in the best interests of all parties in the supply chain. In addition to training, salespeople must receive feedback on their performance. Salespeople cannot possibly improve their performance unless they know whether their forecasts tend to be high or low, and by how much. Such feedback is a critical part of helping salespeople recognize how important forecasting is to their organization.

Another important emphasis area for a company to enhance salesperson forecasting effectiveness is to **minimize "game-playing."** Game-playing can result in bias from either an upward or downward direction. Upward bias most frequently occurs when salespeople perceive that supply of goods and services may be limited, and they intentionally inflate forecasts to ensure receiving adequate supply for their customers. Downward bias most frequently occurs when salespeople perceive that forecasts influence quotas. Companies can minimize both of these types of bias. First, it is critical to constantly measure forecast accuracy so that either form of bias is identified. When such measurement occurs and feedback is given, then bias can, over time, be reduced. Second, it is critical to separate forecasts from quotas in the minds of salespeople. This can be done in a variety of ways. One way is to encourage salespeople to forecast in physical units (the most useful type of forecast for downstream planning purposes) while quotas are assigned in dollars, points, or some other unit. Another way is to assign quotas quarterly, or annually, but to make forecasting a normal part of a salesperson's monthly, or in some cases weekly, job assignment.

Another key strategy for enhancing the effectiveness of salespeople's forecasting efforts is to **keep it simple.** One observation that we have made after working with dozens of companies and their salesforces is that salespeople are generally not very good at forecasting. However, they can be *very* good at adjusting forecasts. The best way for a company to "keep it simple" for their salespeople is to provide those salespeople with an initial forecast, generated through statistical models, which they can then adjust. What we have seen in world-class forecasting companies is a process whereby time series and regression models are employed to generate quantitative forecasts, which are then provided to the sales staff for them to review, often with their customers, and make adjustments based on what they know about expected changes to previous demand patterns. When salespeople are ineffective is when they are given a "blank piece of paper" and expected to generate initial forecasts on their own. Whenever possible, companies should use salespeople as adjusters, not forecasters.

A final strategy that companies can use to enhance salesperson effectiveness is to **keep it focused.** By this, we mean that for most salespeople, the "80/20" rule is a reality along two dimensions: customers and products. In other words, 20% of a salesperson's customers generate 80% of his or her business. Similarly, 20% of a salesperson's product portfolio generates 80% of his or her business. When either or both of these concentration principles are in effect, then those salespeople should be forecasting only those 20% of customers, or 20% of products, that generate the bulk of their business. If a salesperson has 100 total customers, and 100 products in his or her portfolio, then that salesperson would theoretically be responsible for 10,000 forecasts. But when a company "keeps it focused," then that salesperson might only pay attention to his or her top 20 customers, and top 20 products, resulting in a forecasting workload of (at most) 400 forecasts per month. Such a process has several advantages. First, when salespeople perceive that the magnitude of the forecasting job is enormous, they are likely to resist and do a poor job on all forecasts. Second, salespeople are likely to have very limited information on those 80% of customers and/or products that do not generate significant revenue. When they are forced to provide forecasts in those situations where they have limited information, they are likely to turn in forecasts that are simply not very good. The bottom line is that salespeople should forecast *only* those customer/product combinations where they can really add value. In one chemical company that has participated in the audit research, the goal is for salespeople to look at, and think about, around 10% of the customer/product combinations for which they are responsible. For this company, salespeople do not see the forecasting task as onerous, and they provide excellent insights that enhance the overall accuracy and effectiveness of forecasts.

The bottom line concerning sales force composite forecasting is that when companies use some of these strategies to enhance the effectiveness of salespeople's forecasts, those companies can increase accuracy by as much as 50%. Remember, a forecast is a best guess about what customers will demand in future time periods, and no one is closer to customers than salespeople. If companies **make it part of their jobs, minimize game playing, keep it simple, and keep it focused**, then salespeople can greatly enhance the overall forecasting process.

Supply Chain Partner Forecasting. In many situations, salespeople participate in the forecasting process through their interaction with a company's supply chain partners. Many manufacturers never directly experience end-user demand and rely on supply chain partners both to satisfy end-user demand and to provide forecasting information about anticipated future end-user demand. Enlightened supply chain partners realize that effective supply chain management requires a clear understanding of demand; in other words, accurate forecasts are critical. However, even though such accurate forecasts greatly enhance the overall effectiveness of the supply chain, political pressures between organizations can lead to inventory game playing between manufacturers and distributors. In some cases, distributors fail to view the participation in the sales forecasting process with the manufacturer as an opportunity to enhance supply chain performance by accurately forecasting future sales. Instead, they view forecasting as an opportunity to manage their inventory, either increasing distributor inventory in response to trade promotions, increasing manufacturer inventory as a distributor "safety stock," or avoiding "pipeline" inventory for new products. When distributors take this attitude, they undermine, and make a mockery, of the sales forecasting process. Manufacturers possessing a certain level of sophistication in their sales forecasting process realize that conventional supply chains (i.e., those consisting of independent organizations) are, in general, characterized by manifestations of power and conflict (Keith, Jackson, & Crosby, 1990; Gaski, 1984), such as inventory game playing, and take this into account by qualitatively adjusting the forecasts they receive from supply chain members.

In order to reduce the unreliability of distributor-generated sales forecasts, manufacturers should recognize the effects of trade promotions on this process. We have found that trade promotions can play havoc with the sales forecasting process, creating promotion-driven "seasonality" in historical sales data when distributors increase their inventories in response to periodic price promotions from manufacturers, rather than anticipated increases in consumer demand.

One possibility for reducing the forecasting error that is caused by trade promotions is to include the effects of these promotions within quantitative forecasting models. Using another approach, many consumer packaged goods manufacturers have begun to embrace the concept of "everyday low prices" (EDLP), which eliminates trade promotions, along with the problems these promotions cause for the sales forecasting process.

A related approach to managing the reliability of distributor-generated sales forecasts is the vendor-managed and co-managed inventory relationships many manufacturers and distributors are developing. In these relationships, manufacturers and distributors alter the nature of their relationship from the conflict-ridden, competitive relationship characteristic of a conventional channel to what are essentially strategic alliances (Stern, El-Ansary, & Coughlan, 1996). Generally, the cooperation and collaboration that characterize these altered supply chain structures extend to the forecasting process, thereby reducing the political pressures that introduce bias into the forecasts.

When distributors deliberately under-forecast demand because they do not want to assume liability for new product inventories, it is, to a large extent, simply another manifestation of the competitive nature of conventional supply chain relationships. This situation can be mitigated to some extent by improved product research and development on the part of the manufacturer. In one manufacturer whose personnel we interviewed, new product ideas come exclusively from upper management, and there is little or no market research undertaken before introducing the products. Skepticism of independent distributors regarding new product introductions causes distributors to deliberately underforecast sales for this manufacturer's new products until sales convinces them that the product concept is sound. Contrast this with a similar manufacturer that conducts extensive new product research and shares the results with its distributors. The result is more confidence in the supply chain in new products and more informed forecasts of their demand.

Both manufacturers and supply chain members must adopt a supply chain mentality. Organizations that adopt such a mentality acknowledge that overall supply chain performance depends on a free flow of information concerning future demand. Such information helps to reduce inventory across the supply chain and allows suppliers, manufacturers, and retailers to be more responsive to the needs of end consumers. Point-of-sale data can be used by manufacturers to quantitatively model end-user demand, and sharing such data is one way that supply chain partners can help the entire supply chain to forecast effectively. Further, when supply chain partners commit to working collaboratively with manufacturers by providing qualitative information about their future marketing and promotional plans, then manufacturers can more effectively predict demand fluctuations, have adequate inventory available during peak demand, and minimize overall supply chain inventories during slack periods.

❖ MARKET RESEARCH TOOLS FOR QUALITATIVE FORECASTING

The information obtained through market research efforts can, in many cases, enhance qualitative forecasts. For example, assume a jury of executive opinion is attempting to formulate a long-range forecast to guide corporate capacity and budget planning. One possibility is to simply extend or extrapolate the sales trends for the company's product lines, which were derived using quantitative techniques such as time series analyses. Remember from Chapter 3 ("Time Series Forecasting Techniques") that sales trends are continuing patterns of sales increases or decreases and that those patterns can take the form of either straight lines or curves.

Simply extending a sales trend is fine, as long as we are sure that the pattern will not change. But what if there are changes? How can we forecast these? Remember that an advantage of qualitative forecasting techniques is their ability to forecast changes in existing patterns. Using these techniques, trend extensions may be made with the benefit of input from individuals or groups of people with the knowledge and expertise to correctly modify existing trends. Providing additional information obtained through marketing research enhances these decisions.

Information obtained from market research can be provided to a jury of executive opinion; to members of a panel participating in the Delphi method; to salespeople, sales managers, or independent distributors participating in a sales composite technique; that is, to anyone involved in qualitative forecasting. Market research can be conducted using primary data, secondary data, or a combination of primary and secondary data. A company collects primary data for a specific purpose, such as focus groups conducted specifically to obtain information on the demand for a new product. Secondary data have been previously collected, either by the company using the data or by some other source, for example, syndicated volume tracking data collected by A.C. Neilson (Malhotra, 1996).

Market Research Using Primary Data. If a company has sufficient resources to undertake market research, it can conduct surveys to obtain primary data. These data can provide information on antici-pated product demand or anticipated economic activity to assist in qualitative mid-range (e.g., monthly or quarterly) or long-range (e.g., 1 year to 5 years) product or industry sales forecasts, or for qualitative adjustments to short-range product forecasts. For example, a company could survey (using face-to-face interviews, telephone surveys, or mail survey methodology) a sample of its business/institutional customers to obtain information on anticipated purchases of new or existing products. A manufacturer could use this methodology to systemati-cally secure sales forecasts from independent distributors. A company could survey a sample of households or consumers to obtain infor-mation on purchase intentions for new or existing products. Still another example of using surveys involves a company surveying a sample of economic experts for forecasts of national economic activity or economic activity within an industry.

Another means for obtaining primary data that contribute to the forecasting process is to conduct focus groups. Focus groups are small groups of people (seven to ten), gathered together to exchange ideas on a specific topic. This methodology requires a moderator to conduct the focus groups and is relatively time consuming (Krueger, 1994). However, focus groups can be an effective method of gathering infor-mation to aid in qualitative forecasts, particularly for new products. Focus groups can be used to solicit new product ideas, as well as to obtain feedback on products that are in the development process. One manufacturer with whom we have worked uses focus groups very effectively as an adjunct to its new product forecasting process. The focus groups consist of potential users of new products that are under consideration, and they give excellent insights into adoption rates and patterns for new products.

Market Research Using Secondary Data. An alternative to a company gathering specific data for the purpose of enhancing qualitative forecasting decisions is the use of secondary data, that is, data that has been gathered previously, either within a company or by sources external to the company. For example, instead of conducting its own surveys when attempting to forecast changes in sales trends, a company can obtain information from surveys conducted by external sources, two of which are detailed below.

- A survey of household/consumer attitudes and anticipated purchases (CABP) is conducted regularly by the Survey Research Center at the University of Michigan.
- Surveys on anticipated inventory levels are conducted by the Office of Business Economics of the Securities and Exchange Commission (Granger, 1980).

Another source of secondary data is tracking data in the form of leading and/or simultaneous (coincident) indicators. Economic indicators for the United States are available monthly in the *Business Conditions Digest*, published by the U.S. Department of Commerce (Granger, 1980). When trying to forecast changes or turning points in a company's product sales, knowledge of the behavior of business cycles in the aggregate economy is a valuable input. Of course, the rationale underlying leading indicators, for example, is that some sectors of the economy will expand ahead of others, thus signaling changes in the overall level of economic activity (Granger, 1980). Consequently, it is important that each company possesses and maintains a sufficient level of intelligence and expertise with respect to its own industry. This will enable the company to recognize which indicators are leading and which indicators are coincident for its industry, thereby providing information pertinent to the company's forecasting decisions.

During the benchmark studies, we observed that a characteristic of companies with highly sophisticated forecasting processes was their ability to conduct ongoing analyses of their business and industry. This ability to successfully analyze their business resulted from selecting employees who possessed (or could acquire) expertise in both analysis tools and knowledge about the company and the industry. In addition, upper management was willing to support the business analysis process with systems (e.g., hardware and software) and continuous training. An ongoing program of business analysis is the only way to understand not only which economic indicators are pertinent to a company but also, for example, the effects of trade and consumer promotions and price elasticity of demand for a company's products (including the effects of competitors' price changes).

Keeping in mind that it is up to you to decide which indicators are leading for your particular industry, common leading economic indicators include:

- Average work week (production and manufacturing workers)
- New manufacturing orders
- Durable goods orders
- Construction contracts
- Plant and equipment purchases
- Capital appropriations
- Business population
- After-tax corporate profits
- Stock price indices
- Level and changes in business inventories
- Consumer spending
- Growth in durable goods industries
- Growth in capital equipment industries
- Level and changes in money supplies (e.g., M1, M2)
- Bond prices

The rationale underlying simultaneous or coincident indicators is that these statistics will roughly correspond to changes in aggregate economic trends, essentially serving to confirm that a change in trend, anticipated on the basis of leading indicators, is actually occurring. As with leading indicators, the ability of these statistics to contribute to qualitative forecasting decisions depends on how well a company understands which simultaneous indicators are significant for it and its industry. Some examples of simultaneous indicators:

- Unemployment rate
- Index of help-wanted advertising in newspapers
- Index of industrial production
- Gross Domestic Product
- Personal income
- Retail sales
- Index of wholesale prices

The secondary data sources discussed in this section are appropriate for enhancing long-term forecasting (e.g., 1 to 5 years). There are, however, a number of syndicated services that regularly make available secondary data in the form of consumer point-of-sale data (i.e., volume tracking data) for a subscription fee. The information provided by these services can serve as an appropriate input to mid-range forecasts (e.g., monthly or quarterly). Sources of syndicated volume tracking data include A.C. Neilson (National Scan Track); the Newspaper Advertising Bureau (NABSCAN); and Tele-Research, Inc. (TRIM) (Malhotra, 1996). Several of the consumer package goods manufacturers that we have worked with use these syndicated data sources, along with information from independent distributors, to estimate market share and existing product inventories, respectively. This information is valuable in producing qualitative forecasts of product line demand for the coming month and/or quarter.

❖ DECISION ANALYSIS TOOLS FOR QUALITATIVE FORECASTING

The purpose of using the tools of decision analysis is to structure the qualitative forecasting decision process in such a way that participants are required to examine and state the assumptions used in their decisions. The discipline and structure imposed by these decision tools minimizes bias in qualitative forecasting by (1) diminishing overconfidence in the forecasters' ability to forecast accurately; (2) forcing them to seek out and consider information that is relevant to the forecasting decisions; and (3) enhancing their ability to process large amounts of complex information. The tools discussed in this section include decision tree diagrams and simulation.

Decision Tree Diagrams. The advantage of decision tree diagrams is that they enable participants to visualize the context of a complex decision, thereby reducing biases that occur because of limitations on forecasters' abilities to process complex information. Constructing the diagrams forces decision makers to consider all alternatives and to assign probabilities to each alternative, based on their experience and knowledge of their company and industry. When combined with a statistical concept known as Bayesian analysis, the estimates of probabilities for future events in decision tree diagrams can be revised based on experience, judgment, and/or additional information, such as that gained from market research (Granger, 1980).

The tree diagram in Figure 5.1 illustrates these concepts. This tree diagram helps analysts focus their forecast of sales of a new product. Suppose that for national sales of a new product, analysts can only forecast (without any additional information) a 50–50 probability of high sales versus low sales. However, suppose that, based on past experience with other new products, forecasters know that when the results of market research (e.g., surveys of prospective customers) have forecast success for a product, 80% of the time high sales actually do occur. On the other hand, when a new product has been introduced in the past and market research forecast product failure, 85% of the time low sales, in fact, occurred.

Using Bayesian analysis, the probabilities of both high and low product sales for national introduction of the new product can be revised from their former (and uninformative) 50–50 probabilities. As Figure 5.1 indicates, the probability of market research indicating

Figure 5.1   Decision Tree Diagram

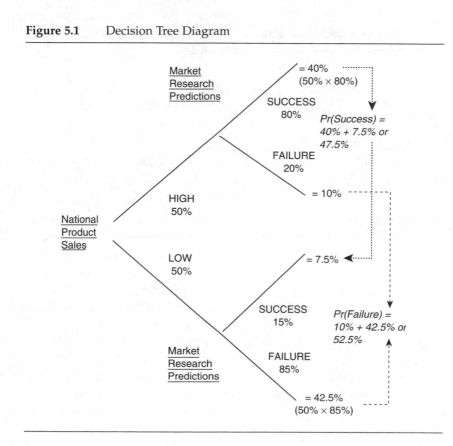

product success (*Pr(Success)*) is the sum of 40% (the probability of market research forecasting product success when national sales will, in fact, be high) and 7.5% (the probability of market research forecasting product success when national sales will, in fact, be low), or 47.5%. On the other hand, the probability of market research indicating product failure (*Pr(Failure)*) is the sum of 10% (the probability of market research forecasting product failure when national sales will, in fact, be high) and 42.5% (the probability of market research forecasting product failure when national sales will, in fact, be low), or 52.5%. From these forecasts, the probabilities of both high and low national sales can be revised as indicated below:

- The probability of high national sales when market research forecasts success is 84%, that is,

    Pr(High Sales/Success) = 40%/47.5% = 84%

- The probability of low national sales when market research forecasts failure is 81%, that is,

    Pr(Low Sales/Failure) = 42.5%/52.5% = 81%
    (Hanke & Reitsch, 1995).

Thus, through this decision analysis, we have improved our ability to forecast success in our new product introductions if we heed the input from market research.

Simulations. Another decision analysis tool that can be used in the qualitative forecasting decision process is simulation. Like decision tree diagrams, simulation requires forecasters to structure their decision making by examining and stating their assumptions. Essentially, simulation demands that the system under investigation be defined, enabling that system to be manipulated so that "what-if" analyses can be performed to explore alternatives (Pritsker, 1986). For example, forecasters predicting sales for a new product could use simulation to explore alternative outcomes based on the probabilities of various economic conditions occurring. Simulation software is currently available that greatly facilitates the use of this decision tool, requiring, for example, that the user merely create a graphical diagram of system components (similar to what is done for a decision tree diagram) (Pritsker, Sigal, & Hammesfahr, 1989).

However, simulations do not necessarily need to involve the computer or complex software. One consumer products company simulates the introduction of new products by giving them away at a test mall. Subjects are given a free sample of the product, asked to try it, and told they will be sent a short questionnaire to complete. Several days later, each subject receives the questionnaire asking what he or she thought of the product. The subject also receives a form to order more of the new product. Various prices are tried with different subjects to see how likely customers are to order more of the product. In this way, the company can simulate new customers' price sensitivity and, thus, forecast new product sales at various introductory price levels.

❖ SUMMARY

This chapter has focused on the use of qualitative forecasting techniques that turn the opinions of experienced people into formal forecasts. The information presented included an overview of the advantages inherent in qualitative forecasting analyses, with the discussion of problems focusing on the sources of bias that cause inaccuracies in qualitative forecasts. Qualitative forecasting techniques that were discussed as methods for tapping the knowledge and intuition of experts included: the jury of executive opinion, the Delphi method, the sales force composite, and supply chain partner forecasting. In addition, we presented a number of tools that are important adjuncts to the qualitative forecasting process, primarily because of their ability to enhance qualitative forecasting decisions through the reduction of the effects of the biases that can affect the accuracy of qualitative forecasts.

Chapter 6 discusses the systems (hardware and software) that surround the forecasting process we use to efficiently and effectively conduct the business of developing and using sales forecasts.

APPENDIX

In order to gain a more complete understanding of how salespeople actually forecast in business organizations, the authors conducted a survey to explore salesperson forecasting practices. The primary objective of the research was to supplement the extensive qualitative research that has been conducted through working with a large number of companies, and to offer some generalizations and a "state of practice" view of salesperson forecasting. To accomplish this objective, a survey of salespeople was conducted across a variety of industries and sales settings. A sample of 1,024 salespeople was taken from a commercially purchased mailing list. Each of the salespeople in this sample indicated that he or she was involved in selling products and/or services to companies (in other words, *not* retail sales or sales to individuals). From this initial mailing, 382 salespeople returned a postcard indicating they were appropriate respondents and expressing willingness to complete the survey. The survey was mailed to these individuals, and 262 completed surveys were returned from business-to-business salespeople (a response rate of 68.6%). The survey was developed to collect information regarding the salesperson's role in sales forecasting, the level of satisfaction with and seriousness placed on the forecasting process, and the presence of situational variables that impact forecasting performance. In addition, demographic data were collected to further explore possible patterns among variables.

Results indicate that, among the 262 respondents, 214, or almost 82%, have forecasting responsibilities. This is consistent with the evidence accumulated through years of working with dozens of organizations, the vast majority of which use their salespeople to assist in their forecasting efforts. The remaining results reported in this Appendix pertain only to those 214 respondents who reported that they are engaged in the forecasting process.

Approximately 86.4% of the respondents are employed by the company for which they sell products or services, and 13.1% are independent manufacturer representatives. Among the industries represented, 47.1% sell consumer goods, 37.1% sell industrial products, 8.2% sell consumer services, and 7.7% sell industrial services. The majority of companies are manufacturers (56.9%), followed by transportation and distribution companies (10.5%), wholesalers (8.1%), retailers (4.8%), and the remaining 19.6% are from other industries (e.g., advertising, health care, publishing, market research, telecommunications, and finance). The typical firm included in the survey has sales volume ranging from less than $10.0 million to more than $5.0 billion, with an average sales volume between $201 million and $500 million. The number of employees ranges from less than 100 to more than 1,000, with the majority of companies (52.9%) having less than 100 employees (see Table 5.2).

A typical respondent is male (83.6%), has an average age of 35 to 44, has been employed in sales for an average of 10 to 15 years, and has a college degree with an educational background in business (see Table 5.2). Of the respondents, 46% are compensated with a combination of salary and bonus, followed by 15.3% who are compensated with straight commission, 12.8% with salary and commission plus bonus, 12.2% with salary plus commission, and 10.8% with straight salary.

Forecasting Responsibilities

The number of hours spent per month on the forecasting process ranges from zero (n = 2) to 100 (n = 1), with an average of 3.0 hours per month (see Table 5.3). A total of 11.7% of respondents forecast on a weekly basis, 46.3% of respondents forecast on a monthly basis, 29.9% forecast on a quarterly basis, and 46.3% forecast annually. The most common time horizon for which respondents are asked to forecast is 1 year (62.1%), followed by a quarterly horizon (42.1%), and a monthly horizon (33.2%), with all other horizons forecast by fewer than 10.0% of the respondents (see Table 5.3). Results indicate that 71.0% of respondents forecast dollars, 53.0% forecast units, and 10.7% indicated that they forecast "other" volumes, such as weight, price per pound, market share, product mix, orders, shipments, call volume, FTEs, referrals, board square footage, profit, and company product equivalents. The most common level at which forecasts are created is the customer level (68.2%), followed by product level (54.2%), SKU (23.8%), and SKUL (7.0%). For those forecasting at the customer level, 70.5% treat some customers differently than others in the forecasting process, and 29.5% treat all customers the same. Similarly, 70.0% of respondents indicated that they treat some products differently than others, while 30.0% treat all products the same.

Regarding resources provided for forecasting by their companies, 65.0% of respondents are given account or territory buying history, 15.9% have access to a forecasting computer program, and 14.0% have received formal forecasting training. In response to a question asking what resources respondents use in the forecasting process, 90.7% indicated they use sales history, 86.9% use their own judgment, 79.4% use

Table 5.2   Sample Descriptive Statistics

Annual Sales in Dollars	Frequency	Percent	Number of Employees	Frequency	Percent
< $10M	35	16.9	Under 100	35	16.9
$11M–$50M	30	14.5	1001–5000	30	14.5
$51M–$100M	16	7.7	5001–10,000	16	7.7
$101–$200	16	7.7	> 10,000	16	7.7
$201M–$500M	22	10.6	Total	22	10.6
$500M–$1B	24	11.6			
$1B–$5B	33	15.9			
> $5B	31	15.0			
Total	207	100.0			

Age	Frequency	Percent	Years Employed in Sales	Frequency	Percent
18 to 34	35	16.5	5 or less	21	9.8
35 to 44	96	45.1	6 to 9	20	9.3
45 to 54	50	23.5	10 to 15	72	33.8
55 or over	32	15.1	16 to 20	43	20.2
Total	213	100.0	21 or More	57	26.8
			Total	213	100.0

Level of Education	Frequency	Percent	Educational Background	Frequency	Percent
HS to Some College	35	17.1	Business	126	59.7
College Grad	119	58.0	Engineering/ Tech	23	10.9
Grad School	51	24.9	Liberal Arts	39	18.5
Total	205	100.0	Other	23	10.9
			Total	211	100.0

information resulting from conversations with customers concerning future buying, and 40.7% use general market research provided by their employer, such as industry trends and economic forecasts. A total of 13.6% of respondents use time series, 4.7% use regression, and 84.6% indicated they do not use quantitative forecasting techniques.

Table 5.3   Forecasting Descriptive Statistics

Hours Spent Per Month of Forecasting	Frequency	Percent	Forecasting Horizon[a]	Frequency	Percent
1 hour or less	45	21.0	Weekly Horizon	14	6.5
1.1 to 2.0 hours	46	21.5	Monthly Horizon	71	33.2
2.1 to 3.0 hours	22	10.3	Quarterly Horizon	90	42.1
3.1 to 4.0 hours	27	12.6	1-Year Horizon	133	62.1
4.1 to 5.0 hours	13	6.1	2-Year Horizon	11	5.1
5.1 to 10.0 hours	28	13.1	5-Year Horizon	9	4.2
10.1 to 20.0 hours	11	5.1	Other Horizon	26	12.1
20.1 or more hours	22	10.3			
Total	214	100.0			

a. Note: There are multiple responses.

Forecasting Environment Within Company

More than 12% of respondents indicated that they have "very little" to "no" knowledge of what is done with their forecasts after they are submitted, 35.2% have "some knowledge," 28.2% have "lots of knowledge," and 23.9% have "extensive knowledge." While 76.5% of respondents receive feedback on the accuracy of their forecasts, only 59.4% believe the feedback is adequate. A total of 43.7% of respondents indicated that forecast quality impacts their performance evaluations, and 24.4% indicated that forecast quality is tied to their compensation.

Respondents were asked how seriously they regarded their forecasting responsibilities, as well as how seriously others in the organization regarded the forecasts the respondents provided, measured on a 5-point Likert-type scale ranging from "Not at all seriously" to "Extremely seriously." Results show that the level of seriousness placed on the forecasts by the respondents is strikingly similar to that of the organization for which they provide the forecasts, with most responses being "fairly seriously" (37.3% and 35.3%, respectively) to "quite seriously" (35.8% and 35.3%, respectively; see Table 5.4). In terms of the overall forecasting process, 24.3% of respondents are "extremely satisfied" to "quite satisfied," 44.8% are "satisfied," and 31.0% are "somewhat dissatisfied" to "extremely dissatisfied" (see Table 5.5).

Table 5.4   Level of Seriousness Placed in the Forecast

	Extremely Seriously	Quite Seriously	Fairly Seriously	Not very Seriously	Not at all Seriously
How seriously do you take your forecasting responsibilities?	17.5%	35.8%	37.3%	8.5%	0.9%
How seriously are your forecasts taken by others in the organization?	19.8%	35.3%	35.3%	8.2%	1.4%

Table 5.5   Level of Satisfaction with Forecasting Process

	Extremely Satisfied	Quite Satisfied	Satisfied	Somewhat Dissatisfied	Extremely Dissatisfied
How satisfied are you with the forecasting process?	1.9%	22.4%	44.8%	26.7%	4.3%

Results indicate that there is considerable involvement of the sales force in sales forecasting, but there is also considerable room for improvement in many companies.

6

Sales Forecasting Systems

❖ ❖ ❖

We have been amazed at the number of companies in the benchmark studies that have little, or no, systems connectivity. The sales forecasters often do not have access to the management information system—when they need data for forecasting, they have to type it into their computer. Further, users of the forecasts do not have direct access to the sales forecasting system. When the user needs the forecast, the sales forecaster prints out the results and someone carries it to the user's office and types it into the user's planning system. Such manual data transfers are time consuming, frustrating, and prone to input errors. In addition, the users of the forecast cannot provide electronic input to the sales forecast. As one software company remarked to us, "Remember, the most popular forecasting system in the world today is Excel® . . . billion-dollar companies are running their sales forecasting processes on hundreds of unconnected spreadsheets!"

However, not all companies suffer from such lack of systems connectivity.

"I was working on a spreadsheet for one of our product forecasts," said a sales forecasting analyst for a large manufacturer of automotive parts. "As I worked, a message came across the bottom of the screen that said, 'I used to be responsible for forecasting the same product and I have seen this situation before.' The sender went on to suggest ways I could adjust the system forecast to improve its accuracy."

When we asked her if she followed the sender's advice, she said, "Well of course! The message was from the CEO!"

❖ INTRODUCTION

While not everyone gets such "helpful hints" from the CEO as the sales forecaster in this example, it is just this type of systems connectivity that is a necessary component of forecasting systems. Forecasting systems are not just the personal computer on which the forecasting software package resides. Rather, **sales forecasting systems are all the computer and communication systems used by the developers and users of the sales forecasts**—they are the integrating template that overlays all of the processes, procedures, and reporting associated with sales forecasting.

How these computer and communications systems should be designed is the topic of this chapter. In discussing this topic, we will be guided by **the seven principles of sales forecasting systems** that we have developed from working with a number of companies in defining, developing, and refining sales forecasting systems. These seven principles are:

1. The sales forecasting system should serve as a communication vehicle between users and developers of the forecasts.

2. The tool should fit the problem, not the other way around.

3. Complex forecasting systems do not have to look that way to the user.

4. Think in terms of a "suite" of time series techniques, not just one technique.

5. Think in terms of time series, regression, *and* (not or) qualitative analysis.

6. Let the system tell you which techniques to use.

7. You tell the system which forecasts are important.

We discuss each of these principles individually. This is followed by a description of a system, which personifies these principles and is used by a number of companies, to illustrate how these principles can be put into practice.

❖ THE SALES FORECASTING SYSTEM AS A COMMUNICATION VEHICLE

As we mentioned at the opening of this chapter, we have been surprised in the benchmark studies (discussed in later chapters) with the number of companies that reported "system disconnects" and "islands of analysis" in their sales forecasting process. **System disconnects** exist when the information needed to develop sales forecasts is not electronically available to the developers of the sales forecasts. When market research information, inventory levels, confirmed orders, EDI input from suppliers and customers, and sometimes even historical demand information are not available to the forecasters, they simply do not have the information necessary to do their jobs. No one can forecast in the absence of information. Conversely, the more information that is available, the better the forecast that can be developed. When the information is available, but not in an electronic form, a considerable amount of error creeps into the forecasting process as a result of mistakes in manual data entry. Thus, "system disconnects" can be cured by providing forecasters with electronic access to the systems that contain the information necessary to develop informed sales forecasts.

The second systems communication problem is **islands of analysis**, which exist when the **users** of the sales forecasts do not have electronic access to the sales forecasting system. As we discussed in Chapter 1, managers in all the functional areas of a business (marketing, sales, finance, production, and logistics) need sales forecasts. When these managers cannot obtain electronic access to the sales forecasts, at the very least the same types of manual data entry mistakes occur when these functional managers enter the forecasts into their systems. At the worst, the functional managers become frustrated with the inability to interact with the forecasting process and to provide their input to the forecasts while they are being developed. This frustration often results in each functional area independently developing their own forecasts for their own use. These "islands of analysis" result in duplication of effort, each function forecasting without access to all the information they need, and no function having input from the other functions.

The cure for both system disconnects and islands of analysis is an open-systems architecture, both internal and external. Internally, an open-systems architecture means that all the systems used by the functional areas, sales forecasting, and the management information systems (MIS) area are tied together through a central system, which has access to the corporate "data warehouse." The data warehouse means that all information gathered by MIS is stored in a central location so that all information relevant to sales forecasting can be easily and electronically accessed by anyone in the system (i.e., the "open" system). The "open" system means that all functional systems (including the sales forecasting system) can be accessed by all other functional systems through this central system.

Such an internal open-systems system means that anyone involved in **developing** the sales forecasts can electronically access whatever information is needed—whether this information is sales history, order history, market research information for regression analysis, financial plans, production schedules and/or capacity, or inventory levels. Further, this means that anyone involved in **using** the sales forecasts can electronically provide input to the developers of the sales forecasts and conduct their own analyses and planning based on the existing sales forecasts.

External open-systems architecture, often called CPFR or Collaborative Planning, Forecasting, and Replenishment (VICS, 2004), means that the corporate system has access to the corporate systems of as many customers and suppliers as possible. The reason for access to your customers is to provide more accurate and timely information on the demand your customers are receiving from their customers and the inventory your customers are carrying to meet it. With this information, independent demand, derived demand, and dependent demand can be identified; thus, more accurate forecasts can be derived by each major customer, reducing overall forecasting error. The reason for access to suppliers is to provide more accurate information on the availability of materials for the production system (dependent demand) and to improve the forecasting accuracy of the suppliers (an improvement that should eventually lower their costs and price).

Figure 6.1 illustrates this internal and external open-systems architecture. To the degree that this complete architecture can be achieved, communication between the functional areas and sales forecasting is improved, manual data entries are minimized, islands of analysis eliminated, and sales forecasting becomes a much more informed and accurate process.

The Tool Should Fit the Problem

Principle 2 relates to a basic systems principle that business systems exist to serve the business, not the other way around. Unfortunately, the philosophy of many software vendors is essentially, "If you can just make your company run the way our system operates, then we can solve all your problems."

It ought to be the other way around—the sales forecasting system (or any business system, for that matter) should be customized to meet the forecasting needs of the company. If the company wants to forecast

Figure 6.1   Sales Forecasting Systems Open-Systems Architecture

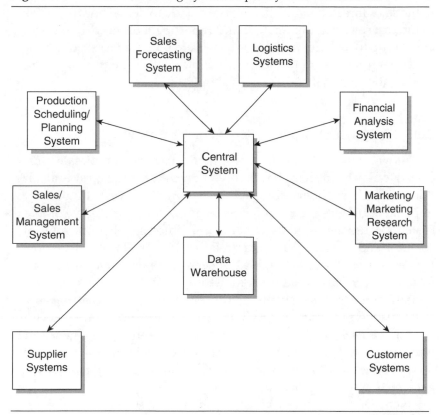

weekly, with monthly, quarterly, and yearly roll-ups, the system should be customized to provide forecasts for these intervals and horizons. If the company wants to forecast at the stock keeping unit by location (SKUL), the stock keeping unit (SKU), the product line, and the corporate level, with adjustments at any level automatically reconciled at all other levels, the system should accommodate this. If the company wants analysts and managers to be able to make qualitative adjustments to the forecasts and capture the effect of each on forecasting accuracy, this should also be possible. Too often, requests such as these are met with the response, "but the system does not work that way."

A sales forecasting system for the sales forecaster is much like the toolbox for a mechanic—the toolbox exists to provide the tools for the mechanic to do his or her job. If the mechanic needs a screwdriver, the toolbox should not have only hammers. In the same sense, it is up to the sales forecasting function in a company to define how they want to forecast sales, and the analytic and reporting tools needed to do this job. It is up to the sales forecasting system to provide these tools. As we go through the rest of the seven principles and through the example system, the potential of these tools should be clearer.

Complex Systems Do Not Have to Look That Way

As we observed in Chapters 2 through 5, the job of sales forecasting can get a bit complex. Involved procedures, logic, and calculations may be necessary to arrive at the final forecast. In addition, implementing these seven principles can involve incredibly complex systems solutions—solutions that access information from multiple sources, and then perform hundreds of thousands of calculations. However, none of this complexity needs to be apparent to the sales forecaster. The job of the sales forecaster is to understand the uses and limitations of the two quantitative groups of sales forecasting techniques (time series and regression), and to understand how each is used in their sales forecasting system to arrive at the system-generated forecast. From this understanding, sales forecasters should bring their own experience to bear to qualitatively improve the quantitatively generated system forecast.

None of this requires an in-depth understanding of the actual systems functions or the mathematical calculations that must be conducted to bring the quantitative forecast to them. The systems functions are the responsibility of the information systems group. The mathematical calculations are the responsibility of the developers of the actual sales forecasting system. What the sales forecaster should see is the quantitative forecasts, laid out in a format that is easy to understand and lends itself well to the analysis the sales forecaster may want to do while making qualitative adjustments. We have found that the best environment to accomplish this is a spreadsheet environment. As the example system described later will illustrate, the complex systems functions and mathematical calculations can all be performed without direct input from the sales forecaster. All the sales forecaster needs to do is access a spreadsheet and follow some straightforward instructions to finalize the sales forecasts. This is also the case with the demonstration software described later in this chapter and should be the case for any sales forecasting software.

A "Suite" of Time Series Techniques

Time-series-based forecasting systems have traditionally been centered around one time series technique. The state of computer technology historically only allowed a computer system to have one of the time series techniques discussed in Chapter 3. As a result, companies had to go through considerable analysis prior to selection or development of their sales forecasting system to determine which time series technique worked best for the largest number of their products. Alternatively, companies simply purchased a software package and hoped the one time series technique included would work for their products.

Modern computer technology has eliminated the need for such a narrow focus on one time series technique. With the availability of systems similar to the demonstration system discussed later in this chapter, there is no reason why a company should use a naïve, one-time-series-technique system today.

Rather, modern sales forecasting systems include a "suite" of time series techniques—that is, all the techniques discussed in Chapter 3 are available in the system. Any and all of these techniques can be brought to bear in forecasting each individual product. For example, exponential smoothing with an α of 0.14 might be best for the first product forecast, the same technique with a different α might be best for the next product forecast, exponential smoothing with trend and seasonality might be best for the next product, and so on until the best technique is selected for each product to be forecast.

As we discuss in a later section, this selection of which technique for each product can be automatic or conducted by the forecaster. The demonstration system discussed later in this chapter, in fact, gives you both these options. The ability to select the technique for each item to be forecast is usually not a necessary characteristic of large systems that are designed to forecast thousands of products in any given period. Regardless of whether the system selects the technique or you select one, however, the point of this principle is that a "suite" of time series techniques must first be available in the system. There is no excuse today for using a sales forecasting system that does not offer this feature.

Time Series, Regression, and (not or) Qualitative

In this book, we have talked about qualitative techniques, time series techniques, and regression analysis separately—each in its own separate chapter, in fact. Unfortunately, these techniques are also treated as separate in many sales forecasting systems—if you use one, then you do not need to use the others. This leads to systems that "take a time series approach" or "are regression based"—both of which often make it difficult or impossible to make qualitative adjustments to the quantitative forecasts.

In fact, time series, regression, and qualitative techniques each have their own unique advantages and disadvantages with respect to sales forecasting (as we discussed in Chapters 3, 4, and 5). However, these advantages and disadvantages are largely complementary. Time series techniques are designed to identify and forecast trends and seasonal patterns in data and to adjust quickly when the trend or the seasonal patterns shift. The disadvantage to times series techniques is that they do not consider external factors.

Regression analysis does a poor job of identifying trends and seasonality and an even poorer job of adjusting to changes in either. (Remember: Regression analysis requires a considerable amount of data, so it does not adjust "quickly" to anything.) What it does do well is consider external factors and their impact on the forecast (that is, after all, what it is designed to do).

What neither time series nor regression does well is deal with changes in the business environment that have never happened before or have happened before but we have no data in the system that describes what happened (in other words, we have no previous data to analyze). This is exactly what experienced forecast analysts and managers do well—take various "feelings," "impressions," and "inter-action" from themselves, others in the company, suppliers, and cus-tomers and translate that into a qualitative adjustment to the quantitative forecast. Often, this translation is based on a keen analysis of the business environment, but involves no quantifiable data. What forecast analysts and managers do not do well is look at masses of data and precisely identify trends, seasonal patterns, or relationships with external factors.

Thus, each of the three approaches to sales forecasting does some-thing well that the other two do poorly. We call this the "three-legged easel" of sales forecasting systems (Figure 6.2). Just like a three-legged easel where one of the legs is cut off, in a forecasting system that does not use the three forecasting technique groups ("legs") of time series, regression, and qualitative, forecasting accuracy will suffer (or fall over completely). For this reason, we have found that the most effective sales forecasting systems start with a time series forecast (using the "suite"

Figure 6.2   The "Three-Legged Easel" of Sales Forecasting Techniques

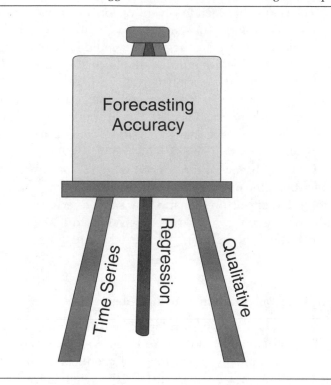

approach we just discussed) to develop an initial forecast, use regression analysis of external factors to improve this initial forecast, and then make it easy for the sales forecasters to analyze the resultant forecasts and make qualitative changes based on information they have that was not considered by the time series or the regression analysis.

A brief example might help. Suppose we are forecasting a product that has a definite trend and for which we run a trade promotion every May. However, suppose we also run consumer price promotions at various times during the year for this product. Time series will very effectively identify and forecast the trend and the effect on demand of the May trade promotion (this promotion that happens at the same time every year will show up in time series analysis as a seasonal pattern). What time series will not figure out is the impact on the forecast of consumer price promotions because they do not happen at regular times each year. Time series will treat this pattern as "noise."

It is precisely this pattern that regression analysis will identify (by finding a correlation between the event of consumer price promotions and the jump in demand). Thus, we have a quantitative forecast that is better than either time series or regression could have obtained alone.

If we make this information available to the sales forecaster—identifying the trend, the seasonal trade promotions, and the consumer price promotion effects so the sales forecaster can understand them—we can build on this forecast. For example, suppose the sales forecaster knows that a special order will be coming from a key customer that will increase demand next month by 50%, but decrease demand for the subsequent three months by 15%. Knowing how the system identified the historical trend, trade promotion, and consumer price promotion effects on demand, the sales forecaster can use this knowledge that is not available to the system to make a qualitative adjustment. Thus, the accuracy of the resultant forecast is further improved.

Let the System Tell You Which Techniques to Use

Back in the 1980s, we developed a **sales forecasting expert system**. This system allowed the user to answer a series of questions about his or her company, the number of products the user forecast, whether trend and seasonality existed, the availability of external information, the sophistication of personnel and computer systems, and a host of other questions. Based upon the answers to all these questions, the expert system made specific recommendations regarding which forecasting techniques should be used for each product in the company.

After more than 300 companies had used this expert system and provided us with feedback on its usefulness, we realized the one thing the system did not need was the person sitting at the computer answering the questions. If we could design a sales forecasting system that had the access to corporate information depicted in Figure 6.1, the system could automatically select the best forecasting technique for each situation—all without input from the user. This resulted in the development of a number of sales forecasting systems that follow this principle. The demonstration system discussed later in the chapter is an example of this process.

The embodiment of Principle 6 simply means that a system that has access to demand history for all the products to be forecast can take each product, one at a time, try a number of different time series techniques on that one product, and select the technique that provides the best forecast for that one product. The system can then go on to the second product and repeat the process until all products to be forecast have been analyzed. The result is the selection of the most accurate time series technique to use for each product to be forecast.

The system should also have access to data on all the variables that might affect demand for any of the products (see the discussion of variable selection in Chapter 4). With this access, the system can automatically follow the process outlined in Figure 4.3 in Chapter 4 to find the variables that do the best job of improving each time series forecast for each product (the variables used may be different for each product).

The result is that the sales forecaster sees a quantitative forecast—with the trend, seasonality, and regression effects identified—without going through the tedious process of trying different times series techniques and regression variables for each product. The user trusts the system to do this analysis, using the criterion of increased accuracy for time series technique selection and the criteria presented in Figure 4.3 of Chapter 4 for regression analysis. The users can then concentrate on what they do best—qualitatively improving the system forecast.

Tell the System Which Forecasts Are Important

The previous section pointed out that modern sales forecasting systems can do much of the analysis for you concerning which techniques to use. However, you still need to tell the system which forecasts are important and which are not. In many cases, sales forecasting systems in large companies make thousands (or hundreds of thousands) of forecasts per month. Of these thousands of forecasts, which should be analyzed qualitatively and which are "good enough" and do not require valuable and limited sales forecaster time?

Effective sales forecasting systems assist the sales forecaster in answering this question with a **management by exception** approach. In Chapter 8, we identify a number of criteria by which sales forecasting managers can decide which products need more accurate forecasts and which can tolerate less accuracy. The management by exception approach to sales forecasting systems dictates that, for each product to be forecast, management agrees on what constitutes an acceptable level of MAPE. Any product for which the system achieves a MAPE lower than the acceptable level does not show up on the exception report. Any product for which the MAPE achieved with time series and regression analysis is greater than the acceptable level shows up on the exception report. This report lists all the products for which the system is not automatically achieving acceptable MAPEs and, thus, those which need to be qualitatively analyzed by the sales forecasters.

This does not mean the sales forecaster cannot also analyze other products that are not on the exception report. It simply means that the majority of the attention of the sales forecaster is focused on the products that need it most—those for which the system is not already achieving acceptable levels of accuracy.

Summary: Sales Forecasting Systems Principles

We have presented seven principles that should be embodied in any sales forecasting system today. Given the considerable savings resulting from lower supply chain costs, higher customer service levels, improved coordination between business planning functions, and improved coordination with suppliers and customers, the cost of implementing these principles is well worth the effort.

To demonstrate how these principles can be implemented, an example of a sales forecasting system (MULTICASTER® Forecasting Systems [MFS]) that embodies all seven of these principles is presented. Again, to demonstrate the benefits from such a system, one company using this system reported a monthly improvement in sales not lost due to stockouts of $6,000,000—a direct result of improved forecasting accuracy (Mentzer & Schroeter, 1993). This is followed by a more detailed description of a demonstration version of this system that can be used with this book.

MULTICASTER®

MULTICASTER® (MFS) is that basis upon which many modern forecasting systems are built today—forecasting systems that provide a communications vehicle for the sales forecasting function by interacting with the management information system (MIS) to obtain data on past demand, forecasts, and exogenous events, and by providing access to the forecasting results for the sales forecasters and the users of the forecast.

Although MFS provides a sophisticated forecasting environment, all the user sees is a spreadsheet (in fact, most modern versions of MFS actually work in an Excel® environment). Thus, the complex system does not look that way to the user.

MFS uses a suite of 19 times series techniques and selects the one technique that provides the lowest MAPE for each product to be forecast. This is followed by use of regression analysis to forecast that part of the demand pattern that time series could not. The results of the time series and the regression forecasting are then placed in the spreadsheet for the user to analyze; this combines time series, regression, and qualitative forecasting techniques and lets the system select which techniques to use. Finally, an exception report is available to direct the attention of the sales forecasters to those forecasts that most need qualitative adjustment (see Figure 6.3 for an illustration of this process).

Figure 6.3   MFS Systems Flow

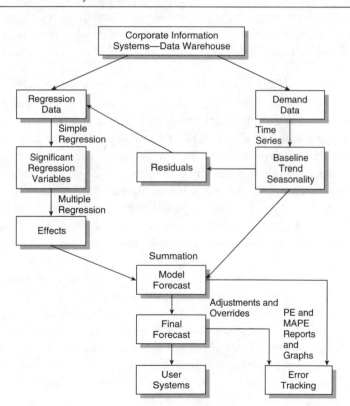

MFS is designed to forecast down to a level of detail equal to each stock keeping unit at each distribution location (SKUL), but forecasts can be made and reconciled at any level above this. At the beginning of each forecasting period, a data file that contains all changes to the product list and the prior month's demand history is loaded into MFS. This process triggers MFS to reforecast all products that have additional demand data, and creates a spreadsheet for each product, allowing the sales forecasters to see the latest demand history and forecasts available. Once the sales forecasters have finished examining and qualitatively adjusting the spreadsheets, the final forecasts are released to the users' systems. However, during this qualitative forecasting stage, the ability exists for users to view the spreadsheets and, electronically, make suggestions for adjustments. In this way, the system facilitates involvement of all the functions in Figure 6.1 in the sales forecasting process.

Thus, MFS is designed to be a system that interacts with the other information systems illustrated in Figure 6.1, provides relevant analysis of historical data using a suite of time series techniques and regression analysis, and communicates the analysis to the sales forecaster and users of the forecasts in a convenient analytical environment, i.e., a spreadsheet.

MFS uses any of up to 19 time series forecasting techniques to determine base line (level), trend, and any seasonal patterns in the data for each product forecast. Table 6.1 provides a descriptive list of these techniques. The first three techniques are naïve techniques, and the next four are variations of a moving average. The remaining 12 techniques are exponential smoothing techniques. Techniques 8, 9, and 10 are variations of exponential smoothing (Brown & Myer, 1961). Techniques 11, 12, and 13 are adaptive smoothing (Trigg & Leach, 1967). Techniques 14 through 19 are variations of extended exponential smoothing (Winters, 1960; Mentzer, 1988). Notice that this list includes all the techniques discussed in Chapter 3.

The technique that produces the lowest error in forecasting the existing data for each product is selected each period by MFS to produce the time series forecast for that product. Each product has its own unique spreadsheet where the forecast baseline, trend, and seasonality are recorded separately. Although the MFS techniques calculate baseline, trend, and seasonality multiplicatively (as was discussed under FMTS techniques in Chapter 3), the components are recorded in the spreadsheet as separate components to be added together for the purpose of displaying each time series component for the sales forecaster.

Table 6.1   Multiple Forecasting System Time Series Techniques

Technique

1    $Actual_t = Forecast_t + 1$

2    $Actual_t + (Actual_t - Actual_{t-1}) = Forecast_{t+1}$

3    $Actual_{t-11} = Forecast_{t+1}$

4   Moving Average (User specifies number of months in average)

5   Moving Average with Multiplicative Seasonality (User specifies number of months in average)

6   Weighted Moving Average (User specifies number of months in average and weights)

7   Weighted Moving Average with Multiplicative Seasonality (User specifies number of months in average and weights)

Numbers 8 through 19 are exponential smoothing

	Alpha	Beta	Gamma	Code
8	F	N	N	F = Fixed
9	F	F	N	N = Not Included
10	F	N	F	A = Adaptive
11	A	N	N	H = Heuristic
12	A	F	N	
13	A	N	F	
14	F	F	F	
15	A	A	A	
16	A	F	F	
17	H	H	H	
18	H	F	F	
19	H	N	N	

NOTE: 8 = Exponential Smoothing, 9 = Exponential Smoothing with seasonality, 10 = Exponential Smoothing with trend, 11 = Adaptive Smoothing, 12 = Adaptive Smoothing with seasonality, 13 = Adaptive Smoothing with trend, 14 = Winters Technique, 15 = Adaptive Extended Exponential Smoothing with calculated smoothing constants, 16 = Adaptive Extended Exponential Smoothing, 17 = Adaptive Extended Exponential Smoothing with heuristic selection of smoothing constants, 18 = Adaptive Extended Exponential Smoothing with fixed beta and gamma and alpha heuristically selected, 19 = Exponential Smoothing with alpha heuristically selected.

For example, suppose Technique 14 is selected by MFS and the times series components are calculated by the technique to be as follows:

Base Line = 1,000

Trend = 150

Seasonality = 1.15

The formula from Chapter 3 for the final forecast in Technique 14 is:

Forecast = (Base Line + Trend) × Seasonality

and, thus, the forecast would be ((1000 + 150) × 1.15) or 1,323. However, this information would be presented in the first three lines of the spreadsheet as:

Base Line = 1,000

Trend = 150

Seasonality = 173

which still equals 1,323. For techniques that do not consider trend or seasonality, those lines in the spreadsheet are simply left blank.

The part of the data not explained by the time series forecast (the residual or, in time series terminology, the noise) is further subjected to multiple regression analysis. Data on up to 500 potential exogenous variables are stored in the regression module of MFS, and each variable is compared to the residual for each product. Up to 10 of these variables that are significantly related to the residual of each product are selected by the regression module to forecast the residual portion of the demand for that product, using the stepwise approach discussed in Chapter 4. Once this analysis is completed, the regression-based forecast of the residuals is also recorded in the spreadsheet for that particular product. The base line, trend, seasonality, and regression forecasts of the residual are then added together in the spreadsheet to present the MFS forecast. Thus, time series and regression forecasting are combined automatically to provide the advantages of each technique to each individual forecast.

The sales forecaster is now in a position to view each spreadsheet and analyze the MFS forecast and its four components (time series base line, trend, and seasonality, plus the regression forecast of the residual). Based upon previous experience with the company and its business environment, with MFS, and knowledge of future events, the sales forecaster has the ability to adjust the MFS forecast to arrive at the final forecast.

To capture a record of the logic for these adjustments, each spreadsheet has a unique notepad attached that can contain up to 30 pages of text. This feature augments the qualitative forecasting process. A conversion button is also available that can convert a spreadsheet with forecasts in units (something production typically wants) to dollars (something often needed by marketing, sales, and finance), or to cubic volume (something often needed by distribution center managers) or to weight (something often needed by transportation planning).

Because these different areas may need the forecast at different forecast levels, the spreadsheet can be aggregated up or broken down to any level in the "forecasting hierarchy" that is defined by the company. For example, a forecasting hierarchy may go from SKUL to SKU to product to product line to division to corporate. MFS allows the sales forecaster to analyze and make changes at any of these levels, with the changes reconciled with the other levels.

A number of graphs are available to assist the sales forecaster in qualitatively forecasting and in analyzing forecasting performance. These include graphic comparisons of: (1) sales forecaster's forecasts versus actual demand, (2) MFS forecasts versus actual demand, (3) management-adjusted forecasts versus actual demand, (4) sales forecaster's forecasts versus MFS forecasts, (5) sales forecaster's forecasts versus management adjusted forecasts, (6) actual demand, (7) sales forecaster's forecasts versus MFS forecasts versus actual demand, (8) percent errors, (9) MAPE, and (10) YTD MAPE.

To make the process of adjusting forecasts easier, graphs should allow the forecaster to "click and pull" the forecast. In other words, rather than having to enter forecast adjustments in each future period of the spreadsheet, the forecaster can use the cursor to reshape (draw) the forecast into a line that the forecaster believes is more accurate. When this process is completed, MFS calculates the actual values from the new line and enters them into the spreadsheet. In this manner, the forecaster can enter adjustments directly into the spreadsheet or enter values that visually seem more accurate.

MFS also allows for "looks like" forecasting of new products. This feature allows the user to specify for a new product that the demand for the first year will "look like" another product, an aggregate of several products, or a line drawn on the screen by the user. MFS uses this "looks like" forecast until one of the time series techniques has sufficient data to produce more accurate forecasts.

MULTICASTER® Book Version

Although we were involved in developing a number of mainframe-based sales forecasting systems back in the 1970s, in 1982 we developed one of the first PC-based, commercial sales forecasting software packages. This system, called EASY CASTER®, worked on the old two-floppy disk computers—hard disks were not even available yet. The system had eight different time series techniques, plus simple and multiple regression analysis. You could select one technique at a time, and it took a considerable amount of time to make one forecast.

Because the system was designed to make one forecast at a time for one product at a time, it was really designed to analyze techniques to help the user decide which techniques to use in larger, mainframe-based systems. In fact, the analytical capabilities of EASY CASTER® made it very popular for teaching forecasting techniques in college courses.

EASY CASTER® led to us working with a number of companies in the 1980s to develop customized, in-house, PC-based sales forecasting systems, which eventually led to the development of the customizable system, MULTICASTER®.

We have now come full circle by going from a PC-based system designed to analyze and forecast a small number of products (EASY CASTER®), to a large-scale PC-based system designed to forecast many products (MULTICASTER® Forecasting System, [MFS]), back to a PC-based system for analyzing a small number of products (MULTICASTER Book Version, [MBV]), which is a supplement for this book.

During this circle, of course, the system has become much more powerful. MBV has built into it all the sophistication of large-scale MFS versions, but is available for you to try what you have learned in this book on your own demand data.

The rest of this chapter is really a "walk through" of how to use this demonstration version (MBV) of world-class sales forecasting software (this software can be downloaded from the Profiles section of www.jtmassociates.com). The purpose of this software is to allow you to read the book, turn to your computer, and try what you have learned to forecast some of your own data.

MBV has four major components: a set of data files, the worksheet, the Settings screen, and the Notes screen. These four components are used together in a straightforward process to produce forecasts of your data. This process is described first, followed by an in-depth explanation of how to use each of these four components.

MBV PROCESS

As illustrated in Figure 6.4, MBV starts with downloading the system on your computer. The next step is loading your data into the MBV Template spreadsheet data file. This is a "csv" file that is included on the www.jtmassociates.com website. You can download and access this data file through Excel® and replace the sample data with your own data. We will discuss the format of this data sheet later, but the purpose of this step is to enter your data in an environment that is readily available and easy to use.

Once the data are correctly entered into the spreadsheet, this file should be saved as a comma-delimited (or "csv") file—with the name of the file associated with the name of the product (i.e., productname.csv)—in the same directory where you have previously installed MBV.

If you have already downloaded MBV, you enter MBV by double clicking the MBV icon on your desktop screen. When you enter MBV, you will see a screen like the one in Figure 6.5. Click OK and you will then be asked to enter one of the passwords from the Appendix to this chapter. Once you have successfully entered the password, the next screen (shown in Figure 6.6) will offer you the option of loading a file you have already imported (by clicking the right mouse button or pressing F5), or importing a new file. The MBV system comes with data files for 10 products already imported (five files have only a history of demand for that product—for five products from a variety of companies—and five files have the demand history for various products of a furniture manufacturer and regression variables that might be useful for forecasting demand for these products).

To import a new file, click the File | Import menu, and the screen in Figure 6.7 will appear. Click the Import Product button, then select the csv file you wish to import from the screen shown in Figure 6.8. When you are finished importing data files, you may click the Done button and you will be returned to the screen in Figure 6.6.

If you wish to load a file you have already imported, click the right mouse button from the screen shown in Figure 6.6, or press F5, and

Figure 6.4   MBV Process

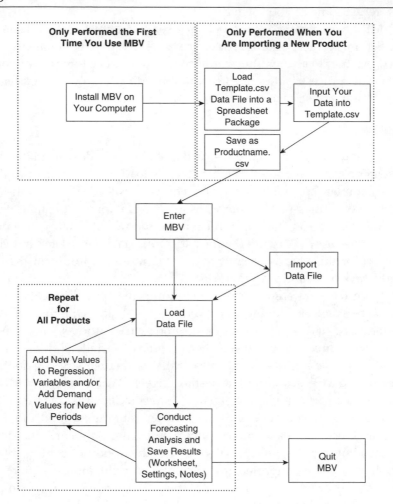

then indicate the file you wish to load. Once you have loaded a file, you will see a screen similar to Figure 6.9. This is the worksheet component of MBV. From this screen, you can make adjustments to forecasts, analyze graphs, and perform various other functions we will discuss later. Also, notice in the lower-left corner of Figure 6.9 the buttons labeled "Worksheet," "Settings" (Figure 6.10), and "Notes" (Figure 6.11). By clicking any of these three buttons, you can move between these three components of MBV.

Figure 6.5   MBV Opening Screen

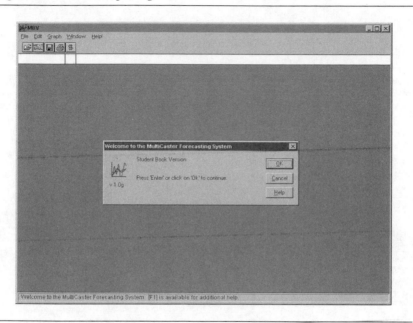

Figure 6.6   MBV File Load Selection Screen

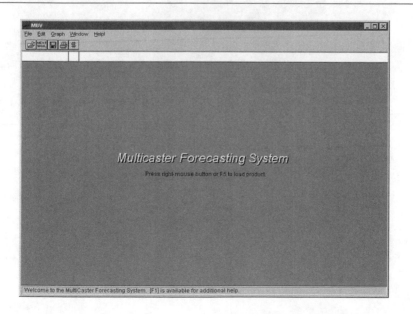

Figure 6.7   MBV File Import Screen

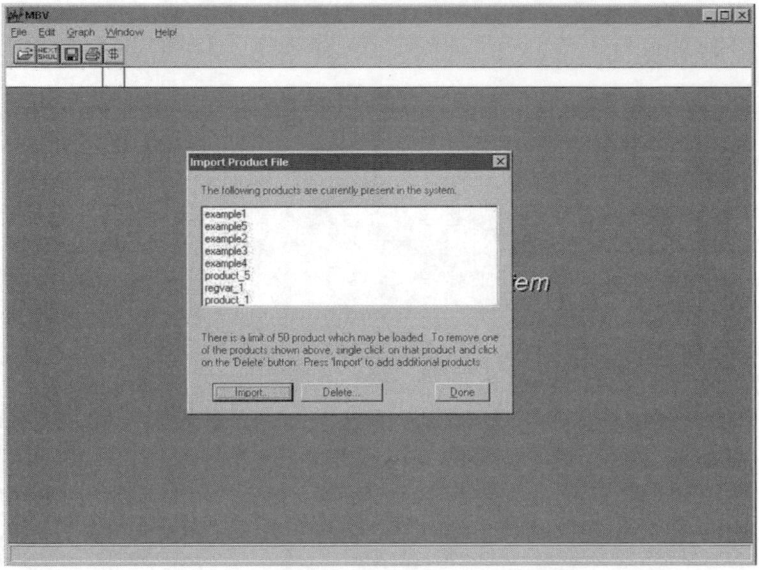

Figure 6.8   MBV File Import Selection Screen

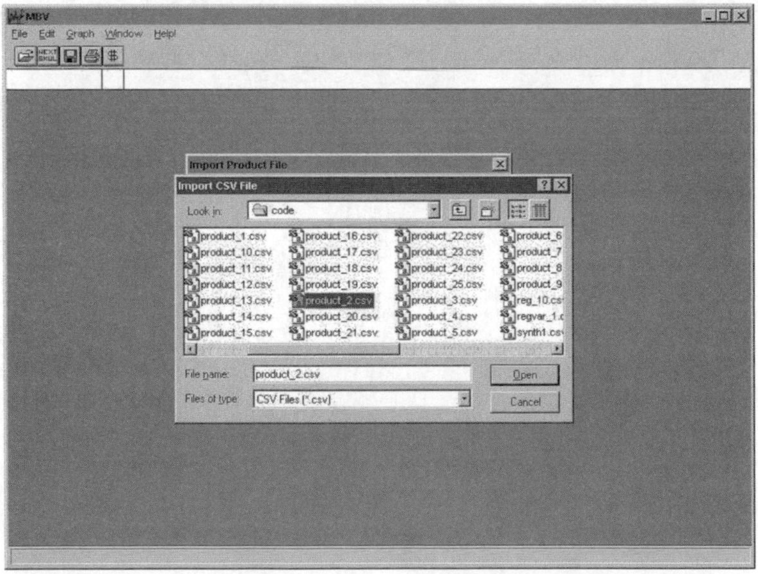

Figure 6.9   MBV Worksheet

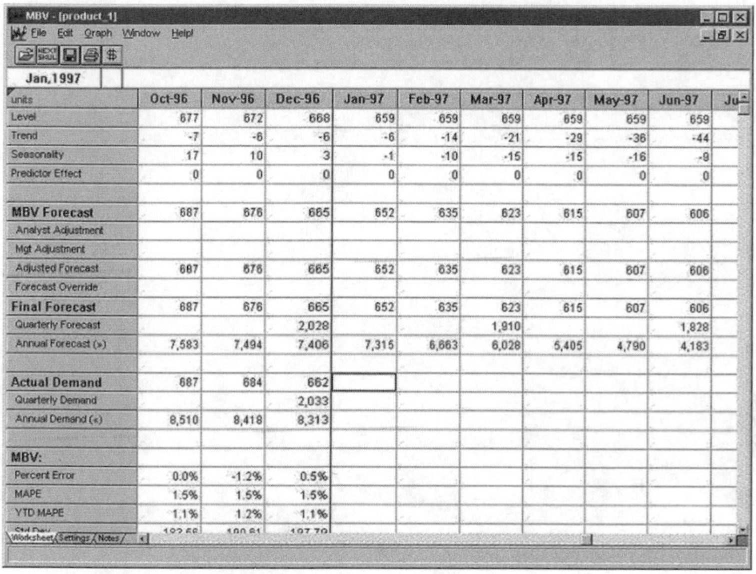

Figure 6.10   MBV Settings Screen

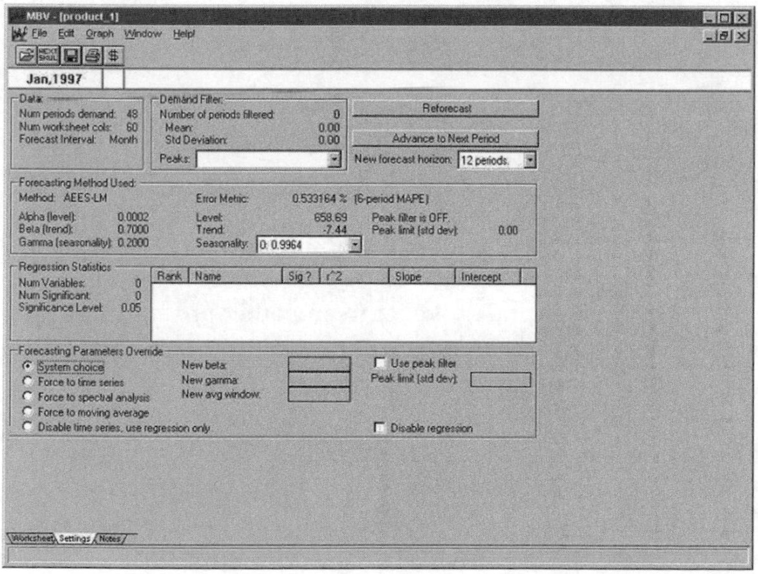

Figure 6.11   MBV Notes Screen

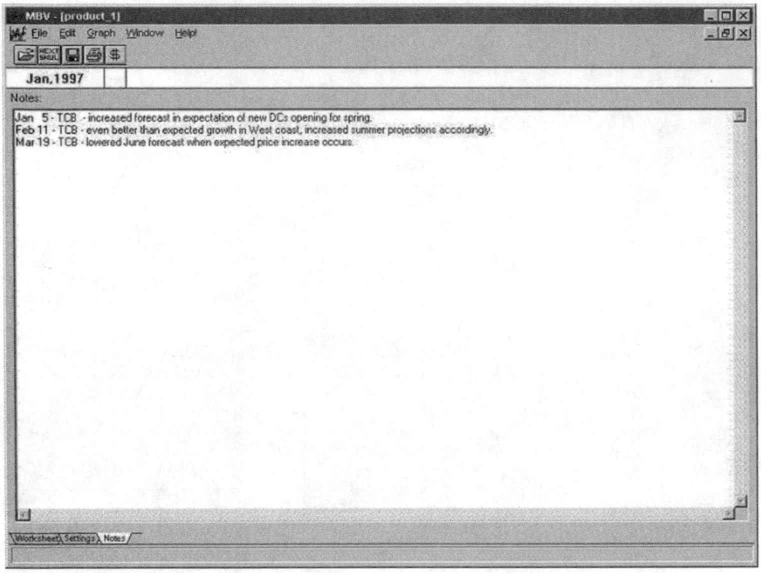

Briefly, the settings screen is used to specify how you wish to forecast this particular product and to create the forecast (when you first import and load a data file, there are no forecast numbers in the worksheet until you access the Settings screen and "Reforecast"). The Notes screen is available to keep notes on the logic you used to make any forecasts.

When you have finished analyzing a particular product, you can save your changes from the File | Save menu, close the worksheet with the File | Close menu, and move on to any other products you wish to load and forecast. At this point you can also add new, future values to any of the regression variables by typing those values directly into the worksheet. To make these new values a permanent part of the worksheet, again follow the File | Save menu.

When you are finished forecasting all of your products for the current period and you wish to move on to the next period (i.e., load a new period's demand for each product), you must access each product's Settings screen and select "Advance to Next Period." Because this process "locks" all information in the current period, MBV will ask you to confirm that you wish to continue. If you select "continue," MBV will ask you to enter the demand value for the new "current period." You need to repeat this procedure for every product. Note: Because a production version of MULTICASTER® (MFS) is designed to deal with a much larger number of products, this procedure for updating each period is automatic.

When you have finished forecasting and updating all the products you wish, you simply exit the system through the File | Quit menu.

Data Files

Our intention in creating the data files in a spreadsheet environment was to make it easy for the user to create, change, and import into MBV any of their own data. To create you own data file, use Excel® to access the MBV template spreadsheet data file (csv file) on the www.jtmassociates.com website. Your data file should have the generic form illustrated in Figure 6.12. Your company name, your name, and ID are optional. However, it is important to enter in this data file the number of periods per year (12 if the data are monthly, 4 if quarterly, 52 if weekly), the period in which you are presently developing a forecast (the Current Period is one period past the last period with actual demand data), how many periods into the future you wish to forecast (Forecast Horizon), and the price per unit of the product.

You need to label the periods (columns), because these labels will be imported into the MBV worksheet. The next row is the actual history of demand that is to be forecast, followed by the names and values per period of any regression variables (up to a total of 10) you wish to try. Again, it is important to include the regression variable names, because these will be imported into MBV.

The data, which start in the second column, should be the information for the first period of the first year in which you have demand history that you wish to include in the forecasting analysis. For example, if your data begin in August of 2001, the second column should start with January of 2001, with blanks in the columns until you reach the column for August of 2001 (where the actual demand values begin). Ordinarily, the more history the better, especially because regression and some of the time series techniques need at least 2 years of data to work well. The total number of periods of history, plus the months into the future to forecast, can be up to 256. Because MBV uses spreadsheet packages to import the data, it is limited to the number of columns allowed in such packages (i.e., 256) and, thus, has an upper limit to the number of periods that can be considered.

Figure 6.12   Example of CSV File to be Imported into MBV

Company Name	ABC Inc						
User Name	John Nemo						
User ID	42	Note: This example contains eight demand points, ten regression variables, and will produce forecasts out through Feb 97 (6 period forecast horizon). An actual product would typically contain at least 2 or 3 years of demand points. Only cells shown in bold-italics are used by the program, other cells may contain notes, other numbers, graphs, etc.					
Number Periods/Year	12						
Current Period	9						
Forecast Horizon	6						
Unit Price	1.23						
Period	1	2	3	4	5	6	7
	Jan-96	Feb-96	Mar-96	Apr-96	May-96	Jun-96	Jul-96
Demand (Units)	12	43	21	23	65	23	45
RegVar 1	2	3	4	6	7	4	3
RegVar 2		4					4
RegVar 3		3	2	1	4	6	
RegVar 4	6	1			2		
RegVar 5	1	3	4	6	2	3	4
RegVar 6	2	1					
RegVar 7	1	1	4	6			4
RegVar 8	1	2	2	3	3	2	2
RegVar 9	3	2	1	3	4	6	2
RegVar 10	4		2		1		

The regression values must be entered as integers. For example, price (which would normally be recorded in dollars), must be entered in cents ($235.10 should be entered as 23510). This will not affect the accuracy of regression forecasting.

When you have included all the information in your new spreadsheet, simply save it as a "csv" file and it is ready to be imported into MBV.

Worksheet

The worksheet (Figure 6.9) is an environment in which the forecast specified in the Settings screen can by qualitatively analyzed, adjusted, and/or overridden. If time series is used and level, trend, and/or seasonal components are identified, they are each placed in the corresponding first three rows in the worksheet. Even though the formulae in Chapter 3 described multiplying together the various components to get the forecast, to take advantage of the convenience of a worksheet, these three components are displayed in a fashion that allows them to be added together to arrive at a forecast (thus showing the impact of each component on the forecast).

The effects of all the significant regression variables for any given period are added together and placed in the fourth row of the worksheet (labeled Predictor Effect). Under this row, all regression variables that were included in the data file can be displayed. For each regression variable in each period, both the value of that variable in that period and the effect that value has on the forecast can be displayed. If the value of the variable is displayed, but the line below it is blank (the line for the effect on the forecast), it means that this variable did not have a significant effect on the forecast and, therefore, was not used. By default, this detailed information is displayed in the worksheet. If you wish to suppress this detail, click the green arrow in the Predictor Effect row label. If you wish to bring this detailed information back, click again on the same arrow.

For each period, the Level, Trend, Seasonality, and Predictor Effect are added together to arrive at the MBV Forecast. For all periods previous to the current period (i.e., all periods where actual demand exists), the forecast recorded is the forecast made one period before that period. In other words, for all the previous periods, the recorded forecast was a one-period-into-the-future forecast. This is the forecast on which the error statistics are calculated. For future periods, you can forecast as far forward as you want (specified in the data file). This is a deviation of MBV from MFS. In MFS, the user should be able to specify how far into the future each forecast is important, and calculate the error statistics based upon this "critical forecast horizon."

Different individuals within a company may make different qualitative adjustments to forecasts and, therefore, it is important to capture the impact of those adjustments separately. For this reason, three rows are provided in the worksheet to make changes to the systems forecast. Notice that if you try to make changes on any of these rows during previous periods, a "padlock" icon appears, reminding you that you cannot make changes to forecasts in periods where the actual value is already known (sorry, but this would be cheating).

In an actual company, the first adjustment row (Analyst Adjustment) would typically be made by a forecast analyst and constitutes adding or subtracting from the system forecast. The second row (Mgt Adjustment) would typically be made by a forecasting manager (hopefully, considering a broader range of factors as discussed in Chapter 5) and, again, constitutes adding or subtracting from the total of the system and the analyst forecast. The third row is an override of the system forecast and any adjustments that have been made to it. The result of these qualitative adjustments (overrides) is the Final Forecast. Again, this is a deviation of MBV from MFS—MBV has only two adjustment rows and the override row, whereas MFS should have as many adjustment rows as the user wishes to specify, and only certain people can make adjustments on certain rows.

The next two rows provide a summation of the last 3 months or 13 weeks (the Quarterly Forecast row) and the last 12 months or 52 weeks (the Annual Forecast row).

The next three rows in the worksheet provide the same detail of information for the actual demand. If the actual demand in any period has been "filtered" (explained later under the Settings section), a green triangle will appear in the upper left-hand corner of the actual demand cell for that period.

The rest of the worksheet displays error statistics discussed in Chapter 2: (1) for the MBV forecast, (2) for the forecast as adjusted by the analyst, and (3) for the final forecast (which includes either the management adjustment or the override).

A considerable number of additional options and information are available in the pull-down menus and toolbar. The File menu allows new worksheets to be loaded (also possible from the toolbar), saving or quitting currently loaded worksheets (also possible from the toolbar), importing additional data files, printing a copy of the worksheet (also possible from the toolbar), exporting the existing file to Excel® for more sophisticated graphing options, and quitting the MBV environment.

From the File | Load Product menu, two options exist. The user can select the list of all the products loaded into MBV and select the product to analyze (Directly option). The Directly option is typically sufficient for MBV, but MFS often has thousands (or hundreds of thousands) of products to forecast, so this list can become unwieldy. For this reason, the "from Exception List" option is provided. The Exception List contains products in decreasing order of a metric (called the Weighted PE), which is equal to the total demand volume for that product for the last three periods times its three-period MAPE. The higher this error metric (or the worse the error), the earlier the product appears on the list. In MFS, this Exception List should be adapted so that only those products with error rates higher than what is considered acceptable by management appear on the list. Remember Principle Seven earlier in this chapter: You tell the system which forecasts are important (in this case through the Exception List).

Because many popular spreadsheet packages have much more sophisticated graphing options than MBV, it may be desirable to export the worksheet once you have completed your analysis (production versions of MFS typically work in Excel®, so this option is not necessary). As with most worksheet-like environments, MBV allows you to "copy" and "paste" to and from other spreadsheet packages. To select a range of cells to copy, first move to the first cell in the range, then press the period (".") key. Continue to move the cursor using the arrow keys. A black rectangle will surround a range of cells. When you have the range that you wish to copy selected, select the "Copy" option in the "Edit" menu. The cells will revert to the normal, non-highlighted appearance and the range will be copied to the clipboard. Now you can switch to another application and select "Paste" from *that application's* "Edit" menu. The range selected will appear.

The above process may also be used to bring a range of cells from another package into MBV. However, because MBV only permits changeable values in the "Adjustment" and "Override" rows, only these two rows will be affected. Because you cannot paste something that has not already been defined, the "Paste" option in the "Edit" menu will only be able to be selected if the clipboard already contains a "cut" or "copy" from another application.

If you would prefer to create a copy of the current worksheet and save it as a file, you can select the "Export" option in the "File" menu. You can select either a text or Excel® format. The text format uses commas or tabs to separate the columns of worksheet information and may then be read into a word processing package. The "Excel" format permits you to create a file, which may be loaded using Microsoft Excel®.

Either format allows you to select a subset or range of rows and columns of the entire worksheet. To select only a few columns to be exported, click the All button below the Column Start/End section of the Export to File dialog box. After clicking, you will be able to select a start and an end column. Individual rows may be similarly chosen. Click the All button below the Row(s) section. Again, after clicking you may single-click to highlight individual rows to be exported. If you choose to export all rows or columns, you may still click the All button and select all rows and columns.

When you have finished selecting the worksheet range to export, click the Export button. A dialog will appear that allows you to choose the filename and location for the exported file. Click OK to generate the file.

Although most of the toolbar buttons are self-explanatory, one toolbar button needs explanation. If the data loaded in the data (csv) file consisted of units and a dollar value was entered in the file (in cell B8 of the csv file), the forecasts will be developed in units, but the toolbar button with the dollar sign on it allows quick conversion of all numbers to dollars. Thus, users (such as production personnel) can look at forecasts in units or quickly convert the forecasts to dollars if desired (which marketing, sales, and/or finance personnel might want). In MFS, this option should be expanded to also allow quick conversion to product volume (a form in which a logistics manager might want to see the forecast for distribution center capacity planning), weight (a form in which a transportation manager might want to see the forecast for transportation vehicle planning), price, cost, or gross margin (forms in which financial managers and/or accounting might want to see the forecast).

If we are in a large worksheet with hundreds of columns, it can be tedious to look for the current month, that is, the one in which we are developing the next forecast. To alleviate this inconvenience, the "Jump to Current Period" option in the Edit menu moves the cursor to the month in which we are trying to develop the forecast. (You can accomplish the same thing directly by pressing Ctrl+N.)

Under this same Edit menu is the option for forecasting new products through the "Looks Like" option. Selecting this option produces the screen shown in Figure 6.13. This option produces a forecast for a user-specified number of periods (up to a maximum of all the periods in the first year). Once the number of periods is specified, you must also enter several qualitative assessments:

1. Your forecast of the total demand for these initial periods,

2. Your qualitative assessment of what the growth in demand per period (trend) will be during these periods,

3. Your assessment of when this demand will begin (the "Insert at" section of the screen), and

4. Your assessment of the initial seasonal pattern.

Figure 6.13   "Looks Like" New Product Forecasting Screen

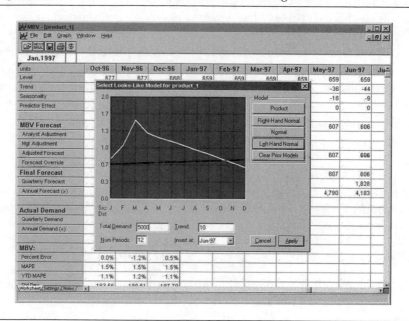

You have several options for specifying the initial seasonal pattern. The "Product" button allows you to select the seasonal pattern of any other products loaded into MBV. The next three options are variations on a seasonal pattern that follows a normal curve. The Clear Prior Models button removes any Looks Like settings that have previously been saved for this product (i.e., it gives you a "clean slate" from which to start reevaluating this new product). When you have completed your analysis, press the "Apply" button to apply the results to this product in the worksheet. This will cause the Looks Like results to be displayed on the MBV Forecast row with a green triangle in the upper-left corner of each affected cell. These Looks Like forecasts will override any MBV forecasts for the affected periods (those displaying the green triangle).

By accessing the Graph menu (or using ALT-#), any of nine graphs can be displayed. These are the various graphs sales forecasters typically use to assist in their analysis of system forecasts to make qualitative adjustments. Users should familiarize themselves with each of these graphs and decide which is the most helpful to them.

A particular feature of Graph 5 should be discussed. When in this graph, if the user "feels" the forecast needs to be adjusted, it is not necessary to flip back to the worksheet, make an entry, and then flip back to the graph to see its effect. If you simply place the cursor on the Final Forecast line for the month you wish to change, click the left mouse button, then move the cursor to where you think the forecast should be, the system will redraw the graph, calculate your change, and put that change in the Forecast Override cell for that period. In this way, you can "pick and point" your forecast changes.

You will notice when you do this (or when you make any qualitative adjustment, for that matter), the worksheet displays an icon of a finger with a string tied around it. This is to remind you to enter the Notes screen and record your logic for making this qualitative adjustment.

Settings

This component provides various forecasting status information and allows selection of forecasting methods and options through the screen illustrated in Figure 6.10. The Data section of this screen provides information on the number of periods in which actual demand data are available. The number of worksheet columns adds to this the number of periods in the initial year that have no actual demand values and the number of periods specified to forecast into the future (i.e., the forecast horizon). The "Forecast Interval" should be in weeks, months, quarters, or years.

The Demand Filter section of this screen is used only if you specify a peak filter in the lower-right box on this screen. A peak filter is used when there are large peaks or troughs in the data that are not representative and, therefore, should not be included in the MBV forecast. When you enable the peak filter (by specifying the filter in terms of the number of standard deviations of the demand from the average), MBV takes any period in which demand is outside this range and "filters" the demand—that is, MBV still records the actual demand value, but uses the value that is the specified number of standard deviations above or below (depending upon whether it is a peak or a trough, respectively) the average up to that period in the forecasting calculations. MBV displays in the Demand Filter section the number of periods in which demand was filtered and the mean and standard deviation as of the current period. The specific periods in which this filtering occurred, the actual demand value, and the filtered value are also displayed. Further, MBV indicates the filtered periods in the worksheet by placing a green triangle in the upper-left corner of the Actual Demand cell for that period.

The Forecasting Method Used section displays information on the forecasting method currently being used in the MBV forecast. Method simply indicates the technique chosen either by MBV or the user. When you allow MBV to pick the "best" forecast, MBV tries a variety of techniques and selects the "best" based on the lowest MAPE for the last half year (the Error Metric). The Error Metric achieved for the technique chosen is displayed in this section. The lower-left corner of this section displays parameters relevant to the technique chosen. The center of the section displays information on the level, trend, and seasonality values, and the right side of the section displays the peak filter status.

If regression variables were included in the data file and regression analysis is enabled (at the bottom of this screen), the Regression Statistics screen displays relevant information on each regression variable. The left side of this section displays the number of variables that were included, and the number that were found to be significant through stepwise regression at the 0.05 level of significance. The remainder of this section displays information on each variable included. Rank is the order in which the significant variables were selected during the stepwise process, followed by the nonsignificant variables in order of decreasing r^2. Slope is the b-value and intercept is the b_0-value in Equation (2) in Chapter 4.

The Forecasting Parameters Override section is where the user specifies how MBV should forecast this particular product. Selection of the System Choice option allows MBV to try:

1. Moving average (with the different numbers of periods included in the average ranging from 2 to the number of periods in a year),

2. Naïve (a moving average with an N of 1),

3. Exponential smoothing,

4. Exponential smoothing with trend,

5. Exponential smoothing with seasonality,

6. Exponential smoothing with trend and seasonality,

7. Adaptive smoothing of 3, 4, 5, and 6,

8. OMTS in the form of spectral analysis, and

9. Stepwise regression analysis,

where all of these techniques are defined in Chapters 3 or 4. MBV selects which of Techniques 1 through 8 produces the lowest error metric, and then uses Technique 9 to forecast the residual.

You can select "Force to time series" if you want to try only exponential smoothing techniques (Numbers 3, 4, 5, 6, and 7 above). Because the values of beta and gamma must be between 0 and 1 in exponential smoothing, you can "turn off" a certain time series component by setting the smoothing constant for that component equal to zero. In other words, to use exponential smoothing only (Number 3 above), set the values of beta and gamma both equal to zero. This "turns off" trend (beta = 0) and seasonality (gamma = 0). Similarly, trend or seasonality can be left on or turned off to obtain Number 4 or 5 above. If you do not enter anything for beta and gamma, MBV will find the optimal values of each (the values that minimize the error metric). Thus, when the "Force to time series" option is chosen, you can still allow MBV to find the best values of beta and gamma, you can enter your own (values between zero and one), or you can simply "turn off" either the trend and/or seasonality components. The reason for doing either of the latter two is to analyze the effect of each of these on forecasting accuracy.

You can select "Force to spectral analysis" if you want to try only OMTS (Number 8 above). When this option is chosen, you can still allow MBV to find the best values of beta (smooths annual trend) and gamma (smooths seasonality), or you can enter your own (analyzing the effect of each of these on forecasting accuracy).

You can select "Force to moving average" if you want to try Numbers 1 and 2 above. When this option is chosen, you can still allow MBV to find the best number of periods to include in the moving average (from 1 [which is really the naïve technique] to the number of periods in a year), or you can enter your own (analyzing the effect of each of these on forecasting accuracy).

For any of these options, you can enable regression analysis—which allows regression analysis to forecast the part of the demand that the time series could not (i.e., the noise or residual) in the same way as described for MFS earlier—or disable regression analysis. The option of "Disable time series, use regression only" is the converse of this. That is, MBV will not try to forecast demand with any of the time series techniques. Rather, the actual demand is analyzed and forecast with regression analysis. The value of this option is that the information displayed in the Regression Statistics section pertains to how strongly each regression variable is related to the actual demand, not the residual after time series has forecast actual demand.

Notes

Any time a qualitative forecast is made or a qualitative adjustment is made to a quantitative forecast, it is crucial for sales forecasters to document their logic. The value of this is to review this logic when similar situations occur at a later date and/or to learn from the documented logic of other sales forecasters.

The Notes component of MBV assists in this documentation by providing a notebook attached to each product (Figure 6.11). Whenever you make qualitative adjustments and/or overrides, we encourage you to fully describe the logic that went into that change. For guidance in the types of factors to consider in this logic, please review Chapter 5.

❖ SALES FORECASTING SYSTEMS: SUMMARY

In this chapter, we have presented seven principles that should be followed by any organization in its sales forecasting system. To the degree that a company can implement all of these principles, the sales forecasting system becomes a valuable tool to the sales forecaster, rather than a hindrance. Although many systems exist that, to various degrees, accomplish these principles, one particular system (MFS) that is the basis for many modern sales forecasting systems was presented here as an example of how all seven principles can be accomplished.

A description of a demonstration version of this system (MBV) was also described. MBV is a special version of MFS that was created to accompany this book. As such, the passwords to enter MBV are related to the Appendix to this chapter (we do not encourage anyone to use MBV without first learning the advantages and disadvantages of different forecasting techniques as described in this book).

Although MFS is designed to handle a much larger number of product forecasts, MBV has the same analytical power of a larger, production version. The intent of MBV is to allow the reader of this book to quickly and easily apply what they have learned about sales forecasting techniques and systems to their own products in a realistic forecasting system environment.

APPENDIX

MBV Passwords

We do not encourage anyone to use MBV without first reading this book. It is inadvisable to try forecasting with a system such as MBV without first understanding the logic of the sales forecasting techniques used. For this reason, we have provided a password screen in MBV that is tied to the book.

Each time you enter MBV, you will be asked for one of the passwords listed below. Simply type in the password that corresponds to the number below and continue to use MBV.

1 = system	21 = reason
2 = number	22 = without
3 = button	23 = continue
4 = addition	24 = phrase
5 = spread	25 = sheet
6 = continue	26 = windows
7 = procedure	27 = import
8 = product	28 = particular
9 = chapter	29 = briefly
10 = directly	30 = click
11 = done	31 = screen
12 = finish	32 = month
13 = larger	33 = version
14 = production	34 = forecast
15 = select	35 = marketing
16 = update	36 = label
17 = finance	37 = columns
18 = detail	38 = logistics
19 = multiply	39 = stepwise
20 = sales	40 = application

7

Benchmark Studies

The Surveys

❖ ❖ ❖

The impetus for the benchmark studies was borne primarily out of frustration. In the 1970s and early 1980s, it seemed every time we worked with a company, the question got asked, "What are other companies doing?" This question was usually aimed at what techniques were being used or what level of accuracy was being achieved, but we always had to answer with what the dozen or so companies we had worked with at that time were doing. Of course, the response was always, "That's fine, but what are other companies (besides these few) doing?"

After being asked this repeatedly, we decided to find out—thus, the benchmark studies were born (although we did not call them benchmark studies back then because the term had not been invented yet—we were doing benchmarking before we knew what to call it). What is now called Phase 1 of the benchmark studies was conducted in the early 1980s, and it was a mail survey completed by 157 companies. It primarily dealt with what techniques companies were using, the accuracy they were achieving, and their satisfaction with the techniques.

Ten years later, Dwight Thomas at AT&T approached us and asked us to repeat the Phase 1 study to see how things had changed. We agreed, but told Dwight that our thinking about sales forecasting management had changed as well—we not only wanted to look at techniques, but at forecasting systems

211

and management and the effect of the three on accuracy and satisfaction. This mail survey of 208 companies became Phase 2 of the benchmark studies.

It is the results of these first two phases that will be addressed in this chapter. Phase 3, the in-depth analyses of 20 companies, and Phase 4, the audit database containing 23 companies, will be discussed in Chapter 8.

❖ INTRODUCTION

This chapter discusses the results of Phases 1 and 2 of the benchmark studies. We will begin this discussion by reviewing other studies besides Phase 1 and 2 that have also assessed the state of the art of sales forecasting. Because part of Phase 2 was a replication 10 years later of Phase 1, we will follow this description of the literature with a comparison of the results from Phases 1 and 2. Because much of what we learned in Phase 2 was new, we will then provide the new findings—in particular, an examination of a question many executives have asked us: What is the difference between forecasting for consumer markets and industrial markets?

❖ STUDIES PRIOR TO PHASE 1

Phase 1 built upon previous studies (see Table 7.1) to examine the relationship between sales forecasting and the issues of technique familiarity, satisfaction, usage, and application. These four Phase 1 issues were characterized as:

1) Familiarity: how familiar executives are with various forecasting techniques and what avenues are used to learn about new methods and applications;

2) Satisfaction: how satisfied managers are with using different forecasting techniques;

3) Usage: which forecasting techniques are most commonly used for different time horizons and forecast levels;

4) Application: the decision-making to which forecasts are applied, the criteria used to evaluate forecasts, and the rate of adoption of new techniques.

As shown in Table 7.2, the results of Phase 1 (Mentzer & Cox, 1984a; 1984b) received general support from subsequent studies by Fildes and Lusk (1984), Sparkes and McHugh (1984), Dalrymple (1987), Wilson and Daubek (1989), and Drury (1990). However, Fildes and Lusk (1984) reported greater practitioner familiarity with Box-Jenkins (open model time series) analysis, while Dalrymple (1987) and Wilson and Daubek (1989) found increased application of computer-based forecasting.

Between Phases 1 and 2, additional issues associated with sales forecasting were investigated. As shown in Table 7.3, such issues included the evaluation of forecasting performance across business functions (Lowenhar, 1984); the influence of forecasters (Sparkes & McHugh, 1984); software support, academic/experience background, forecaster salary, and number of products forecast (Davidson, 1987); needs in forecasting research and forecasting research interests (Armstrong, 1988); and sources of forecast error and forecast improvements needed (Drury, 1990). Interestingly, all subsequent studies continued to overlook the issue of satisfaction, which Phase 1 noted as overlooked prior to 1984. The importance of examining satisfaction is that it "should give an idea of which techniques have been most successful in real world applications" (Mentzer & Cox, 1984a). Consequently, the replication of Phase 1 was part of the goal of Phase 2 (Mentzer & Kahn, 1995; Mentzer & Kahn, 1997; Kahn & Mentzer, 1994; Kahn & Mentzer, 1995). Such a replication effort was valuable for providing better evidence to substantiate the Phase 1 findings and indicate changes in forecasting management over the ensuing decade.

❖ PHASE 2 METHODOLOGY

A mail survey comprising an eight-page questionnaire, cover letter, and a list of forecasting technique definitions was sent to a random sample of forecasting executives in 478 companies. The questionnaire included measures of familiarity, satisfaction, usage, and application of forecasting techniques, paralleling those used in Phase 1. In addition, questions about forecasting systems and management were included. The cover letter directed the questionnaire to the manager responsible for the sales forecasting function, asking for their participation in the study. Prior to the initial mailing, a pretest was undertaken with forecasting managers from nine companies to check the appearance and comprehensibility of the questionnaire, cover letter, and technique definitions.

Table 7.1 Surveys on Sales Forecasting Practices Prior to Phase 1

	Reichard 1966	Sales Management 1967	National Conference Board 1970	National Conference Board 1971	Dalrymple 1975	Wheelright and Clarke 1976	Pan, Nichols, and Joy 1977
Date of Survey	Not Reported	Not Reported	Not Reported	Not Reported	1975	1975	1974
Sample Size (No. of firms responding)	126	182	161	93	175	127	139
Population	Leading business firms	Not Reported	Conference Board's marketing executives panel	Primarily companies with fewer than 2000 employees in U.S. and Canada	Midwestern business people	Fortune 500 firms	Fortune 500 firms
Response Rate	42%	Not Reported	Not Reported	Not Reported	35%	25%	55%
Representativeness of Sample	Not claimed to be representative	Not Reported	Not Reported	Not Reported	Claimed to be representative	Not claimed to be representative	Some data given to indicate representative
Type of Instrument Used	Mail questionnaire	Not Reported	Mail Questionnaire	Mail Questionnaire	Mail Questionnaire	Mail Questionnaire	Mail Questionnaire

Table 7.2   Comparison of Phase 1 to Other Surveys on Sales Forecasting Practices

	Mentzer and Cox (1984a and 1984b)—Phase 1	*Fildes and Lusk (1984)*	*Sparkes and McHugh (1984)*	*Dalrymple (1987)*	*Wilson and Daubeck (1989)*	*Drury (1990)*
Population	U.S. Forecasting Managers	U.S. and U.K. Forecasting Academics and Practitioners	British Cost and Mgt Accountants	Marketing and Forecasting Managers	American Marketing Association Members	Officers of Canadian Companies
Response Rate	160 (32%)	(31%)	76 (25%)	134 (16%)	168 (11%)	234 (23%)
Methodology	Mail Survey	Mail Survey	Mail Survey	Mail Survey	Mail Survey	Mail Survey
Familiarity	Majority of respondents familiar with all techniques except Box-Jenkins, Life Cycle Analysis, and Classical Decomposition Techniques learned from 1) conferences, 2) textbooks, 3) trade journals	Box-Jenkins models well known to respondents U.S. and U.K. responses similar except for Bayesian methods, where U.K. respondents more familiar	General lack of awareness of Box-Jenkins time series, Delphi method, and cross-impact analysis Bias towards more subjective techniques	Most popular forecasting techniques were sales force composite and jury of executive opinion Most popular extrapolation forecasting method was naive approach Industrial firms have a strong preference for sales force composite methods	Survey and opinion polling judge as the most important method followed by jury of executive opinion	

(Continued)

215

Table 7.2 (Continued)

	Mentzer and Cox (1984a and 1984b)—Phase 1	Fildes and Lusk (1984)	Sparkes and McHugh (1984)	Dalrymple (1987)	Wilson and Daubeck (1989)	Drury (1990)
Satisfaction	Majority satisfied with regression, exponential smoothing, moving average, trend line analysis, classical decomposition, simulation, jury of executive opinion Majority dissatisfied with Box-Jenkins time series					
Usage	Majority use subjective techniques for short range forecasts (less than 3 months) Jury of executive opinion favored across all time horizons and corporate levels of forecasts		The more sophisticated the techniques, the lower the level of usage Executive opinion was most widely used by those familiar with it	Naïve method most popular method for short range forecasts Identified differences between this study and Mentzer and Cox (1984)		Management judgment, or a variant thereof, remains highly used (86% of respondents) U.K. firms appear to use more forecasting techniques than companies in the U.S. or Canada

	Mentzer and Cox (1984a and 1984b)—Phase 1	Fildes and Lusk (1984)	Sparkes and McHugh (1984)	Dalrymple (1987)	Wilson and Daubeck (1989)	Drury (1990)
Application: Accuracy	Accuracy generally decreased as forecast level moved down to individual product forecasts

Accuracy decreased significantly as time horizon increased

Avg accuracy across forecast levels and forecast periods was 85% | Box-Jenkins ranked as most accurate for short lead times, while trend analysis ranked first for longer lead times

Exponential smoothing considered more accurate than adaptive smoothing

Familiar techniques judged more accurate | Moving averages rival executive assessments for short term forecasts

No trends found across time horizons

Executive assessments judged as having an acceptable level of accuracy | Typical one month forecast error was 9.5% with a variance of 7.7%

Typical one year forecast error was 9.9% with a variance of 7.9%

Computers, firm size, and use of seasonal adjustments all appeared to reduce forecast error | Multiple regression judged as most accurate followed by survey and opinion polling

Naïve models judged as least accurate

Strong association between importance and accuracy | |

(Continued)

Table 7.2 (Continued)

	Mentzer and Cox (1984a and 1984b)—Phase 1	Fildes and Lusk (1984)	Sparkes and McHugh (1984)	Dalrymple (1987)	Wilson and Daubeck (1989)	Drury (1990)
Evaluative Criteria	Ease of use top criteria		Ease of use most mentioned			
Management Considerations	Production planning and budgeting top application areas				38% of respondents always or frequently combined forecasts	62% of respondents always or usually combined forecasts
Technology Diffusion	Some use of computer modeling				64% of respondents always or frequently used computers	87% of respondents used computers to forecast

218

Table 7.3   Other Findings From Past Surveys on Sales Forecasting Practices

	Lowenhar (1984)	Sparkes and McHugh (1984)	Davidson (1987)	Armstrong (1988)	Drury (1990)
Population	Sales Forecast Users and Preparers	British Cost and Mgt Accountants	Sales Forecasters of U.S. and Canadian Manufacturing Firms	Members of the International Institute of Forecasters	Officers of Canadian Companies
Response Rate	32	76 (25%)	?	113	234 (23%)
Methodology	Mail Survey	Mail Survey	Mail Survey	Mail Survey	Mail Survey
Findings	*Evaluations of Forecasting Performance Across Business Functions:* Departments rated themselves better on accuracy criteria than did other departments rating them.	*Influence of Forecasters:* 75% of companies using executive assessment considered their influence to be extensive.	*Software Support:* 90% of respondents regularly relied on software for forecasting. *Academic and Experience Background:* A college degree was found to be most important for sales forecasting.	*Needs in Forecasting Research:* Wide variety of responses, however, implementation of forecasts was most frequently mentioned. *Research Interests:* Strong interest in applications, not only by practitioners, but by academics also.	*Sources of Forecast Error:* Unexpected events was the top reason for forecast error. *Forecast Improvements Needed:* A top need is for systems and procedures to analyze forecast error.

(Continued)

Table 7.3 (Continued)

Lowenhar (1984)	Sparkes and McHugh (1984)	Davidson (1987)	Armstrong (1988)	Drury (1990)
		Forecaster's Salary: Average salary was $33,875, ranging from $17,000 to $60,000. *Number of Products Forecast:* Where a bottom-up approach was used, the forecaster was responsible for an average of 1,122 products (range was 100 to 5,000). Where a top-down approach was used, the forecaster was responsible for 40 products on average (range was 1 to 80).		

Two survey waves provided 208 completed questionnaires for a 43% response rate. This response rate was deemed acceptable in comparison to response rates of the previous studies (see Tables 7.1 and 7.2). A review of business cards enclosed with survey responses confirmed that surveys were completed by forecasting managers.

Analysis revealed no demographic differences between each wave of respondents. The majority of responding firms were consumer products manufacturers. Like Phase 1, there was a slight bias toward larger companies, but the range of corporate demographics indicated a representative sample. On average, responding firms had sales of $1.375 billion (range of $1,000,000 to more than $10,000,000,000), assets of $1.984 billion (range of $1,000,000 to more than $10,000,000,000), and employment of 12,032 individuals (range of less than 100 to 100,000 employees). Geographically, 91% of the responding firms were U.S. firms, with 28% of these coming from the Great Lakes region, 24% from the Mideast region, and 20% from the Southeast region.

❖ FINDINGS COMPARING PHASE 2 TO PHASE 1

T-tests on proportions were used to compare findings of Phase 2 to those of Phase 1. Cases where statistical differences were identified ($p < = 0.05$) suggested possible changes in sales forecasting practices over the ensuing years between Phases 1 and 2.

Familiarity

Similar to Phase 1, moving average, exponential smoothing, straight-line projections, and regression remained very familiar techniques (Table 7.4). To reflect emerging forecasting technique trends, two additions to the Phase 1 list of techniques were expert systems and neural networks. However, a majority of respondents in Phase 2 were unfamiliar with neural networks.

The differences in familiarity across the two Phases concerned the techniques of jury of executive opinion, sales force composite, customer expectations, moving average, exponential smoothing, regression, life-cycle analysis, decomposition, and Box-Jenkins analysis. Surprisingly, respondents to Phase 2 were less familiar with jury of executive opinion than respondents to Phase 1. However, respondents in Phase 2 were more familiar with exponential smoothing and somewhat more familiar

Table 7.4   Familiarity

Technique	Sample Size		% Familiar		% Somewhat Familiar		% Not Familiar	
	P1	P2	P1	P2	P1	P2	P1	P2
Qualitative:								
Jury of Executive Opinion	158	204	*81*	*66*	*6*	*16*	13	18
Sales Force Composite	159	203	79	71	5	14	16	15
Customer Expectations	158	205	73	64	7	19	20	17
Quantitative:								
Moving Average	158	201	*85*	*92*	7	6	*8*	*2*
Straight Line Projection	157	204	82	85	11	11	7	4
Exponential Smoothing	157	201	73	*90*	12	6	*15*	*4*
Regression	157	206	72	78	8	10	*20*	*12*
Trend Line Analysis	75	205	67	73	16	16	17	11
Simulation	156	205	55	50	22	26	23	24
Life Cycle Analysis	153	205	48	50	*11*	*22*	*41*	*28*
Decomposition	151	205	42	43	9	20	*49*	*37*
Box-Jenkins (OMTS)	156	205	*26*	*38*	9	23	*65*	*39*
Expert Systems		204		33		29		38
Neural Networks		201		19		23		58

Key: Items underlined are statistically different at p < = .05
     P1 = Phase 1
     P2 = Phase 2

with the techniques of moving average, regression, life-cycle analysis, classical decomposition, and, in particular, Box-Jenkins analysis. These findings support the findings of Fildes and Lusk (1984) and suggest that firms have a better understanding of quantitative forecasting techniques than qualitative techniques.

A second issue of familiarity considered where respondents learned about sales forecasting techniques. As shown in Table 7.5, it appears that forecasters rely on the same sources for learning about sales forecasting techniques. However, Phase 2 respondents identified several new sources to learn about sales forecasting techniques. Among these, the majority of respondents identified colleagues as an important source.

Table 7.5   Where to Learn About Forecasting

	Sample Size	% Important	
Source	P2	P1	P2
Conferences	204	68	59
Books	204	56	65
Trade Journals	203	49	59
Consultants	204	38	46
Colleagues	204		65
College Courses	204		45
Public Seminars	204		35
Company Seminar	205		23

Key: P1 = Phase 1
P2 = Phase 2

Satisfaction

As in Phase 1, only Phase 2 respondents who were familiar with each technique were included in the satisfaction analysis for that technique (Table 7.6). Phase 2 respondents were most satisfied with exponential smoothing (72%), followed by regression (66%) and decomposition (61%). Respondents were most dissatisfied with straight-line projections (42%).

As for contrasts, Phase 2 respondents were less satisfied with jury of executive opinion and moving average than those in Phase 1. Phase 2 respondents also were more satisfied with exponential smoothing and somewhat more satisfied with simulation, life cycle analysis, decomposition, and Box-Jenkins analysis. These differences suggest that quantitative techniques are more successful in forecasting today than in the 1980s.

In Phase 1, only 7.8% of respondents were familiar with and satisfied with Box-Jenkins analysis. In Phase 2, 16.72% of respondents were familiar and satisfied with this approach. Although this increase is probably indicative of improved Box-Jenkins software, the consistently low level of application and satisfaction led us to give limited treatment in Chapter 3 to Box-Jenkins as an open model time series technique.

Table 7.6   Satisfaction

	Sample Size		% Satisfied		% Neutral		% Dissatisfied	
Technique	P1	P2	P1	P2	P1	P2	P1	P2
Qualitative:								
Jury of Executive Opinion	118	131	*54*	*35*	*24*	*36*	22	29
Sales Force Composite	112	140	43	34	25	27	32	39
Customer Expectations	95	130	45	46	23	32	32	22
Quantitative:								
Moving Average	112	179	*58*	*40*	*21*	*35*	21	25
Straight Line Projection	93	169	32	28	31	30	37	42
Exponential Smoothing	104	172	*60*	*72*	19	24	*21*	*4*
Regression	99	156	67	66	19	29	*14*	*5*
Trend Line Analysis	40	145	58	48	28	40	15	12
Simulation	65	100	54	50	*18*	*42*	*28*	*8*
Life Cycle Analysis	52	99	40	36	20	46	*40*	*18*
Decomposition	71	84	55	61	*14*	*28*	*31*	*11*
Box-Jenkins (OMTS)	47	78	30	44	*13*	*45*	*57*	*11*
Expert Systems		66		45		47		8
Neural Networks		37		38		49		13

Key: Items underlined are statistically different at p < = .05
P1 = Phase 1
P2 = Phase 2

Usage

Table 7.7 reveals statistically significant differences in usage for all given techniques except simulation. The direction of these differences suggests that firms in Phase 2 have a greater tendency to forecast 3 months to 2 years in advance. Phase 1 did not reflect such a tendency.

Table 7.7 also indicates the popularity of techniques across time horizons. In the 3-month to 2-year time horizon, the majority of respondents preferred exponential smoothing (92%), jury of executive opinion (77%), sales force composite (77%), regression (69%), and trend line analysis (57%). In the greater than 2 years time horizon, the majority of respondents preferred jury of executive opinion (55%).

Analysis across forecast levels found few statistically significant differences between Phase 1 and Phase 2 (Table 7.8). This suggests that forecasters are applying techniques to the same forecast levels as they

Table 7.7   Usage Across Time Horizons (Percent of Respondents)

Technique	<= 3 months		3 months to 2 years		> 2 years	
	P1	P2	P1	P2	P1	P2
Qualitative:						
Jury of Executive Opinion	37	4	42	77	38	55
Sales Force Composite	37	4	36	77	8	21
Customer Expectations	25	5	24	38	12	15
Quantitative:						
Moving Average	24	9	22	45	5	11
Straight Line Projection	13	5	16	35	10	10
Exponential Smoothing	24	8	17	92	6	16
Regression	14	4	36	69	28	30
Trend Line Analysis	21	2	28	57	21	22
Simulation	4	1	9	6	10	12
Life Cycle Analysis	1	1	5	24	12	18
Decomposition	9	2	13	40	5	10
Box-Jenkins (OMTS)	5	2	6	19	2	7
Expert Systems		1		6		8
Neural Networks		2		17		6

Key: Items underlined are statistically different at p < = .05
   P1 = Phase 1
   P2 = Phase 2
   P1 Sample Size = 160
   P2 Sample Size = 186

were in 1984. There were only **three** significant differences: greater use of exponential smoothing for corporate level forecasts, greater use of life-cycle analysis for product-line forecasts, and less use of customer expectations for product forecasts. Note that the categories of forecast level vary slightly from those used in Phase 1. The categories used in Phase 2 were preferred by managers in the pretest and, thus, were incorporated into the questionnaire.

Application

The overall degree of forecast accuracy (defined in both studies as one minus the Mean Absolute Percent Error experienced) across both

Table 7.8   Usage Across Forecast Level (Percent of Respondents)

Technique	Industry P1	P2	Corporate P1	P2	Product Group P1	Product Line P1	P2	Product P1	P2	SKU By Location P2
Qualitative:										
Jury of Executive Opinion	26	26	41	47	32	32	37	22	17	11
Sales Force Composite	5	5	20	31	25	27	29	24	22	18
Customer Expectations	8	5	12	15	18	18	16	23	12	10
Quantitative:										
Moving Average	4	3	9	12	18	19	17	20	20	15
Straight Line Projection	6	5	10	11	11	10	12	11	12	9
Exponential Smoothing	4	8	6	23	14	14	28	23	34	25
Regression	18	17	22	26	21	19	24	12	22	16
Trend Line Analysis	13	9	20	19	20	21	21	22	20	14
Simulation	7	4	9	5	7	4	5	4	3	2
Life Cycle Analysis	4	8	4	12	4	4	14	6	6	3
Decomposition	2	4	4	12	8	7	12	9	14	13
Box-Jenkins (OMTS)	2	3	3	9	3	2	7	6	5	4
Expert Systems		4		4			2		3	2
Neural Networks		3		5			5		6	5

Items underlined are statistically different at p < = .05
P1 = Phase 1
P2 = Phase 2

P1 Sample Size = 160
P2 Sample Size = 186

phases is almost equivalent, reflecting a weighted average of 85% for Phase 1 and a Phase 2 weighted average of 84% (see Table 7.9). There is a noticeable difference in accuracy, that is, greater than 10%, for product forecasts in the greater than 2-year time horizon. This indicates that respondents in Phase 2 are experiencing greater accuracy

Table 7.9   Percent Accuracy

Forecast Level	<= 3 months		3 months to 2 years		> 2 years	
	P1	P2	P1	P2	P1	P2
Industry	92 (n = 61)	90 (n = 1)	89 (n = 61)	88 (n = 16)	85 (n = 50)	87 (n = 36)
Corporate	93 (n = 81)	72 (n = 2)	89 (n = 89)	90 (n = 64)	82 (n = 61)	88 (n = 42)
Product Group	90 (n = 89)		85 (n = 96)		80 (n = 61)	
Product Line	89 (n = 92)	90 (n = 4)	84 (n = 95)	86 (n = 83)	80 (n = 60)	88 (n = 25)
Product	84 (n = 96)	82 (n = 14)	79 (n = 88)	79 (n = 89)	74 (n = 54)	86 (n = 10)
SKU by Location	76 (n = 17)		75 (n = 58)		87 (n = 5)	

		P1	P2
	Weighted Average:*	85	84

Key: P1 = Phase 1
   P2 = Phase 2

*Weighted average calculated by weighting each cell accuracy by the number responding.

when forecasting long-term for individual products. While there is also a noticeable difference for corporate-level forecasts in the less than 3-month time horizon, the cell's small sample size in Phase 2 prohibits any general conclusions.

In a related question, Phase 2 investigated how firms measured forecast accuracy (see Table 7.10), which Phase 1 did not explore. It was revealed that the majority of respondents relied on mean absolute percent error (MAPE). A quarter of respondents relied on mean absolute deviation (MAD).

Akin to the findings of Phase 1, the majority of Phase 2 respondents identified accuracy (92%) and credibility (92%) as top criteria for evaluating sales forecasting effectiveness (see Table 7.11). The majority of Phase 2 respondents also identified customer service performance (77%), ease of use (75%), and inventory turns (55%) as criteria for evaluating sales forecasting effectiveness. Interestingly, Phase 2 respondents considered cost (41%) and return on investment (35%) as lesser criteria to evaluate forecasting effectiveness. This suggests that forecasting techniques are often not evaluated based upon financial measures.

Table 7.10   Measures of Forecast Accuracy

	# of Respondents in Phase 2*
Mean Absolute Percent Error	122 (52%)
Mean Absolute Deviation	59 (25%)
Mean Squared Error	23 (10%)
Deviation	9 (4%)
Percent Error	8 (3%)
Forecast Ratio	2 (< 1%)
Inventory Statistic	2 (< 1%)
Standard Deviation	2 (< 1%)
Other	9 (4%)

*Some respondents listed more than one measure.

Table 7.11   Criteria for Evaluating Sales Forecasting Effectiveness

Criteria	Sample Size P2	% Important
Accuracy	205	92
Credibility	206	92
Customer service performance	199	77
Ease of use	206	75
Inventory turns	198	55
Amount of data required	205	46
Cost	205	41
Return on investment	199	35

❖ CONCLUSIONS FROM COMPARING PHASE 1 AND PHASE 2

This comparison sought to answer the question "Have sales fore-casting practices changed over the past 10 years?" Regarding the issue of familiarity, forecasting executives are more familiar with quantitative techniques than they were 10 years ago. Practitioners are, in particular, more familiar with the technique of exponential smoothing. Practitioners were less familiar with the qualitative technique of jury of executive opinion than they were 10 years ago. This finding is especially noteworthy in light of other studies indicating higher familiarity with the jury of executive opinion technique (Dalrymple, 1987; Wilson & Daubek, 1989).

Findings concerning satisfaction somewhat parallel findings associated with familiarity. Forecasting executives were more satisfied with exponential smoothing, indicating exponential smoothing was a more successful technique than it was 10 years ago. Conversely, respondents in Phase 2 were less satisfied with jury of executive opinion, suggesting that it was a less successful technique. While this would suggest a positive relationship between familiarity and satisfaction, this was not always the case. Respondents in Phase 2 were quite familiar with the technique of moving average, but were less satisfied with this technique.

As for usage, Phase 2 respondents appear to be concentrating on sales forecasting in the 3-month to 2-year time horizon. This contrasts the Phase 1 findings, where respondents were generally likely to use techniques across all time horizons. The most popular, that is, greatest degree of usage, forecasting technique was exponential smoothing applied in a 3-month to 2-year time horizon. Within this same time horizon, a majority of respondents also used jury of executive opinion, customer expectations, regression, and trend line analysis. Interestingly, jury of executive opinion was shown to be a popular technique in this time horizon, as it was in Sparkes and McHugh (1984) and Drury (1990). However, jury of executive opinion reflected less satisfaction than each of the other four "popular" techniques. This is further evidence that satisfaction is an important factor.

Accuracy still remains a top criterion for evaluating sales fore-casting effectiveness. With particular regard to achieved accuracy, the Phase 2 study found little change in the accuracy of forecasting techniques over the past 10 years. This finding suggests that the forecasting techniques discussed in the first few chapters of this book will not, alone, necessarily improve accuracy. Managers should consider other issues associated with forecasting, including the forecast environment, data collected, computer systems used, and management of the forecasting process.

While part of the intent of Phase 2 was to assess changes in sales forecasting practices since the early 1980s, it also provides a new baseline or benchmark for sales forecasting practices. With this benchmark goal in mind, a number of questions were asked in Phase 2 that were new since Phase 1. We will discuss these results next.

Phase 2 Results

Although the previous studies we reviewed in Tables 7.1, 7.2, and 7.3 examined sales forecasting technique issues, no study prior to Phase 2 had looked at the broader sales forecasting issues regarding the types of systems used to support the sales forecasting techniques or how the sales forecasting function is managed. This is surprising because (as we discuss throughout this book) forecasting systems and management have as much, if not more, potential to affect the ultimate effectiveness of sales forecasts as does the proper selection of the forecasting technique.

Thus, although the systems within which sales forecasts are developed and the management processes by which the role of sales forecasting is defined are integral parts of the sales forecasting function, previous surveys of sales forecasting have largely ignored these topics. This led to the questions that drove part of Phase 2: "What are the characteristics of sales forecasting systems and management approaches to sales forecasting?" and "What is the level of management satisfaction with these systems and management approaches?" To address the two components of the research question, the findings are divided into the two main areas of interest: sales forecasting systems and sales forecasting management.

❖ SALES FORECASTING SYSTEMS

Companies on average employed 1.82 sales forecasting computer systems. In other words, many companies have more than one computer system for developing the sales forecast. In 30% of the responding companies, these systems were contained entirely on personal computers and in 29% they were entirely on mainframes. More often, however, these systems consisted of both a personal computer system and mainframe system (41% of respondents). This is probably indicative of the proliferation of personal computer-based sales forecasting software packages, combined with the availability of much of the necessary information still residing on the mainframe.

The majority of respondents' systems were not on a distributed data network (55%). This indicates a lack of electronic integration of the sales forecasting function with the various functions using the sales forecasts (marketing, sales, finance, production, and logistics) and the function providing information (MIS). This finding was reinforced by the fact that almost half (44%) of the responding companies did not have electronic connections between forecasting systems and the production and inventory planning (DRP/MRP) systems, and more than one-third (36%) were not even electronically linked to the management information system (MIS). These findings indicate the potential for "islands of analysis." As discussed in Chapter 6, islands of analysis exist when the different areas involved in the sales forecasting process make their calculations/analyses on separate systems and, therefore, may inadvertently not share all this information with other systems. Islands of analysis often lead to contradictory assumptions, analyses, and results.

For the companies whose sales forecasting systems were electronically linked to MIS, less than half of the respondents had access to the type of information that could be used for regression-based forecast modeling (see Table 7.12). In fact, the only information that was electronically available in a majority of companies was sales and/or demand history. Particularly disturbing were the number of companies trying to forecast with no access to market research information (89% of the responding companies).

Computer systems software was divided between commercial software (48%) and software that was custom built for the company either internally (41%) or by an outside developer (11%). This indicates that about half of the responding companies find software that is customized to their particular sales forecasting needs more effective than generalized software. This provides growing support for the idea expressed in Chapter 6 of, "let the tool fit the problem, instead of the other way around."

All of these findings, taken in aggregate, indicate a typical forecasting function where a personal computer is available, some access to the mainframe is possible, but the type of information readily available for analysis is limited. Perhaps more importantly, electronic access to the users of the forecast is severely limited and, in an alarmingly large number of companies, no vehicle for electronically transmitting the

Table 7.12   Types of Information Input From MIS to the Sales
Forecasting System

	# of Respondents*
Sales	94 (72%)
Demand	77 (59%)
Orders	58 (44%)
Price Changes	49 (33%)
New Product Introduction Information	36 (27%)
Advertising/Promotional Information	25 (19%)
Competitive Information	17 (13%)
Market Research Information	15 (11%)
Economic Information	14 (11%)
Other	11 (8%)

*% based on 131 companies responding to this question—there are multiple responses

resultant forecasts to the users is possible. Clearly, the forecasting function has a long way to go in the area of computer systems integration.

Of particular interest were two innovations in supply chains that have been touted as providing more accurate and timely information to the forecasting system (Kahn & Mentzer, 1996)—electronic data interchange (EDI) and direct customer forecasts. Responses, however, indicate most companies' sales forecasting systems do not have access to electronic data interchange (EDI) from suppliers (82%) or customers (69%). Also, most companies (77%) do not receive forecasts directly from customers (i.e., the customers' forecasts of what their customers plan to buy). These results would indicate that although there does seem to be potential for improving channel-wide forecast accuracy through EDI and direct customer forecast information, these innovations are not currently being realized.

Another aspect of forecasting systems that has considerable potential for improving forecast accuracy is the simple expedient of making it easy for forecasters to adjust technique forecasts based upon their qualitative judgments. This potential is being realized in most (76%) of the responding companies.

The departments most likely to make changes to the forecast were marketing, sales, planning, and product management (see Table 7.13). Not surprisingly, these results largely follow the functions with knowledge of customers and markets. However, combined with the earlier findings of limited electronic integration, this access is apparently interpersonal. These results in combination seem to indicate ease of access for other functional areas and means they can tell the forecaster the changes they want made, but they cannot directly enter these changes into the sales forecasting system.

Various functional areas may need ongoing information on forecasts and forecasting accuracy (i.e., the ability to review the forecasts being developed), even if these individuals are not actually allowed to make changes to the forecasts. In the responding companies, the departments allowed to review but not make changes to the forecasts most often included marketing, finance, production, sales, and planning (see Table 7.14). Again, these are typically personnel with a need for ongoing knowledge of the developing sales forecast. However, it is interesting that for every function listed in Tables 7.13 and 7.14, more companies allow these functions review access to the forecast system (Table 7.14) than allow actual access to make changes (Table 7.13). This would indicate that most companies see these functions as users of (rather than developers of) the sales forecast.

Overall, respondents were neutral about their satisfaction with their existing sales forecasting system—the average response was 4.20 on a scale from 1 (extremely dissatisfied) to 7 (extremely satisfied), with 4 being neutral (see Table 7.15). This, again, could be a function of system improvements brought over the years by improved personal computer-based software, but still limited information and functional area electronic access.

Table 7.13   Functional Personnel with Access to the Sales Forecasting System to Make Changes to the Forecasts

	# of Respondents*
Marketing	95 (49%)
Sales	61 (31%)
Planning	53 (27%)
Product Management	50 (26%)
Logistics	46 (24%)
Finance	18 (9%)
Production	15 (8%)
R&D	2 (1%)

*% based on 194 companies responding to this question—there are multiple responses

Table 7.14   Functional Personnel with Access to the Sales Forecasting
System to Review, But Not Make Changes, to the Forecasts

	# of Respondents*
Marketing	128 (66%)
Finance	120 (62%)
Production	111 (57%)
Sales	105 (54%)
Planning	104 (53%)
Logistics	97 (50%)
Product Management	90 (46%)
Engineering	34 (17%)
R&D	20 (10%)

*% based on 195 companies responding to this question—there are multiple responses

Table 7.15   Satisfaction with Existing Sales Forecasting System

Scale	Number of Responses	Percent	
1	13	6.0%	VERY DISSATISFIED
2	22	11.0%	
3	30	14.5%	
4	33	16.0%	NEUTRAL
5	70	34.0%	
6	30	14.5%	
7	8	4.0%	VERY SATISFIED

Average = 4.20   Standard Deviation = 1.54

❖ SALES FORECASTING MANAGEMENT

To investigate how the sales forecasting process is managed, respondents were asked which of the four fundamental approaches to forecasting management outlined in Chapter 6 were used by their companies:

1. In the first approach, each functional department involved in the sales forecasting process develops its own forecast for its own

internal uses, independently of all other departments. Because this is a self-contained approach, it is called the **Independent** approach. This is a narrow approach to forecasting that ignores the synergistic advantages of input from various perspectives. Further, it lacks any form of coordination of plans based on the sales forecasts.

2. In the second managerial approach, one department is assigned the responsibility for developing the sales forecast and all other departments must use the resultant forecast. Because the responsibility for the forecast is held in one department, this is called the **Concentrated** approach. Although it solves some of the coordination problems of the Independent approach, the Concentrated approach gives the sales forecast a definite bias toward the orientation of the department developing it. For example, if residing in logistics, the forecast will tend to be stock keeping unit by location (SKUL)-oriented. If residing in marketing, the forecast will tend to be product line-oriented. If residing in sales, the forecast will tend to be sales territory-oriented. If residing in production, the forecast will tend to be stock keeping unit (SKU)-oriented. If residing in finance, the forecast will tend to be dollars-oriented. Of course, each of these functional areas has different time horizon orientations, which will in turn affect the orientation of the forecast.

3. In the third managerial approach to sales forecasting, for each product grouping, each functional area makes its own independent forecast, but representatives from each functional area come together each forecasting period to reach a negotiated final forecast. Thus, this is called the **Negotiated** approach, and overcomes some of the bias problems of the Concentrated approach. However, the fact that each function brings its own orientation does create an environment of politics that can bias the results.

4. Finally, in the fourth approach, for each product grouping, a committee is formed with representatives from various functional areas and one person placed in charge of the forecast committee. This committee develops forecasts that have the input of all functional areas. This is called the **Consensus** approach, and overcomes some of the bias problems of the Concentrated approach and some of the political problems of the Negotiated approach. Although superior sales forecasts can result from this management approach, it often requires more personnel resources and more interfunctional coordination than is possible within many companies.

It is a measure of the improved sophistication of sales forecasting management that few companies still follow an Independent approach (see Table 7.16). However, almost half of the responding companies have one department responsible for developing sales forecasts (a Concentrated Approach). A number of companies (more than half) are trying some form of the Negotiated or Consensus approach and, of those who are, companies were more satisfied with the results (see Table 7.17).

Managerial responsibility for inventory (having it available for customer access, but not overstocking) should affect involvement in, and responsibility for, development of tactical forecasts. As indicated in Table 7.18, the production department is most often responsible for raw material inventory (65% of responding firms) and work-in-process inventory (78% of responding firms). Logistics was designated as responsible for finished goods inventory for 46% of responding companies, followed by production with 32%. Combined with earlier results on access to the sales forecasting system (Table 7.13) and review of the sales forecasts (Table 7.14), these results indicate production, planning, and logistics responsibility for inventory does not seem to create a great need to have access to the sales forecasting system, but it does create a strong review-based involvement in the development of the forecast.

Table 7.16   Approaches Used to Develop Sales Forecasts

	# Respondents*
1) Each department develops and uses its own sales forecasts (Independent Approach)	25 (12.2%)
2) One department is responsible for developing sales forecasts (Concentrated Approach)	97 (47.3%)
3) Each department develops its own forecasts, but a committee coordinates a final forecast (Negotiated Approach)	59 (28.8%)
4) A forecast committee/task force is responsible for developing sales forecasts (Consensus Approach)	55 (26.8%)

*Some of the 205 companies responding to this question selected more than one approach, i.e., were using different approaches in different areas of the company.

Table 7.17   Satisfaction with Approach to Developing Sales Forecasts

	n	Dissatisfied	Neutral	Satisfied
(1) Independent Approach	25	44.0%	28.0%	28.0%
(2) Concentrated Approach	96	22.9%	17.7%	59.4%*
(3) Negotiated Approach	59	25.4%	13.6%	61.0%*
(4) Consensus Approach	53	13.2%	17.0%	69.8%*

* = $p < .05$

Table 7.18   Department Responsible for Inventory

	Raw Materials	Work-in-Process	Finished Goods
Production	95 (65%)	110 (78%)	51 (32%)
Planning	38 (26%)	32 (23%)	45 (29%)
Logistics	25 (17%)	24 (17%)	73 (46%)
Product Management	16 (11%)	11 (8%)	41 (26%)
Purchasing	9 (6%)	—	—
R&D	9 (6%)	4 (3%)	6 (4%)
Finance	8 (6%)	7 (5%)	15 (10%)
Engineering	5 (3%)	10 (7%)	4 (3%)
Marketing	3 (2%)	6 (4%)	46 (30%)
Sales	3 (2%)	2 (1%)	42 (27%)
# of Responding Firms	146	141	158

Regarding the role that management plays in the forecasting process, middle managers appear to be actually involved in developing the sales forecast in a majority of companies (68%), followed by 23% of the responding companies where middle managers only review the forecast, and 6% where they only approve the developed forecast. This "hands-on" involvement indicates a recognition of the importance of sales forecasting to middle-management planning and a recognition of the value of middle-management qualitative input to the development of the forecasts. Such recognition appears to carry over to upper management, which has actual involvement in 27% of the companies, review responsibilities in 27%, and approval in 38%. However, in many responding companies (34%) the planning process is backward, that is, the business plan is used to develop the forecast instead of the other way around. Apparently, management in these companies is more concerned with the business plan than the sales forecast, even though the latter should drive the former.

To obtain an overall picture of the sales forecasting management process in responding companies, five statements were presented to respondents, who rated each statement on a scale of 1 (strongly disagree) to 5 (strongly agree). A significant majority of respondents agreed that their forecast was prepared via a formal/routine process with clear and precise instructions (Table 7.19). However, a significant majority disagreed with the statement that forecasting performance is formally evaluated and rewarded. A significant number of respondents also disagreed with the statement that the sales forecasting budget was sufficient. Taken in combination, this produces some interesting conclusions. Apparently, many companies have a formal and documented sales forecasting process, but this process lacks the fundamental aspect of performance measurement. Such a lack ignores the management maxim we introduced in Chapter 2, "What gets measured gets rewarded and what gets rewarded gets done." If sales forecasting performance is neither measured nor rewarded, there is little motivation to improve it. Combined with an insufficient budget, these results alone have more potential to negatively affect forecast performance than the entire process of technique selection.

As an example of the impact of such a lack of motivational incentive to improve forecasting effectiveness, many responding companies (28%) still use shipments as their best measure of demand. Although shipments are clearly an inadequate surrogate for demand (shipments data do not capture the amount of demand that the company received but could not fulfill due to inadequate previous forecasts, that is, shipments equal demand minus lost sales), the lack of incentive to improve the sales forecasting process by gathering this more valuable demand information exists in more than one fourth of the responding companies.

In terms of the qualifications for a sales forecaster (Table 7.20), respondents identified forecasting experience as most important (77%). More than half of respondents also identified experience in statistics (64%), computer systems (61%), marketing (56%), and logistics (51%) as important. A significant number of respondents also viewed experience in sales and managing inventory as important. Although respondents were provided with the opportunity to mention other important qualifications, no others were listed.

Table 7.19   Statements About Company Sales Forecasting Process

	n	Disagree	Neutral	Agree
The forecast is prepared via a formal/routine process with clear and precise instructions	204	27%	18%	55%*
Forecasting performance is formally evaluated and rewarded	205	*56%	19%	25%
The final sales forecast is believed by all concerned	204	40%	29%	31%
The sales forecasting budget is sufficient	201	*38%	39%	23%
There are enough people assigned to develop the sales forecasts	205	37%	21%	42%
Too much money is spent in this company to manage around forecasting error	202	37%	27%	36%

* = p < .05

Table 7.20   Sales Forecaster Qualification Importance

	n	Unimportant	Neutral	Important
Forecasting Experience	204	7%	16%	77%*
Statistics Experience	202	17%	19%	64%*
Computer Systems Experience	203	14%	25%	61%*
Marketing Experience	203	17%	27%	56%*
Logistics Experience	202	25%	24%	51%*
Sales Experience	203	22%	32%	46%*
Inventory Experience	201	31%	23%	46%*

* = p < .05

❖ FORECASTING IN CONSUMER VERSUS INDUSTRIAL MARKETS

Consumer and industrial markets are inherently different. Consumer markets encompass individual consumers and families/households "that buy goods and services for personal consumption" (Armstrong & Kotler, 2003, p. 191). Conversely, industrial markets consist of organizations "that buy goods and services for use in the production of other products or services that are sold, rented, or supplied to others" (Armstrong & Kotler, 2003, p. 215).

These inherent differences influence the market structure characteristics of firms in each of these markets. Firms in industrial markets normally have fewer buyers; firms in consumer markets contend with greater numbers of buyers. Industrial market firms reflect a closer relationship between customers and seller because close relationships are critical for maintaining customers in such a small customer base. Close customer relationships are more difficult in consumer markets due to the sheer volume of customers. Industrial market firms also experience inelastic demand in the short run; consumer market firms traditionally reflect more demand elasticity. Demand in industrial markets is frequently derived from demand in consumer markets. Therefore, the effects of short-term fluctuations in consumer demand can be multiplied back up the channel.

Due to varying market structure characteristics, firms in consumer and industrial markets typically differ in their marketing activities. Consumer market firms often rely more on broad-based advertising across various media outlets. Industrial market firms have more specific advertising aimed at fewer outlets and tend to rely on a sales force because there are fewer customers who can be more easily identified and directly contacted. Industrial market firms also handle larger order quantities, which require greater storage capacity. Consumer market firms contend with smaller quantities that often must be delivered faster, thereby requiring operations that can handle greater throughput. Because of higher volume, industrial market firms offer quantity discounts and negotiate price per contract. Pricing in consumer market firms is typically more stable, as the firm itself often sets the price to be offered.

Because of varying business practices as a consequence of varying market patterns, it has often been suggested that sales forecasting practices also differ between firms in consumer versus industrial markets. In fact, there is some evidence for such differences.

Dalrymple (1987) found that industrial market firms have a stronger preference for the sales force composite method than consumer firms. He speculated that the close relationship between industrial salespeople and their customers encourages industrial firms to use their sales force to forecast. Dalrymple also found industrial market firms to have greater preferences for leading indicators, econometric models, and multiple regression techniques.

Herbig, Milewicz, and Golden (1993) supported Dalrymple's findings by reporting that industrial market firms prefer to use the sales force composite method more than consumer market firms. These authors also found that industrial market firms rated their forecasting process as easier to understand, while consumer market firms found the process harder to comprehend. Interestingly, consumer market firms expressed the belief that their forecasting processes were more accurate, while industrial market firms felt that their forecasting processes were less accurate.

Along with the issues of technique usage and accuracy, other conceivable differences could distinguish the forecasting practices of consumer versus industrial market firms. Firms may differ on technique familiarity as a result of standard sales forecasting practices within consumer versus industrial markets. Satisfaction with techniques also may differ across firms in each market as a result of greater success in predicting market fluctuations—those techniques that can adapt quickly to market fluctuations will provide more satisfaction to consumer markets because demand fluctuates more rapidly at the individual consumer level. In addition, there may be differences in the roles of electronic data interchange (EDI), distribution requirements planning (DRP), materials requirement planning (MRP), and management information systems (MIS) in the forecasting process and how these technologies affect the forecasting process. It is believed that EDI, MRP, DRP, and MIS should be more prevalent in consumer markets because the volatility of consumer markets places a premium on demand foresight.

Phase 2 Findings

T-tests were used to compare the responses of consumer market firms and industrial market firms in Phase 2. Those responses with statistical levels of $p < = .05$ were deemed significant to highlight as key differences between firms in consumer versus industrial markets.

Overall, there were few differences between firms in consumer markets and firms in industrial markets. It appears that (except where otherwise noted) technique familiarity, satisfaction, usage, and accuracy are independent of market type. It does, however, appear that the use of the information technologies of EDI, MRP, DRP, and MIS are used to varying degrees in forecasting for consumer versus industrial markets. Results of the t-test analyses for each of these issues are discussed below.

Table 7.21   Familiarity

Technique	Sample Size Con	Ind	% Familiar Con	Ind	% Somewhat Familiar Con	Ind	% Not Familiar Con	Ind
Qualitative:								
Customer Expectations	108	65	64	65	22	15	14	20
Jury of Executive Opinion	107	65	68	63	15	12	17	25
Sales Force Composite	108	64	71	67	17	14	12	19
Quantitative:								
Box-Jenkins (OMTS)	108	65	35	39	*28*	*15*	37	46
Decomposition	108	65	49	38	18	20	33	42
Expert Systems	107	65	34	26	31	31	35	43
Exponential Smoothing	106	63	88	89	7	5	5	6
Life Cycle Analysis	108	65	52	45	23	25	25	30
Moving Average	108	62	92	90	5	7	3	3
Neural Networks	105	64	21	14	26	22	53	64
Regression	109	65	75	76	11	12	14	12
Simulation	108	65	47	48	28	26	25	26
Straight Line Projection	108	64	*89*	*77*	10	12	*1*	*11*
Trend Line Analysis	108	65	71	74	17	14	12	12

Key: Items underlined are statistically different at p < = .05
       Con = Consumer Market Firms
       Ind = Industrial Market Firms

Technique Familiarity. As shown in Table 7.21, there were three significant differences between consumer and industrial firms regarding technique familiarity. Two of these differences indicate that forecasting executives in consumer firms are significantly more familiar with straight-line projections than their counterparts in industrial firms. A third difference indicates that significantly more consumer firms are somewhat familiar with Box-Jenkins analysis than industrial firms. However, no difference was found between the number of consumer and industrial firms that were unfamiliar or familiar with Box-Jenkins analysis. Thus, this difference (although statistically significant) seems somewhat minor.

Technique Satisfaction. As shown in Table 7.22, three significant differences were also found across consumer and industrial firms regarding technique satisfaction. Two of these differences indicate that forecasting executives in consumer firms are much more dissatisfied

Table 7.22   Satisfaction

Technique	Sample Size		% Satisfied		% Neutral		% Dissatisfied	
	Con	Ind	Con	Ind	Con	Ind	Con	Ind
Qualitative:								
Customer Expectations	69	40	40	57	35	28	25	15
Jury of Executive Opinion	72	38	35	34	36	40	29	26
Sales Force Composite	76	41	26	49	24	24	50	27
Quantitative:								
Box-Jenkins (OMTS)	38	25	42	48	45	36	13	16
Decomposition	50	23	62	61	24	35	14	4
Expert Systems	37	16	46	38	49	50	5	12
Exponential Smoothing	91	51	70	73	23	25	7	2
Life Cycle Analysis	54	28	37	36	48	46	15	18
Moving Average	98	54	39	46	36	30	25	24
Neural Networks	21	9	24	56	62	33	14	11
Regression	80	47	66	68	29	28	5	4
Simulation	50	29	52	55	36	41	12	4
Straight Line Projection	93	47	27	28	30	30	43	42
Trend Line Analysis	75	46	41	65	44	31	15	4

Key: Items underlined are statistically different at $p <= .05$
     Con = Consumer Market Firms
     Ind = Industrial Market Firms

Note: Some familiar respondents did not provide a satisfaction rating.

with the sales force composite technique than forecasting executives in industrial firms. This finding corresponds to the findings of Dalrymple (1987), who noted that sales force composite forecasting was more prevalent in industrial firms. In light of greater satisfaction, it appears that the sales force composite technique is more successful in industrial settings. As also indicated by Dalrymple (1987), this is probably the result of more direct and frequent contact between most industrial firms and their customers, compared to most consumer market firms.

A third difference indicated that industrial firms were more satisfied with trend line analysis. It is possible that industrial market trends may be more stable and lasting than consumer market trends and, thus, the reason for the superior success of trend line analysis in industrial firms.

Technique Usage. Consumer and industrial firms appear to contrast on their usage of forecasting techniques across time horizons. However, they do not appear to contrast much across forecast levels.

Most usage differences between consumer and industrial firms occurred in the 3-month to 2-year time horizon (see Table 7.23). Consumer firms relied on regression analysis, jury of executive opinion, decomposition, straight-line projections, and life cycle analysis more than industrial firms. Conversely, industrial firms relied on sales force composite and Box-Jenkins analysis more than consumer firms, although neither group had a large number using Box-Jenkins. These findings, again, support Dalrymple's (1987) conclusion that industrial firms rely heavily on their sales forces for forecasting.

In the less than 3-month time horizon, significantly more consumer firms used regression analysis and straight-line projections (although, again, the numbers were small). Because these techniques were also found to be preferred by consumer firms in the 3-month to 2-year time horizon and in the greater than 2-year time horizon (although not significantly), it appears that regression analysis and straight-line projections are more favored by consumer firms. This finding contrasts Dalrymple (1987), who found regression to be more popular with industrial firms. It is possible that regression is becoming more popular with consumer firms due to greater accessibility of consumer demographic databases and more firms specializing in individual consumer behavior research. Information from these two sources may provide more independent variables from which to determine regression models.

In the greater than 2-year time horizon, more consumer firms employed jury of executive opinion, while more industrial firms employed neural networks. Because jury of executive opinion was also favored by consumer firms in the 3-month to 2-year category and in the less than 3 months time horizon (although not significantly), it appears that consumer firms generally have a greater preference for jury of executive opinion. Because consumer markets do not have as strong salespeople-to-customer relationships as in industrial markets, it is possible that there is a need to rely on executive opinion more than salesperson opinion when making a judgmental forecast.

As Table 7.24 shows, there were four significant differences in technique usage across forecast level. At the corporate level, more industrial firms preferred using sales force composite than consumer firms. Again, it appears that industrial salespeople are bestowed higher esteem when forecasting. The other three differences were at the SKU level and indicate consumer firms use regression analysis, jury of executive opinion, and decomposition more than industrial firms. As previously mentioned, greater amounts of data on individual consumers may facilitate the use of regression by consumer firms at the SKU level. As for jury of executive opinion, it is somewhat surprising to see executive opinion popular for forecasting at the SKU level (almost one quarter of the consumer firms surveyed use jury of executive opinion at the SKU level). Given the large number of SKUs in consumer firms, it was expected that executives would spend more time on strategic forecasting (industrial, corporate, or product line forecasting) than tactical forecasting at the SKU level. However, this does not appear the case in the consumer firms of Phase 2. It is possible that executives in these firms are using other quantitative techniques to make individual SKU forecasts and then using executive opinion to make broad adjustments to groups of SKUs (such as all SKUs in a product line). Even so, this possible explanation seems an inordinate use of valuable executive time involved in tactical forecasting. It is left to future research to determine if this is the case and, if so, what effect this procedure has on accuracy and cost.

Table 7.23   Percent Usage Across Time Horizons

Technique	<= 3 months		3 months to 2 years		> 2 years	
	Con	Ind	Con	Ind	Con	Ind
Qualitative:						
Customer Expectations	3	3	31	35	13	17
Jury of Executive Opinion	4	2	86	65	68	45
Sales Force Composite	2	5	70	87	20	25
Quantitative:						
Box-Jenkins (OMTS)	3	0	12	32	6	8
Decomposition	3	0	49	30	12	12
Expert Systems	2	0	9	2	10	2
Exponential Smoothing	11	3	91	98	18	12
Life Cycle Analysis	0	0	28	7	17	17
Moving Average	12	5	49	42	6	15
Neural Networks	0	3	15	13	2	10
Simulation	1	0	4	7	12	10
Regression	7	0	77	60	34	22
Straight Line Projection	7	0	46	22	10	8
Trend Line Analysis	4	0	61	58	26	20

Key: Items underlined are statistically different at p <= .05
    Con = Consumer Market Firms (n = 99)
    Ind = Industrial Market Firms (n = 60)

Table 7.24   Percent Usage Across Forecast Level

Technique	Industry		Corporate		Product Line		Product (SKU)		SKU by Location	
	Con	Ind	Con	Ind	Con	Ind	Con	Ind	Con	Ind
Qualitative:										
Customer Expectations	4	5	11	18	11	15	13	5	8	12
Jury of Executive Opinion	30	23	50	47	43	28	23	7	14	7
Sales Force Composite	3	5	24	40	26	35	23	18	19	20
Quantitative:										
Box-Jenkins (OMTS)	4	2	7	13	5	12	3	8	2	5
Decomposition	5	3	15	12	16	10	20	8	15	8
Expert Systems	5	0	5	2	3	2	5	0	3	0
Exponential Smoothing	7	7	25	18	28	28	37	33	27	28
Life Cycle Analysis	7	5	11	7	16	7	8	3	4	2
Moving Average	1	5	11	13	16	18	24	13	18	12
Neural Networks	1	3	4	5	4	5	5	7	3	7
Regression	20	17	24	27	26	17	28	13	21	10
Simulation	4	3	5	3	4	5	3	3	1	2
Straight Line Projection	5	3	12	8	17	7	16	8	13	5
Trend Line Analysis	11	7	19	20	22	20	26	17	16	17

Items underlined are statistically different at p < = .05
Con = Consumer Market Firms (n = 99)
Ind = Industrial Market Firms (n = 60)

Accuracy. As Table 7.25 indicates, the accuracy experienced by consumer and industrial firms across time horizon and forecast level was very similar. The only significant difference was forecasts made in the 3-month to 2-year time horizon at the product (SKU) by location level. This difference showed that industrial firms experience significantly greater accuracy than consumer firms. Although other cells in Table 7.25 reflect differences of greater than 5%, these differences were not significant due to large variances or small sample size.

Even if these other cells had reflected significant differences, the weighted average accuracy collapsed over all cells shows consumer and industrial firms achieve similar levels of forecasting accuracy. Hence,

Table 7.25   Accuracy

		<= 3 months		3 months to 2 years		> 2 years	
Forecast Level		Con	Ind	Con	Ind	Con	Ind
Industry		10	—	85	92	86	85
	n:	1	0	9	5	19	14
Corporate		73	—	90	91	87	86
	n:	2	0	34	22	20	15
Product Line		92	—	85	89	92	80
	n:	3	0	40	32	16	6
Product (SKU)		80	89	78	82	91	83
	n:	10	3	56	24	5	4
SKU by		77	69	73	81	90	78
Location	n:	11	3	35	20	2	2

	Consumer Markets	Industrial Markets
Weighted Average:	83	85

Key: Items underlined are statistically different at p < = .05
   Con = Consumer Market Firms (n = 99)
   Ind = Industrial Market Firms (n = 60)
   n = Sample Size

the market structure unique to each of the two types of companies does not appear to significantly affect forecasting accuracy performance.

Information Technology Use in the Forecasting Process. A significantly greater proportion of consumer firms have integrated their forecasting process with EDI information from their customers (Table 7.26). Industrial firms did not appear to be linking their forecasting and EDI systems. Also, a significantly greater proportion of consumer firms have integrated their forecasting system and their DRP/MRP systems. On the other hand, significantly more industrial firms are taking input directly from their MIS than consumer firms. Together these findings suggest that more consumer firms develop forecasts from EDI information and then electronically transmit these forecasts to the DRP and/or MRP systems. Industrial firms use their MIS system to develop forecasts and then apply these forecasts where necessary.

Table 7.26   Use of Information Technologies

	Percent Responding Yes	
Technology	Consumer Market Firms	Industrial Market Firms
Does your sales forecasting system have access to EDI from your suppliers?	21%	12%
Does your sales forecasting system have access to EDI from your customers?	41%	17%
Is the output from your sales forecasting system electronically transmitted to a DRP/MRP system?	64%	43%
Is the input to your sales forecasting system electronically transmitted from your MIS?	29%	45%

Key: Items underlined are statistically different at $p <= .05$

❖ CONCLUSIONS: INDUSTRIAL VERSUS CONSUMER FORECASTING

Although a surprising number of similarities were found, there are certain differences between consumer and industrial forecasting practices that warrant discussion. As found by previous research and reaffirmed in Phase 2, industrial firms favor the sales force composite technique more than consumer firms. Hence, industrial companies should allot more training time to the implementation of the sales force composite technique when training the sales force and the forecasting personnel. Furthermore, industrial companies should pay special attention to facilitating the collection and aggregation of sales force data through new programs (e.g., greater collaboration between forecasting personnel and the sales force) and new technologies (e.g., the sales force using portable computers to provide daily updates to composite forecasts on a central computer).

This study also found that consumer firms employ regression, straight-line projections, and jury of executive opinion more than industrial firms. It appears that the lack of direct customer information forces consumer firms to identify extrinsic factors that correspond to sales, extrapolate sales history to predict future sales, and depend on company executives for qualitative forecasts. Conversely, the direct contact with a smaller customer base that is common in industrial markets allows industrial firms to rely primarily on sales force forecasts. The implication of these findings is that consumer firms should highlight the techniques of regression, straight-line projections, and jury of executive opinion in their training of forecasting personnel. This implies different training (i.e., the more quantitative procedures of regression analysis) in quantitative techniques and different individuals (i.e., executives instead of the sales force) involved in the training process for qualitative forecasts.

A particularly interesting difference concerns the use of information technologies. More consumer firms appear to integrate EDI, DRP, and MRP into the forecasting process, while more industrial firms rely on MIS. By using EDI, DRP, and MRP, consumer market firms are becoming more dependent on quick-response systems, which require faster forecasting processes and greater levels of accuracy. The interesting point is that consumer market firms and industrial market firms are almost alike in their technique usage patterns (aside from the differences discussed above) and achieved forecasting accuracy. It is possible that forecasting techniques are not being applied properly in consumer markets and/or the volatility of customer demand of consumer markets inhibits better achieved accuracy. In light of consumer firms' greater involvement in quick-response systems, a key concern for these firms should be how to integrate, and possibly improve, forecasting techniques for use in quick-response systems.

❖ CONCLUSIONS FROM PHASE 2

The results of Phase 2 lead to some interesting conclusions about the state of sales forecasting techniques, systems, and management. Regarding our use of techniques over the last two decades, the surprise is in the lack of real changes. Companies in the 1990s are largely applying the same techniques in the same situations, with the same results (satisfaction and accuracy) as companies in the 1980s. The challenge is to improve this forecasting technique application process to match the proper techniques with the situations where they perform best. We partially addressed this topic in Chapter 6 and will return to it in Chapter 9.

On a positive note, companies are improving the sophistication of the process by which the sales forecasting function is managed. Less than one in eight of the responding companies use an Independent approach to sales forecasting management, with the majority using a Negotiated or Consensus approach. These latter two approaches require a greater commitment of managerial resources (indicating an increase in the importance of the sales forecasting function), but can more than compensate for this with sales forecasts improved by a broader range of input from various other functional areas. Recognition of this positive cost/benefit relationship in such a large number of responding companies is encouraging.

What is less than encouraging is the lack of sales forecasting performance evaluation in more than half of the responding companies. In any area of management, a lack of performance evaluation and reward for improved performance will lead to a lack of motivation for continuous improvement. Given this maxim of management, it is not surprising that respondents also showed little enthusiasm for training sales forecasting personnel, for gathering the more valuable but more difficult demand numbers instead of the easier but less accurate shipment numbers as input to the sales forecasting process, or for providing adequate budgets for the sales forecasting function.

This lack of performance motivation is exacerbated by the fact that management in many respondent companies views the sales forecasting process backwards. The sales forecasts should be developed (based upon market and channel information) and, from this base, the sales and financial plans for the company should be derived. Unfortunately, in one out of three responding companies management first develops the sales and financial plans, then uses these plans to derive the forecast.

Regarding sales forecasting systems, improvements seem to have come largely in the area of technology (related strongly to the increased effectiveness of personal computers and the sales forecasting software that operates on them). Regardless of these technological innovations, however, the islands of analysis that still exist, the lack of access to the information necessary to make informed sales forecasts, and the lack of direct demand input from channel members have left respondents largely neutral on their satisfaction with sales forecasting systems.

This, combined with the lack of electronic integration between functional areas involved in the development or use of the sales forecast or between suppliers and customers, leads to a number of challenges for improvements in sales forecasting systems. First, companies need to eliminate islands of analysis in the sales forecasting process. This implies increasing system integration for all the personnel involved in developing the sales forecasts. This will eliminate the use of different numbers as input to the sales forecast, minimize disparate assumptions in each step in the sales forecasting process, and encourage more closely reconciled final forecasts.

Second, sales forecasting system access for marketing, sales, planning, product management, and logistics should be increased. The former four typically have information on the marketplace, and the last has information on the distribution channel disposition and movement of inventory, all of which are valuable input to the sales forecasting process. Rather than just having these functional areas advise sales forecasting personnel, they should be able to make their adjustments directly to the sales forecasting system, with the effect of their changes on sales forecasting performance tracked over time. This would allow more consistent input and allow these functional areas to track their impact on forecast accuracy over time.

Increasing sales forecasting system integration with suppliers or customers is also important. With the advent of EDI and vendor-managed inventory (VMI) systems, it is possible to reduce much of sales forecasting uncertainty created by channel mismanagement. When the retailer orders product based upon its attempt to forecast demand, and the wholesaler orders based on its attempt to forecast retailer demand, and the manufacturer orders based upon its forecasts of wholesaler demand, much "slack" is built into the channel in the form of product ordered in anticipation of incorrect forecasts. When the manufacturer has access to retail point-of-sale demand and can back up that demand through the channel all the way to its suppliers, significant reductions in channel-wide inventory may result.

Finally, each company is a complex system of customer demand, suppliers, channel members, and competitors. The idea that a canned sales forecasting system will deal with this myriad of nuances is unlikely. As companies strive to become more effective in sales forecasting, they will need to move more toward systems that are customized to their unique requirements.

In this chapter, we have tried to provide insight into the characteristics of sales forecasting techniques, systems, and management approaches and sales forecasting managers' satisfaction with these techniques, systems, and management approaches. The findings indicate moderate sophistication in the area of techniques, but we have a long way to go in sales forecasting to reach the same level of managerial sophistication achieved in other functional areas of business. In addition, the systems that support these techniques and management processes need considerable refinement. We will only achieve this potential if more managerial attention is focused not only on the techniques of sales forecasting, but on the management of its processes and the systems that support these processes as well.

To increase this focus, we undertook Phase 3 of the benchmark studies to delve more in-depth into the sales forecasting management practices of a select group of companies. Following Phase 3, we undertook Phase 4 to apply what we had learned to analyze specific organizations, and to help enhance our understanding of forecasting best practices. We will deal with the results of these phases in the next chapter.

8

Benchmark Studies

World-Class Forecasting

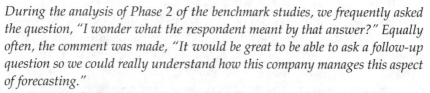

During the analysis of Phase 2 of the benchmark studies, we frequently asked the question, "I wonder what the respondent meant by that answer?" Equally often, the comment was made, "It would be great to be able to ask a follow-up question so we could really understand how this company manages this aspect of forecasting."

We were finding that, although Phases 1 and 2 yielded a wealth of information about the forecasting practices of several hundred responding companies, it also generated a great deal more questions that we wanted answered. These questions were also occurring to companies using the results from Phase 2—companies were reading the results and coming back to us with in-depth questions that we could not answer.

Therefore, in 1994, to gain greater insight into the sales forecasting process and to find out what constituted best practices regarding sales forecasting management, a research team at the University of Tennessee, with the support of Anheuser-Busch, Andersen Consulting, AT&T Network Systems, and Pillsbury, began Phase 3 of the benchmark studies. Phase 3 resulted in a wealth of insight about what is really going on, both good and bad, in forecasting practice. It provided us with the beginning of a "vision" of what world-class forecasting looks like.

Then, in 1996, this research team at the University of Tennessee decided to expand and continually update that vision by launching Phase 4 of the benchmark studies. We developed a methodology for conducting sales forecasting audits at individual companies, and as of this writing, have applied that methodology at 25 companies. The result of this program of research is a clear understanding of what world-class forecasting management is, and a systematic approach to keep that understanding current.

❖ INTRODUCTION

This chapter discusses the results of Phases 3 and 4 of the benchmark studies. The research in Phase 3 began with the selection of 20 companies from those that responded to the survey in Phase 2. We were interested in including companies that had reputations as top performers, though not necessarily top performers in sales forecasting. To understand the variations in sales forecasting management performance, we wanted top performing companies that might still have varying degrees of success in forecasting sales. In addition, we wanted to include companies at various levels of the supply chain.

Site visits were arranged with 15 manufacturers, three distribution firms, and two retailers: Anheuser-Busch, Becton-Dickinson, Coca Cola, Colgate Palmolive, Federal Express, Kimberly Clark, Lykes Pasco, Nabisco, J.C. Penney, Pillsbury, ProSource, Reckitt Colman, Red Lobster, RJR Tobacco, Sandoz, Schering Plough, Sysco, Tropicana, Warner Lambert, and Westwood Squibb.

For each company, any documentation of its sales forecasting management practices was first requested. This documentation included any reports, documentation of systems and/or management procedures, and informal protocols. Once this information was analyzed, an interview schedule was arranged with anyone in the company affiliated with sales forecasting, including developers and users of the sales forecasts. Prior to visiting the company to conduct the interviews, a detailed 11-page protocol was sent to each person to be interviewed (a copy of this protocol is included in the Appendix to this chapter). The interviews were conducted on-site by the research team, with two interviewers in each interview to ascertain interjudge reliability. Interviews were tape recorded and the transcripts from these interviews analyzed for sales forecasting management content.

This in-depth analysis of the documentation and the interview contents of these 20 companies led us to conclude that sales forecasting management can be divided into four dimensions: *Functional Integration,* *Approach, Systems,* and *Performance Measurement.* These four dimensions of forecasting management were then used as the framework for analyzing 25 additional companies (as of this writing) in Phase 4. The Phase 4 research has involved analysis of individual organizations in the context of sales forecasting audits. The companies that have participated in the Phase 4 research to date are: AET Films, Allied-Signal, Alticor, Avery Denison, Bacardi USA, ConAgra, Continental Tire, Corning, Deere and Company, DuPont, Eastman Chemical, Ethicon, Exxon, Hershey Foods, Lucent Technologies, Michelin North America, Motorola, Orbit Irrigation Products, Pharmavite, Philips North America, Sara Lee, Smith and Nephew, Union Pacific Railroad, Whirlpool, and Williamson-Dickie. Chapter 9 is dedicated to an in-depth discussion of the process involved in conducting a Sales Forecasting Audit, so that is not addressed here. However, the insights gained from analysis of these 25 companies have helped us to continually refine our understanding of best practices in forecasting management, as well as understand the common pitfalls into which companies fall.

The four dimensions of forecasting management revealed by the analysis of Phase 3, and refined in Phase 4 of the benchmark studies, are also the four major parts of this chapter. Within each dimension, we identify and discuss four stages of sophistication regarding sales forecasting management. In addition to identifying stages within each dimension, we provide guidelines to enable companies to progress toward a higher level of sophistication for each forecasting dimension. Following these four sections, some general conclusions regarding Phases 3 and 4 are addressed.

Although discussed separately, the reader should keep in mind that all four of these dimensions are inextricably intertwined, and discussion of one dimension sometimes refers to aspects of another dimension. Further, although we refer to companies in certain stages, remember that a particular company can be in one stage on a certain dimension and in a completely different stage on another dimension. However, progress in one dimension is usually related to progress in the others. Finally, among the 20 companies in Phase 3 and the 25 companies to date in Phase 4, there were no companies that were in Stage 4 on all four dimensions.

For managers involved in forecasting, this chapter should facilitate determination of what stage their company is in on each forecasting dimension, as well as provide guidelines on what actions are necessary to progress to higher stages in each dimension. For students studying forecasting, this chapter should provide an in-depth understanding of the processes involved in correctly managing the forecasting function.

❖ FUNCTIONAL INTEGRATION

There are three themes articulated in the Functional Integration dimension, each of which is critical to effectively managing the forecasting process. The first involves a concept we term Forecasting C^3—Communication, Coordination, and Collaboration. Communication encompasses all forms of written, verbal, and electronic communication between the functional business areas of the company—marketing, sales, production, finance, and logistics (including purchasing)—as well as with entities outside the company, primarily customers. Coordination is the extent to which there is a formal process in place, usually manifested through formal meetings, that provides structure to the sharing of information between two or more functional business areas. Collaboration is an orientation among functional areas toward the common goals of forecasting excellence. The second theme found in our discussion of Functional Integration involves the way a company organizes itself around the forecasting function. Finally, the third theme is the extent to which different individuals in different areas of a company are accountable for their contribution to the forecasting process. See Figure 8.1 for a summary of the characteristics of the Functional Integration stages, each of which is now discussed in the context of these three critical themes.

Functional Integration Stages

In **Stage 1** companies, it is common to see major disconnects between various parts of the company. These disconnects refer, in many cases, to a lack of trust between those in demand-oriented departments (i.e., sales and marketing) and those in supply-oriented departments (i.e., production, logistics, purchasing). What we have heard in many of the companies we have worked with are comments from production executives such as, "sales and marketing don't have any grasp of reality. Their forecasts are what they hope will happen, not what they think will happen. All they do is forecast their quotas." At these same companies, individuals from sales and marketing say things such as, "what good does it do me to forecast? They're going to

Figure 8.1   Forecasting Benchmark Stages: Functional Integration

Stage 1

- Major disconnects between marketing, finance, sales, production, and forecasting
- Each area has its own forecasting effort
- No accountability between areas for forecast accuracy

Stage 2

- Coordination (regular meetings) between marketing, finance, sales, production, logistics, and forecasting
- Forecasting located in a particular functional area which dictates forecasts to other areas
- Planned consensus meetings, but with meetings dominated by operations, finance, or marketing - i.e., no real consensus
- Performance rewards for forecasting personnel only

Stage 3

- Communication and coordination between marketing, finance, sales, production, logistics, and forecasting
- Existence of a forecasting champion
- Recognition of the difference between a capacity unconstrained forecast and a capacity constrained operational plan
- Consensus and negotiation process to reconcile demand forecasts and operational plans
- Performance rewards for improved forecasting accuracy for all personnel involved in the consensus process

Stage 4

- Internal functional integration (collaboration, communication, and coordination) as well as external collaboration with key customers
- Forecasting seen as a cross-functional process that serves the entire organization
- Needs of all areas recognized and met by reconciled demand forecasts and operational plans (finance = annual dollar forecasts; sales = quarterly dollar sales territory based forecasts; marketing = annual dollar product based forecasts; production = production cycle unit SKU forecasts; logistics = order cycle unit SKUL forecasts
- Consensus process recognizes feedback loops (i.e., constrained capacity information is provided to sales, marketing and advertising; sales, promotions, and advertising can drive demand, etc.)
- Multidimensional performance rewards for all personnel involved in the consensus process

make what they want anyway, regardless of what I tell them. They just don't understand how dynamic this marketplace really is." Such disconnects often come about because of a lack of Forecasting C^3. There is often little communication, no coordination, and no sense of collaboration that help individuals in these companies understand the needs and concerns of other areas.

Another characteristic of **Stage 1** companies is that they allow each functional area to have its own forecast for its own purposes. As we discussed in Chapter 1, marketing tends to want yearly product line forecasts; sales wants quarterly forecasts by salesperson territory; finance wants yearly dollar forecasts; production wants stock keeping unit (SKU) forecasts tied to the production cycle; and logistics wants stock keeping unit by location (SKUL) forecasts tied to the replenishment cycle. In Stage 1 companies, rather than creating a process where each functional area gets what it needs out of a forecast, often these areas create their own forecasts. In one company, three different departments had installed three different computer systems with three different forecasting packages to address their unique forecasting needs. Of course, the numbers were never the same, and chaos typically ensued. One executive from this company referred to this situation as "black-market forecasting."

A final characteristic of Stage 1 companies is that there is little to no accountability present for forecast accuracy. This lack of accountability breeds mistrust, and leads to comments like, "sales can forecast whatever they want. They don't own the inventory! There is nothing to keep them from forecasting through the roof! I just don't believe what they say." As might be expected, forecasting accuracy and effectiveness are low in Stage 1 companies.

Stage 2 companies have progressed to a recognition of the need for enhanced Forecasting C^3, and they attempt to enhance communication, coordination, and collaboration through a series of formal meetings involving a cross-functional mix of individuals who have insight into future demand. However, in Stage 2 companies, it is often the case that these formal meetings are organized, and sometimes dominated, by the department where the forecasting function is housed. When forecasting is located in one particular functional area, biased forecasts often result. What we have observed is that in companies that locate forecasting in a department responsible for demand (sales or marketing), forecasts tend to have an upward bias. Companies that locate forecasting in a department responsible for supply (production, operations, logistics, or supply chain) tend to have a more downward bias in the forecasts. It is also the case that different departments need different things from forecasts, and they are sometimes unwilling, or uninterested, in providing other departments with different information. For example, marketing and sales find short-range SKU and SKUL forecasts of little use in determining yearly and quarterly product and product line forecasts, whereas production and logistics have little use for longer-term, dollar forecasts. Further, marketing and sales tend to look on forecasts as capacity unconstrained, whereas production and logistics are constantly aware of, and bound by, supply-chain capacity constraints that limit the potential demand that can be fulfilled. Thus, although Stage 2 companies have begun to enhance their level of communication, coordination, and collaboration, the orchestrators of the forecasting meetings can introduce bias and suboptimal forecasts.

Finally, in Stage 2 companies, some progress has been made to enhance accountability. In these companies, performance rewards are available, but only to individuals in the forecasting department. Since in these Stage 2 companies, forecasting is a recognized area within a specific business function, its personnel are evaluated solely on their contribution to the goals of the function in which forecasting is housed. For example, forecasting personnel located in marketing/sales are evaluated on sales goals, whereas forecasting personnel located in operations are evaluated on production/distribution scheduling or inventory control goals. In Stage 2 companies, accountability is not extended to those outside the forecasting group functional area.

Stage 3 companies follow more of a true consensus forecasting approach, with more effective communication and coordination between the functional areas and a recognized forecasting champion. This leads to more effective negotiation between the various functional areas to reach a consensus forecast that recognizes the goals of marketing/sales/finance and the capacity constraints of operations. To achieve more commitment from all personnel involved in reaching the consensus forecast, all consensus team members receive performance rewards for improved forecasting effectiveness.

Stage 4 companies achieve functional integration that stresses Forecasting C^3. In addition, true Stage 4 companies extend their commitment to functional integration to include external collaboration with key customers and suppliers. Whether this is done in a formal CPFR (Collaborative Planning, Forecasting, and Replenishment) context, or whether it is done more informally through regularly scheduled meetings with customers and suppliers, Stage 4 companies enjoy the enhanced forecasting effectiveness that comes from open sharing of information across company boundaries.

Also, Stage 4 companies structure forecasting as a separate functional area, coordinating the forecasting needs of all functional areas and, thereby, reducing the adversarial negotiation approach exhibited by Stage 2 or Stage 3 companies—i.e., a true consensus approach. As a separate functional group that is not accountable to sales, marketing, or operations executives, forecasting can be far more unbiased. This group is often responsible for orchestrating the Sales and Operations Planning process discussed in Chapter 1, and coordinating the flow of information from people who have it (i.e., sales and marketing) to people who need it (i.e., production, logistics, purchasing, and finance). This independent forecasting group is also frequently responsible for maintenance of forecasting systems, which provide full access to information that impacts the forecasting process and outcomes (e.g., capacity constraints, promotions, advertising campaigns). Also, in Stage 4 companies, performance rewards are based on the multidimensional nature of these feedback loops. For example, instead of rewarding on forecasting accuracy alone, rewards are based on division or corporate profitability goals, customer service goals such as improved fill rates, or supply chain goals such as reduced inventory levels.

Improving Functional Integration

Figure 8.2 summarizes the directions necessary to improve functional integration in the sales forecasting process. Companies seeking to improve forecasting effectiveness on the dimension of functional integration can facilitate this improvement by recognizing forecasting as a separate functional area. The primary responsibility of the forecasting function is to bridge the gaps among the orientations of the functional areas within the company (marketing, sales, finance, production, and logistics) by providing sales forecasts at the levels and time horizons required by these functional areas. It is also important that companies move away from independent, concentrated, or negotiated approaches to forecasting management, and toward a consensus approach. Culturally, organizations improve forecasting outcomes if people throughout the company are committed to creating, not the "marketing forecast" or the "sales organization forecast" or the "supply chain forecast," but rather the "company forecast."

Figure 8.2   Improving Functional Integration

To improve forecasting effectiveness on the dimension of
functional integration:

- Recognize forecasting as a function, with adequate organizational clout, that has responsibility to provide forecasts at levels and time horizons useful for downstream users

- Move towards a consensus approach to forecasting management

- Encourage:
  - Common goal setting
  - Communication
  - Free access to relevant information across functional areas, and across organizational boundaries

- Provide performance rewards to all personnel involved in forecasting process

---

Improving functional integration also requires an organizational culture that encourages open communication and common goal setting with regard to forecasting. Not only should this open communication exist inside the boundaries of a company, but it should also extend to the company's key suppliers and customers. These business partners benefit from an open exchange of information, and overall supply chain costs go down and supply chain effectiveness goes up, when demand information is openly shared.

Finally, improving functional integration requires that performance rewards for personnel involved in the forecasting process be based not merely on forecast accuracy, but on the consequences of forecasting accuracy, (e.g., business unit or corporate profitability and/or meeting customer service goals).

❖ APPROACH

The dimension of Approach encompasses what is forecast and how it is forecast. There are seven themes that cut across the various stages of sophistication in the Approach dimension. First is the orientation of the forecast, ranging from plan-driven, to bottom-up, to top-down, to both

Figure 8.3   Forecasting Benchmark Stages: Approach

Stage 1

- Plan driven forecasting approach
- Forecasts based on historical shipments only
- Treat all forecasted products/customers the same
- No defined forecasting hierarchy
- No statistical analysis of historical demand
- No training of forecasting personnel in techniques, and no documentation of the forecasting process

Stage 2

- Bottom up forecasting approach
- Forecasts based upon adjusted demand (e.g., historical shipments plus back-order adjustments)
- Partially defined forecasting hierarchy
- Use of time series-based models to analyze historical demand patterns
- Recognize that marketing/promotion efforts and seasonality can drive demand
- Limited use of statistical tools to analyze historical demand patterns
- Recognize the relationship between forecasting and the business plan, but the plan still takes precedence
- Limited technique training for forecasting personnel, and limited documentation of the forecasting process

Stage 3

- Both top-down and bottom-up forecasting approach
- Forecasts based upon self-reported demand (demand recognized by the organization)

---

top-down and bottom-up, with reconciliation. The second theme is the approach the company takes to conceptualizing historical demand. This ranges from a simple notion of "demand = historical shipments" to a full effort to document all demand, even if that involves orders not placed. The third theme consists of the extent to which companies differentiate between more and less important products or customers in their forecasting process. The fourth theme involves the use of a forecasting hierarchy. The fifth theme considers the level of technique sophistication exhibited by the forecasting company. The sixth theme is the relationship between forecasting and planning. Finally, the seventh theme involves the level of training and documentation of the forecasting process. Each

Figure 8.3 (Continued)

- Use ABC analysis (both customer and product) for forecasting accuracy importance
- Identification of categories of products that do not need to be forecast (i.e., two-bin items, dependent demand items, make to order items)
- Appropriate adjustment of forecasts, given the tendencies of the sales force and the distribution channel to introduce biases (motivation for sales to under-forecast and for distributors to over-forecast)
- Forecast at several levels in the forecasting hierarchy
- Incorporate subjective input from marketing, sales, and operations to the forecast
- Forecasting drives the business plan
- Training in quantitative analysis/statistics, and appropriate documentation of the forecasting process

Stage 4

- Top-down and bottom-up forecasting approach with reconciliation
- Vendor managed and co-managed inventory, along with CPFR customers, factored out of the forecasting process
- Full forecasting segmentation of products and customers based upon strategic importance
- Reconciled forecasts at all levels in the forecasting hierarchy
- Appropriate use of both regression-based and time series-based models to analyze historical demand patterns
- Develop forecasts and business plan simultaneously, with periodic reconciliation of both
- On-going training in quantitative analysis/statistics and an understanding of the business environment—top management support of the forecasting process

of these seven themes is evident in the 4 stages of forecasting sophistication, as documented in Figure 8.3. As a company becomes more sophisticated in each of these seven areas, they advance to higher stages of sophistication in the Approach dimension.

Approach Stages

Stage 1 companies have a forecasting orientation that is driven by the business/profit plan, that is, plan-driven forecasts. In these companies, forecasting personnel are often highly frustrated, since after giving their best efforts to document what they think demand will be in future time periods, their managers simply change the forecast to reflect the amount of demand needed to "make their numbers." Such a forecasting orientation tends to remove integrity from the process, and downstream users of the forecasts come to realize that forecasts represent targets, rather than best guesses of reality. Final forecasts in these companies seldom take into account the impact of economic factors, marketing efforts, or stage in the product life cycle of their product mix.

When it comes to historical demand, Stage 1 companies use the most simple, and most misleading, substitute for true demand, which is historical shipments. When Stage 1 companies analyze historical data, and look for patterns they can project out into the future, they look at what was shipped from their facilities. When a company looks at history in this way, it is forecasting based on its past ability to supply, rather than actual demand in the marketplace.

Also, no recognition is given to the differences in forecasting needs of different products or customers. Most companies have products that are particularly important strategically, or products that by their nature must have more accurate forecasts, but Stage 1 companies use the same procedures and logic for all products in their portfolio. Similarly, most companies have a relatively small number of critically important customers, but Stage 1 companies do not differentiate based upon size or importance of customers. In addition, Stage 1 companies do not have a defined "forecasting hierarchy" in place. Such a hierarchy is important in that it allows people to contribute information to forecasts at the level of their knowledge or expertise, while at the same time, allowing others to take information out of forecasts at the level at which they need it.

In Stage 1 companies, there is no statistical analysis of historical demand. Often, the only forecasting technique utilized is qualitative in nature, and the insights that can be gained from statistically identifying recurring patterns are foregone. A final Stage 1 characteristic is that personnel involved in forecasting receive no training in forecasting techniques, and there is little or no documentation of the forecasting process.

Stage 2 companies take more of a bottom-up approach to forecasting demand. By bottom-up, we mean that forecasting is done at relatively low levels, such as SKU by customer, then rolled up to determine overall demand. This is often done with the involvement of the sales organization, where they are asked to forecast on a customer-by-customer basis. While this approach is superior to a plan-driven approach to forecasting, it is most effective when combined with a top-down approach. Another characteristic of Stage 2 companies is that they have moved closer to forecasting based on actual historical demand. Instead of using only historical shipments as their surrogate for demand, Stage 2 companies use adjusted demand, which is often operationalized as shipments plus backorder adjustments. While this gets the company closer to a measure of actual demand than historical shipments alone, it still does not account for demand that would have occurred had customers actually placed orders. Also, in Stage 2 companies, time series forecasting techniques are prevalent, but more for their simplicity than for their appropriateness in all forecasting situations encountered.

There is greater recognition of the interrelationship between the business plan and forecasting and the effect of marketing/promotion efforts and seasonality on demand. However, profit or other business plans still take precedence over the forecasting process. Stage 2 companies also provide some training for their forecasting personnel in statistical analysis and begin to document the forecasting process. However, individuals outside of the formal forecasting group typically receive little or no training in forecasting techniques.

Stage 3 companies recognize the importance of top-down and bottom-up forecasting approaches. By top-down forecasting, we mean that a company forecasts total industry demand, which when combined with a forecast of the company's market share, results in a forecast of demand for the company's products. Stage 3 companies do both this top-down, as well as a bottom-up approach, but do little to reconcile the discrepancies that often result from these two different approaches. Another Stage 3 characteristic is that companies move even closer to true measures of historical demand. In addition to accounting for shipments and backorder adjustments, Stage 3 companies make some effort to document demand that would have occurred had customers actually placed orders. Consider the following example. In conversation with a salesperson, a customer says, "we'd like 20,000 units of your product next month." Knowing capacity constraints, the salesperson replies, "Well, I could get you 15,000 but not 20,000." An order is then placed for 15,000 units. In a Stage 1 company, demand history would reflect 15,000 units shipped next month. In a Stage 3 company, the salesperson has some mechanism in place to document the 5,000 units of lost sales, and demand history then reflects 20,000 units. Such a procedure is what we refer to as "self-reported demand."

In addition, Stage 3 companies are more sophisticated in their ability to distinguish among both products, and customers, that should be treated differently in the forecasting process. For example, one Stage 3 company tags each customer as an A-, B-, or C-level customer, based on size and strategic importance, as well as all products as A-, B-, or C-level products, based on volume and profitability. In this company, salespeople are asked to make qualitative adjustments only to A-level products demanded by A-level customers. All other product/customer combinations are forecast using the company's statistical forecasting system.

Having moved beyond shipments forecasts or self-recorded demand forecasts, some Stage 3 companies use some point of sale (POS) demand and supply chain timing/inventory information to forecast demand at their position in the channel. Some customers of Stage 3 companies provide projections of future demand needs and current inventory levels, enabling this information to be used for separating these key customers' forecasts from overall forecasts. However, these customers are not required to accept shipments based upon their previously projected demands (i.e., "uncommitted commitments"); therefore, the uncommitted nature of these projections does not allow for vendor-managed inventories.

This differentiation among ways to forecast different products is further expanded by Stage 3 companies to include products that do not need to be forecast. Examples include:

1. Products that move so slowly that they are considered two-bin items. For these products, inventory is kept in two locations (bins). When one bin is empty a replenishment bin is ordered. Since the item moves so slowly, the new order arrives long before the second bin is empty, thus eliminating the need to forecast.

2. Products with dependent demand, that is, products that are sold to manufacturing locations that use a constant and predictable amount per day over a long production scheduling cycle. Such products allow for planned production/procurement and eliminate the need for forecasting.

3. Products that are made to order. Customers expect no inventory and are willing to wait through the production order cycle to receive delivery, eliminating the need to forecast these products.

Another characteristic of Stage 3 companies is that they forecast at several levels of the forecast hierarchy, allowing considerable flexibility in both input to, and output from, the forecasting process. In addition, Stage 3 companies recognize that regression-based forecasting works better for longer-range forecasts at levels higher in the corporation; a "suite" of time series forecasts (discussed in Chapter 6) works better for shorter-range SKU and SKUL forecasts; and experienced business qualitative input is an important component of all forecasts. Thus, subjective input from sales, marketing, operations, and other functional areas in a company are critical to the forecasting process, and procedures are put into place to incorporate that subjective input to final forecasts.

A very important Stage 3 characteristic is that in these companies, planning and forecasting are in their appropriate sequence. In contrast to Stage 1 or 2 companies, Stage 3 companies devise business plans in light of a dispassionate assessment of future demand in the marketplace, which is the role of forecasting. In these companies, plans are much more often achieved, since these plans are based more on a sense of reality. Finally, at Stage 3 companies, training is provided for both forecasting personnel and others involved in the process, and appropriate documentation of the complete process is in place.

Stage 4 companies recognize that top-down and bottom-up forecasting approaches often result in two different answers, and they "dig into the numbers" to reconcile and understand those differences. An example here helps to illustrate these insights. Let's say that a consumer packaged goods (CPG) company first forecasts in a bottom-up approach. Each of this company's major retail customers predicts that demand for the CPG company's products will increase by 5% next year, because of increased marketing activity at the retail level. However, a top-down forecast reveals that demand for this particular product will be relatively flat. The "best" forecast is probably somewhere in between. Not every retail customer will increase demand by 5%, but increased retail marketing support may increase overall demand to some degree. Therefore, a thoughtful reconciliation of the bottom-up and the top-down forecasts gives the CPG company great insight into its marketplace, and results in a more accurate and useful overall forecast.

Stage 4 companies are also more involved in vendor-managed or co-managed inventory arrangements with key customers, as well as formal or informal CPFR arrangements. Forecasts for these customers are managed separately and then ultimately merged into forecasts for non-VMI, CMI, or CPFR customers. Further, a full range of segmentation factors are considered in determining the level of forecasting sophistication and accuracy required for each product and for each customer. These include the factors of ABC analysis, two-bin designations, dependent demand products, and make-to-order products mentioned in previous stages, but also include:

1. Dissimilar seasonal patterns.

2. Products whose demand is largely promotion driven and, thus, should be forecast with regression-based promotional models.

3. Different stages in the product life cycle, which affect the importance of forecasting and the predictability of demand.

4. Whether or not the product has a short shelf life, because the shorter the shelf life, the greater the product obsolescence due to forecasting error.

5. The value of the product, since more valuable products are more costly to hold in inventory, thereby increasing the inventory cost of forecasting error.

6. The customer service sensitivity of the customer, because the higher the customer service sensitivity, the higher the customer service cost of stockouts due to forecasting error.

7. The raw material lead time, because different forecasting horizons (and, consequently, different forecasting techniques) are required for products whose raw materials can be procured in a matter of weeks compared to products whose raw materials may take more than a year to obtain.

8. The production lead time, because—similar to raw material lead times—the length of the lead time for the production schedule and how often this schedule can be changed affects the forecasting time horizon and techniques.

Stage 4 companies have a complete forecasting hierarchy in place, allowing anyone to forecast at the level at which they have information, and allowing all users to extract information from the forecast at the level at which they need it. For example, at a Stage 4 company, salespeople can *contribute* forecasts at the product line level (if that is the level at which they most commonly operate), and distribution planners can *use* forecasts at the SKUL level, without the need for cumbersome manipulation of the data. In addition, Stage 4 companies take full advantage of all the various statistical tools at their command, appropriately using a suite of time-series tools for more short-range, operational level forecasts, and regression tools for mid- to long-range, strategic-level forecasts. With a full appreciation of the intricacies of the business environment comes a recognition that a certain amount of "game playing" will occur in any forecasting process. For instance, salespeople often under-forecast to obtain lower quotas and distributors often over-forecast to cause greater quantities to be produced and held in inventory to be available for their use. Stage 4 companies recognize these natural biases, and appropriately modify forecasts generated by these groups, thus improving overall forecasting accuracy.

Stage 4 companies recognize that the business plan and forecasts are intertwined and should be developed together, rather than allowing one to drive the other. This final point is only achieved in Stage 4 companies through top management's recognition of the importance of forecasting, both to the business plan and to operational planning.

Improving Forecasting Approach

Figure 8.4 summarizes the actions that facilitate improvement in forecasting approach.

There are some important points to highlight from Figure 8.4. First, companies should use both a top-down and a bottom-up orientation to forecasting, and should thoughtfully examine the results of each, reconciling any differences. This provides not only better forecasts, but tremendous insights into the nature of the business and markets being served. Second, companies should adopt an approach to business planning that begins with a realistic, analytical assessment of demand in the marketplace. In other words, forecasting should precede planning, and it should be a constantly iterating process. Third, it is critically important to document, to every extent possible, *true historical demand*, and use that historical demand as the basis for predicting future demand. Fourth, this true demand should constitute the data that are used by appropriate statistical tools to find patterns that can be projected into the future. Fifth, companies should recognize that not all customers, or products, are equal. Some require more care and attention than others, and procedures

Figure 8.4   Improving Forecasting Approach

**To improve forecasting effectiveness on the dimension
of approach companies should:**

- Do both top-down and bottom-up forecasting, and should actively and thoughtfully reconcile the results of each

- See forecasting and planning as processes that are intertwined, and make business plans based on dispassionate assessments of demand in the marketplace

- Make every effort to document *true* historical demand, and use that historical demand as the basis for forecasting future demand

- Appropriately use all tools available, including time series, regression models, and qualitative input from sales and marketing

- Appropriately segment both products and customers, based upon accuracy levels needed, and strategic importance

- Implement a complete forecasting hierarchy

- Commit significant resources to training and documentation, and demonstrate top-management support

---

should be put into place to identify those important customers and products, and routines should be established to devote needed time and energy to making those important product and customer forecasts as accurate as they can be. Finally, it is also important for a company to have initial as well as ongoing training in quantitative analysis/statistics and the business/industry environment in which the firm operates. This training helps forecasting personnel develop an appreciation of the complex nature of their business environment and gives them the tools needed to incorporate these factors into their forecasts.

❖ SYSTEMS

The dimension of Systems encompasses computer and electronic communications hardware and software that support the forecasting process. There are five primary themes that cut across the four stages of sophistication in the Systems dimension: (1) integration of forecasting systems with other corporate systems; (2) how reporting is handled; (3) how historical data are maintained; (4) how performance measures are handled in the systems; and (5) the level of investment in system infrastructure. See Figure 8.5 for a summary of the characteristics of the Systems stages.

Systems Stages

Most companies have a number of systems installed to perform the critical business functions of the company, such as sales systems, marketing systems, financial reporting and analysis systems, materials requirement planning (MRP) systems, distribution requirements planning (DRP) systems, and forecasting systems. In **Stage 1** companies, these various systems are not integrated, and movement of information from one system to another requires manual transfer. In some cases, this manual transfer entails "cut and paste" operations, and in others, it entails re-keying of data from one system to another. In either case, such manual transfer of information is costly, time consuming, and introduces significant errors. Another characteristic of Stage 1 companies is that reports that are needed by forecast users are generated sporadically, and only in hardcopy. More sophisticated companies have reporting systems in place that allow users to design the reports they need, generate reports when they are needed, and have the option of either hardcopy or on-screen reports.

A further Stage 1 characteristic is what we refer to as "islands of analysis"—where different individuals operate different analysis tools, potentially using data from different sources. A very typical example of island of analysis can be found when forecasting personnel use a variety of spreadsheet templates on different computers, with little control over the source of the data used or the assumptions that underlie the various spreadsheet models. At one company involved in Phase 4, such a phenomenon was described by a company executive as "spreadsheet mania." When such islands of analysis are in place, there is often a breakdown in credibility, since forecast users lack confidence in the source of data analyzed, or the existence of adequate controls.

In terms of performance metrics, Stage 1 companies usually fail to include measures of performance in the system. Finally, Stage 1 companies fail to adequately invest in the infrastructure necessary to

Figure 8.5   Forecasting Benchmark Stages: Systems

Stage 1

- Separate marketing, sales, forecasting, and downstream planning systems require manual transfer of data from one system to another
- Reports generated sporadically and distributed only in hard-copy
- "Islands of analysis" exist with lack of coordination between information in different systems
- Lack of performance metrics in any of the systems or reports
- Inadequate system infrastructure such as hardware and technical support for forecasting system

Stage 2

- Separate marketing, sales, forecasting, and downstream planning systems linked by customized interfaces
- Reports periodically generated and distributed online in addition to hard-copy format
- Inconsistent database distributed over multiple systems requires frequent uploads/downloads and data manipulation
- Performance measures calculated off-line and available in reports
- Minimal system infrastructure support for hardware, system maintenance, and upgrades

Stage 3

- Partially integrated supply chain software suite allows forecast updates to be automatically communicated to downstream planning systems
- Routine reports made available on demand online
- System-user interface allows subjective input
- Forecast data resides in central data warehouse and made available in a batch process on a shared drive
- Measures of performance available in reports and online
- Acceptable system infrastructure provided for system maintenance and upgrades

Stage 4

- Integrated supply chain software suite permits both internal and external information access and automatically feeds downstream planning systems
- Electronic linkages with major customers and suppliers support collaborative forecasting
- User-friendly report generator supports both standardized and customized reports for end-users
- Data warehouse design supports forecast updates on a real-time basis
- Notes function captures subjective information in a searchable format
- Performance measures highly visible in reports and easily accessible online
- Superior system infrastructure permits timely upgrades and enhancements needed to support improved forecast management

support forecasting. Such infrastructure takes the form of hardware and technical support. Stage 1 companies constantly need additional hardware capacity to support the forecasting process, and forecasting system upgrades and support are often "at the bottom of the priority list."

In **Stage 2** companies, the various corporate systems are electronically linked through customized interfaces, eliminating the need for manual transfer of information from one system to another. However, since each corporate system has its own patterns of upgrade and enhancement, the custom interfaces require constant maintenance to keep up with the upgrades. In addition, the reporting capabilities of Stage 2 companies are greater than in Stage 1, and forecasting performance is available, although it is calculated "offline," often in separate spreadsheet programs that require manual transfer of information. Stage 2 companies have a database that contains historical demand data, but this database may be distributed over multiple systems requiring frequent uploads and downloads to keep the database up to date. Finally, Stage 2 companies have invested more in infrastructure than Stage 1 companies, although such investment may still be insufficient to achieve forecasting excellence.

Stage 3 companies have moved to an environment where multiple business systems are integrated into a complete software suite, allowing forecasting information to be automatically downloaded to downstream planning systems. There may still be some customized interfaces in Stage 3 companies, most frequently between forecasting systems and upstream marketing or sales systems, but the company has moved away from separate systems with customized integration toward overall integration. Also in Stage 3 companies, report generation is made more "customer friendly" by providing routine reports to users as needed, online. An important Stage 3 characteristic is the existence of a centrally managed data warehouse, which is made available to forecasting systems in a batch process. Although it may not be updated in a real-time environment, its central management brings significantly more integrity to the historical demand data than either Stage 1 or Stage 2 companies. Further, Stage 3 companies include performance measurement functionality directly in the forecasting system, which is available either in printed reports or online. And finally, Stage 3 companies have invested an acceptable level of resources into forecasting system infrastructure.

Stage 4 companies have taken the concept of integrated supply chain software as far as is technologically possible, so that all systems that both contribute to forecasts and use forecasts can do so automatically. In addition, Stage 4 companies use information protocols that allow exchange of forecasting data with both suppliers and key customers. Most Stage 4 companies have implemented, and in many cases progressed beyond, EDI relationships and moved into web-based environments that promote exchange of important forecasting data. Stage 4 companies have also implemented sophisticated report-generation systems that allow authorized personnel to design ad-hoc reports, in real time, and either view or print customized or routine reports as needed.

Another Stage 4 characteristic is the implementation of sophisticated data warehouse systems that allow forecasts to be updated in real time. Because many companies process order data in real time, the ideal way to give users the most up-to-date forecast data is to allow access to that historical data in real time as well. Also, Stage 4 companies have integrated performance measures tightly into their systems, and made them easily available to authorized users, and highly visible in reports. And finally, significant investment has been made by Stage 4 companies in the infrastructure that allows timely and continuous upgrades and enhancements of forecasting functionality, which is needed to support excellence in forecasting management.

Improving Forecasting Systems

Figure 8.6 provides a summary of how to improve the sales forecasting function on the dimension of systems.

To improve on the dimension of Systems, companies should eliminate all manual transfers of data among the various business systems that interact with forecasting. In many companies, this occurs through the implementation of supply-chain systems that are designed to tightly integrate and exchange information seamlessly. Companies should also focus on the integrity of their historical data. To achieve such integrity, companies need to eliminate "islands of analysis," and move to a centralized data warehouse environment. Further, excellence in Systems means the reporting of information becomes as "user friendly" as possible. Authorized users should be able to access relevant forecasting information in whatever way is most useful for them, should it be through online, ad-hoc queries, or regularly scheduled printed reports. Choice of how information is distributed should always be in the hands of the user.

Figure 8.6   Improving Forecasting Systems

To improve forecasting effectiveness on the dimension of systems companies should:

- Eliminate all manual transfers of data from one system to another, and work toward seamless integration of all systems

- Eliminate islands of analysis and support a centralized data warehouse strategy

- Provide access to forecasting information in an ad-hoc, on-screen environment

- Integrate performance measurement directly into the forecasting system

- Invest resource in system infrastructure needed to promote forecasting excellence

---

In addition, forecasting excellence requires that performance measures be kept and made available to relevant users. Companies must provide these performance measures as a part of the forecasting system, thus eliminating manual data transfer and offline performance measurement systems. And finally, companies must acknowledge that forecasting excellence requires an adequate investment in systems infrastructure. Adequate funds must be made available for hardware, software, and technical support to provide the individuals who manage the forecasting function the ability to do their jobs.

❖ PERFORMANCE MEASUREMENT

The dimension of performance measurement addresses what metrics are used to measure forecasting effectiveness and the information gathered to explain that performance. See Figure 8.7 for a summary of the characteristics of the performance measurement stages.

Performance Measurement Stages

Stage 1 companies do not have the systems nor the understanding of the forecasting process to even measure accuracy. In some companies

Figure 8.7   Forecasting Benchmark Stages: Performance Measurement

---

Stage 1

- Accuracy not measured
- Forecasting performance evaluation not tied to any measure of accuracy (often tied to meeting plan, reconciliation with plan, etc.)

Stage 2

- Accuracy measured, primarily as Mean Absolute Percent Error
- Forecasting performance evaluation based upon accuracy, with no consideration for the implications of accurate forecasts on operations
- Recognition of the impact upon demand of external factors (i.e., economic conditions, competitive actions, etc.)

Stage 3

- Accuracy still measured as Mean Absolute Percent Error, but more concern given to the measurement of the supply chain impact of forecast accuracy (i.e., lower acceptable accuracy for low value non-competitive products, recognition of capacity constraints in the supply chain and their impact on forecasting and performance, etc.)
- Graphical and collective (throughout product hierarchy) reporting of forecast accuracy
- Forecasting performance evaluation based upon forecast accuracy and some supply chain metrics, such as inventory levels and customer fill rates.

Stage 4

- Adjust for the fact that unfulfilled demand is partially a function of forecasting error and partially a function of operational error
- Forecasting error treated as an indication of the need for a problem search (for instance, POS demand was forecast accurately, but plant capacity prevented production of the forecast amount)
- Multidimensional metrics of forecasting performance - forecasting performance evaluation tied to the impact of accuracy on achievement of corporate goals (i.e., profitability, supply chain costs, customer service)

---

that have participated in Phases 3 and 4, individuals would respond to questions about forecast accuracy with statements like "well, it's not very good," or "I'd guess it's about 75% accurate." Typically, such responses are in fact embarrassed ways of saying "we don't know because we don't measure accuracy!" Although forecasts are developed and used, no measure of accuracy exists and, not surprisingly, accuracy is not tied to performance evaluation. Typical performance evaluation criteria are based on meeting the business plan or reconciliation of the forecast to the business plan.

Stage 2 companies use some measure of forecast accuracy (generally Mean Absolute Percent Error) as the sole metric of forecasting performance. However, limited understanding of forecasting at this stage leads some Stage 2 companies to incorrectly specify the MAPE formula (a phenomenon discussed more fully in Chapter 2), using forecast rather than demand in the denominator, a formulation that incorrectly inflates the accuracy measure (i.e., the higher the forecast, the lower the MAPE value, regardless of whether the forecast was accurate or not). In this stage, some companies begin to recognize the impact of such external factors as economic conditions, weather, and competitive actions on demand and, thus, on forecast accuracy. However, many Stage 2 companies consider accuracy as the sole indicator of forecasting performance, rather than evaluating the effect that accurate forecasts have on overall supply chain costs and effectiveness. For example, one company that participated in Phase 4 of the research had, over the preceding few years, made significant improvement in supply chain performance. Customer service levels, measured in terms of fill rates, were greatly improved, while inventory levels were down significantly. At the same time, forecast accuracy had improved, but had not reached management's arbitrary target of 80% accuracy. At this company, rather than celebrating the successes of the forecasting group, and working on continuing the excellent momentum, management continued to berate the forecasting group for not achieving the 80% target. The lesson here is that accuracy, while an important measure, is after all a means to an end. Very few, if any, investors buy stock in a company because it has low MAPE figures. Stock is bought and sold because of excellence in overall supply chain management and profitability, and accurate forecasts are one way to achieve those worthy goals.

Stage 3 companies still use MAPE as a measure of forecast accuracy, but concern shifts more to measuring the impact of forecast accuracy on marketing and supply chain activities. The former includes acceptance of lower forecast accuracy for products that are less important to the strategic marketing plan (i.e., lower profit margins and/or customer service sensitivity). The latter includes the consideration of supply chain capacity constraints and the recognition that high levels of forecast accuracy are not as important for low-value products that are cheaper to carry in inventory.

The actual reporting of accuracy measures in Stage 3 companies becomes more sophisticated, with graphical presentations of accuracy and the ability to look at accuracy at various levels in the product hierarchy (from SKUL unit demand all the way up to corporate dollar demand). As discussed in Chapter 2, percent error is an excellent diagnostic measure of forecast accuracy, and it is often more effectively reported in graphical terms. MAPE, on the other hand, is an excellent "report card" measure, and it is more effectively reported in tabular form. So Stage 3 companies use both graphical and collective reporting of forecast accuracy.

Stage 4 companies realize that forecasting error is partially a function of incorrect forecasts and partially a function of the inability of the supply chain to deliver the products when and where they are demanded. It is interesting that this concept was explored in depth more than 25 years ago (Bowersox, Closs, Mentzer, & Sims, 1979), but is still a characteristic only of Stage 4 companies. This recognition leads to treating forecasting error not as an end result, but rather as a symptom of a problem to be investigated further. For instance, investigation of a forecasting error may indicate that POS demand was forecast accurately, but a lack of communication with production failed to alert the forecast system that the demand forecast was beyond the production capacity of the supply chain. The solution to the forecasting "error" in this case is an adjustment to the forecasting information system.

Finally, Stage 4 companies have moved beyond measuring forecasting performance by the unidimensional metric of accuracy (e.g., MAPE). Multidimensional metrics are used that tap accuracy, as well as the impact of the forecast on profitability, competitive strategy, supply chain costs, and customer service.

Improving Forecasting Performance Measurement

Figure 8.8 provides a summary of how to improve sales forecasting performance measurement.

Improvement of sales forecasting performance measurement requires measuring forecast accuracy at all the levels relevant to the functional areas using the forecast. If each functional area using the forecast is not able to track the accuracy of the forecast in terms that are relevant to them (e.g., product line, SKUL), the forecasting function will not be relevant to their business processes. When measuring forecast performance, it is important to use a measure of accuracy with

Figure 8.8   Improving Forecasting Performance Measurement

To improve forecasting effectiveness on the dimension of performance measurement companies should:

• Measure forecast accuracy at all the levels relevant to the functional areas using the forecast

• Use a measure of accuracy with which management is comfortable, but recognize that MAPE is the most popular of such measures

• Provide graphical, as well as statistical, measures of accuracy

• Provide a multidimensional metric of forecasting performance which includes accuracy, as well the impact of the forecast on profitability, competitive strategy, supply chain costs, and customer service

---

which management is familiar and comfortable. We found that MAPE is the most popular of such measures, because it overcomes some of the problems inherent in other measures of forecast accuracy (for a discussion of other measures of forecast accuracy, including mean absolute error, mean squared error, and percent error, see Chapter 2).

Another important step to take when trying to improve sales forecasting performance measurement is to provide graphical, as well as statistical, measures of accuracy. At the risk of using a cliché, a picture really is worth a thousand words. Graphical representations of sales forecasts against actual demand enable users and developers of the sales forecasts to understand forecast performance quickly and clearly.

Finally, companies seeking to improve sales forecasting performance measurement must realize the importance of measuring not only forecasting accuracy, but also understanding and measuring the impact of forecast accuracy on profitability, competitive strategy, supply chain costs, and customer service.

❖ CONCLUSIONS

All companies that participated in Phase 3 of the benchmark studies had some dissatisfaction with their sales forecasting process. Particular areas of dissatisfaction were new product forecasting and the forecasting of low volume, sporadic products. The companies that were at higher stages of sophistication on the four forecasting dimensions were attempting to remedy these problems, whereas companies in lower stages of sophistication accepted these problems as "part of the business." This observation demonstrates that companies that have a relatively high level of sophistication regarding their forecasting function can also be characterized as continuously improving, that is, learning organizations.

In terms of Phase 4 companies, they agreed to participate in the audit research primarily because they recognized that their forecasting practices were inadequate. As we will discuss in Chapter 9, many companies who participated in the audit research proved they were learning organizations by taking the audit findings and using them as an impetus for improvement.

Of the 45 companies we have explored in depth through Phases 3 and 4 of the benchmark research, no one company was found to be primarily in Stage 4 on all of the forecasting dimensions. It was surprising how often companies that performed well on other measures of business success (e.g., profitability, market share) were Stage 1 or Stage 2 companies when it came to forecasting. However, the companies whose sales forecasting functions were identified as being relatively sophisticated realized that failing to improve their sales forecasting process led to problems in the long term (e.g., tactical inventory and production problems, as well as strategic marketing and planning problems).

This benchmark study provides clear steps of progression within each dimension to move a company to a level of excellence in forecasting, a progression that is indicative of the learning organization orientation mentioned above. The rewards of such an orientation and the forecasting excellence it encourages are considerable and include: lower inventory levels, lower supply chain costs, higher customer service levels, and higher morale.

APPENDIX

SALES FORECASTING AUDIT PROTOCOL

❖ QUESTIONS ABOUT SALES
  FORECASTING ADMINISTRATION

Start with a general request, which may answer many of the specifics given below:

Please describe the process you go through to develop each sales forecast.

Specific Questions

To what extent are various functional departments involved in the development of sales forecasts?

Examples: engineering, finance, logistics, marketing, planning, product management, production, R&D, sales, sales forecasting.

What approach is used by these functional departments to develop sales forecasts?

1. Do these departments use their own separate forecasts, or

2. Does one department develop a single forecast that all departments use, or

3. Does a forecast committee develop a single forecast that all departments use, or

4. Does each department develop its own forecast and a committee develops a final compromise forecast?

If #2, which department develops the forecast?

If #3 or #4, which departments are on the committee?

How satisfied are you with this approach?

What is middle management's role in developing sales forecasts? (Example: review only, approval only, actual involvement, combination of these.)

What is upper management's role in developing sales forecasts? (Example: review only, approval only, actual involvement, combination of these.)

At the beginning of each forecasting period, how does the sales forecasting process begin? (Example: sales forecasts developed by computer system, sales force, both computer system and sales force, marketing, forecasting/planning group.)

Is the business plan based upon the sales forecast or sales forecast based upon the business plan?

To what degree do you make the forecast agree with the business plan?

Which department(s) are responsible for managing inventory? (Examples: engineering, finance, logistics, marketing, planning, product management, production, R&D, sales, sales forecasting.)

Do you think the process for preparing a forecast is clear and routine with precise instructions available? Please be specific.

Is forecasting performance formally evaluated and rewarded? How?

Is the sales forecasting budget sufficient for the personnel, computer hardware/software, and training required?

Too much money is spent in this company to manage around forecasting error. Do not specifically ask this, but look for examples to be pursued in the conversation.

Are the sales forecasts developed and reported in:

Units, then converted to dollars

Units only

Dollars, then converted to units

Dollars only

What is forecast? (Examples: distributor orders, shipments, sales, customer demand.)

How do you deal with the following special events: new products, promotions, variety in product/package details?

What percent of your business is in the following categories:

Consumer products

Industrial products

Consumer services

Industrial services

Company Type: To be determined from company documents and general discussion.

Manufacturer

Logistics/transportation

Telecommunications company

Wholesaler

Utility

Retailer

Health care company

Publisher

What is the length and variability of production lead times for your company?

What is the length and variability of raw material lead times for your company?

What is the length and variability of cycle times to your customers?

Are products primarily made to order or made to forecast?

Do you have a specified goal for level of logistics customer service?

Inventory turns?

What is the achieved level for both of these?

How would you describe the level of competition in your industry?

Is the demand for your products primarily driven by marketing efforts of your company and its competitors?

Describe the typical channel of distribution for your products (length).

What is the shelf life for your products?

To what degree do you use the same forecasting management processes in different countries?

If the answer is low, is this something you are trying to accomplish?

❖ QUESTIONS ABOUT SALES FORECASTING SYSTEMS

Start with a general request, which may answer many of the specifics given below:
Please describe the information systems and forecasting computer systems you use to develop each sales forecast.

Specific Questions

The number and type (hardware, software) of forecasting systems?

How long has each been in use?

Is your forecasting system on a distributed data network (LAN/WAN)?

Is your forecasting system on personal computers, a mainframe, or both?

Was your software (1) developed by vendor, (2) custom built by your company, or (3) a commercial software package?

If #1, who was the vendor and please describe the development process.

If #3, what is the name of the package?

Is the output from the forecasting system electronically transmitted to a DRP/MRP system for production and inventory planning? Are forecasts used to determine ROP and OQ?

Is the input to your forecasting system electronically transmitted from the corporate Management Information System?

With what other systems does the forecasting system interact?

How automated is the integration?

What information is input from the MIS to the sales forecasting system? (Examples: sales, demand, orders, price changes, new product introduction information, advertising/promotional information, competitive information, market research information, economic information, past forecast accuracy.)

Does the sales forecasting system have access to EDI (electronic data interchange) information from suppliers?

Does the sales forecasting system have access to EDI (electronic data interchange) information from customers?

Does the sales forecasting system receive demand information directly from customers?

If yes, are forecasts adjusted based upon this information?

How easy is it for users to enter adjustments to sales forecasts directly into the forecasting system?

Which functional personnel have access to the sales forecasting system to review, but not make changes, to the forecasts?

Which have access to the sales forecasting system to make changes to the forecasts? (Examples: engineering, finance, logistics, marketing, planning, product management, production, R&D, sales, sales forecasting.)

To what degree are your forecasting systems in different countries compatible?

If the answer is low, is this something you are trying to remedy?

How satisfied are you with your existing sales forecasting system?

A copy of all system specifications, reports, and graphs should be requested.

❖ QUESTIONS ABOUT SALES FORECASTING TECHNIQUES

At what level of product detail do you forecast? Why?
    (Examples: SKUL, SKU, product, product line, division, corporate.)

For what forecast interval do you forecast? Why?
(Examples: weekly, monthly, quarterly, yearly.)

For what time horizon do you forecast? Why?
(Examples: 6, 9, 12 months, 2 years.)

For what geographic breakdown?

For each of the levels, intervals, horizons, and geographic breakdowns just described, what forecasting technique(s) is used? Examples:

Regression

Jury of executive opinion

Exponential smoothing

Moving average

Sales force composite

Box-Jenkins

Trend line analysis

Decomposition

Straight-line projections

Customer expectations

Life cycle analysis

Simulation

Expert systems

Neural networks

How credible are the subjective technique values you receive from:

1. Salespeople?

2. Channel members?

3. Executives?

To what degree does each of the above groups "game play" when providing forecasts?

How do you forecast "slow movers," "spikes," and "blips?"

❖ QUESTIONS ABOUT SALES FORECASTING PERFORMANCE

We will need documented information on the following:

Percent Error by Forecasting Level

Percent Error by Time Horizon

Percent Error Goal by Time Horizon and Forecasting Level

What criteria are used for evaluating sales forecasting effectiveness? (Examples: accuracy, ease of use, credibility, cost, amount of data required, inventory turns, customer service performance, return on investment, impact of forecast error on safety stock/logistics customer service, operating costs of forecast error.)

Are performance statistics weighted by volume?

What graphical reports are available? (Example: plot of PE over time.)

What measures of forecast error are used? (Examples: Mean Absolute Percent Error (MAPE), mean absolute deviation, mean squared error, deviation, percent error, forecast ratio, inventory statistics, standard deviation.)

9

Benchmark Studies

Conducting a Forecasting Audit

❖   ❖   ❖

In the summer of 1996, the research team had just completed Phase 3 of the benchmark studies, and articulated for the first time the framework described in the previous chapter. An executive summary of the research had been published and distributed to a wide range of academic researchers and forecasting practitioners. One of the forecasting practitioners who received that executive summary was intrigued by the framework, and recognized the potential to apply it in his own organization to pinpoint areas of weakness. He contacted the research team to discuss his ideas, and from the discussion came the concept of conducting a formal audit of his company.

We gathered a team of faculty and Ph.D. students from the University of Tennessee and traveled to this company's location and began interviewing people. We collected data from a wide range of people over several days and then began to piece together a picture of what we saw. The framework discussed in the previous chapter gave us a template within which to work, and we were soon able to show this company where it stood relative to our vision of world-class forecasting. What they saw was that they had many challenges facing them in terms of their forecasting practices.

This company was fortunate enough to have the type of leader who, when presented with a challenge, developed a calm and methodical approach to prioritizing, developing strategies for improvement, and then executing those strategies. We worked closely with this company over the next several years, and it went from a company that was primarily in stage 1, to a world-class forecasting company. Throughout that journey, it was this individual's leadership, along with the blueprint for change that we provided in the audit, which helped the organization improve dramatically.

Since that first summer, we have worked with 25 other companies, many of which had the leadership and foresight to embark on a similar journey of continuous improvement. Throughout these experiences, the research team has been able to continuously learn about best (and worst!) practice, and continuously update our vision of world-class forecasting.

❖ INTRODUCTION

In the previous chapter, we articulated a vision of world-class forecasting, and we presented a framework that was designed to help a company identify where it stands relative to that vision of world-class. Many companies have benefited from an introspective look at their own forecasting practices and used this framework to guide their own thinking about what they are doing right and wrong. But for a number of other companies, there was recognition that a formalized process to evaluate current forecasting practices, and identify areas for improvement, would be extremely beneficial. In these companies, those who were driving forecasting process improvement recognized that they needed two things in order to really drive meaningful change. The first thing they needed was information. They needed unbiased, expert judgment to assess where their problems were and what needed to be done to solve them. Second, they needed a spark. In many instances, senior managers need to have visible, credible, outside experts provide documented evidence of needed process improvement to serve as an impetus for change. In those organizations, a formalized forecast audit fills their needs very well.

The purpose of this chapter is to describe a methodology for conducting a *sales forecasting audit* that has been tested in 25 companies as of this writing (August 2004). Such an audit has three purposes: it is designed to help a company (1) understand the current status of its forecasting management practices (the *"as-is"* state); (2) visualize the goals it should be striving to reach in the various dimensions of sales forecasting management (the *"should-be"* state); and (3) develop a roadmap for achieving these goals (the *"way-forward"* process). The following companies have participated in the sales forecasting audit research: AET Films, AlliedSignal, Alticor, Avery Denison, Bacardi USA, ConAgra, Continental Tire, Corning, Deere and Company, DuPont, Eastman Chemical, Ethicon, Exxon, Hershey Foods USA, Lucent Technologies, Michelin North America, Motorola, Orbit Irrigation Products, Pharmavite, Philips North America, Sara Lee Intimate Apparel, Smith and Nephew, Union Pacific Railroad, Whirlpool, and Williamson-Dickie. This list indicates that a broad range of industries and positions within their respective supply chains have been represented in the sales forecasting audit research.

❖ THE ROLE OF AUDITING

An audit has been defined as "a formal evaluation of performance to predetermined standards and the use of that evaluation to induce improved performance" (Arter, 1989). While auditing is typically thought of in relation to preparation of financial statements, other areas of business use auditing as a way to arrive at an unbiased assessment of current performance, as well as identify areas of needed improvement. Examples include marketing audits (Tybout & Hauser, 1981), sales management audits (Churchill, Ford, & Walker, 1993), human resource management audits (Hussey, 1995), and quality audits (Dew, 1994).

One of the characteristics of a successful audit emphasized by each of these authors is the unbiased nature of the auditors themselves. Each author encourages engagement of credible experts from outside the organization to both collect and analyze the data. There are three reasons for this. First, outside experts have knowledge of accepted standards against which current management practice can be compared. As Fildes and Ranyard (1997) point out, external consultants "have a wide knowledge of business practices across a range of organizations, as well as relevant knowledge of competitor operations. They may also have specialist knowledge and skills that few in-house groups can sustain" (p. 339). Second, individuals from outside the organization have no incentive to overlook areas that might prove sensitive or embarrassing to current management. Third, data collection, particularly when such data collection involves interviews with individuals currently involved in a management process, can be more successful when those collecting the data are from outside the organization. Individuals tend to be more willing to share their true experiences with unbiased, outside experts, particularly with assurances of confidentiality. Or, as Fildes and Ranyard (1997) point out, for an internal project or audit team, "confidentiality may be perceived as more problematic compared to an external consultancy" (p. 339).

As mentioned above, an audit can be seen as a "formal evaluation of performance to predetermined standards." While outside experts may employ a variety of "pre-determined standards," such standards should always be based on published, documented research. The "pre-determined standards" that we have employed in our audit research are the standards as set forth in the previous chapter, which were initially introduced by Mentzer, Bienstock, and Kahn (1999), and implemented by Moon, Mentzer, and Smith (2003).

The Audit Process

The audit process developed in this research was used to assess practices and recommend actions to improve forecasting management performance at 25 large, diverse organizations. Table 9.1 shows the diverse nature of the organizations that have participated to date in the audit research. While these organizations are diverse in terms of products and services they offer, one important commonality they all shared was a realization that their forecasting practices needed improvement. Each of the 25 organizations agreed to participate because they felt the audit could help them identify and rectify fundamental problems with their forecasting practices. As a result, while it is impossible to easily characterize the "typical" company that has participated in the audit research to date, one characterization is that, on each of the four dimensions of forecasting management discussed in the previous chapter, the "typical" company is in stages one or two on all four dimensions. It is in this way that this Phase 4 research diverges from the Phase 3 research. In Phase 3, the research team was investigating companies possessing a wide range of forecasting proficiency on each of the four dimensions, but in Phase 4, the purpose of this research was to focus on companies with a recognizable deficiency in one or more of the dimensions. Our purpose was to see if these dimensions could serve a diagnostic tool to help companies improve their forecasting performance.

The process used to conduct a forecasting audit is graphically depicted in Figure 9.1. This process begins with identification of the liaison person within the company. Because the companies that agree

Table 9.1   Characteristics of Audited Companies

Company	Consumer	Business to business	Direct sales	Sales through distributors
AET Films		X	X	
Allied Signal	X			X
Alticor	X		X	
Avery Denison	X			X
Bacardi USA	X			X
ConAgra	X			X
Continental Tire*	X	X	X	X
Corning		X		X
Deere and Company	X			X
DuPont		X		X
Eastman Chemical		X	X	
Ethicon		X		X
Exxon		X	X	
Hershey USA	X			X
Lucent Technologies		X	X	
Michelin North America*	X	X	X	X
Motorola**	X	X	X	X
Orbit	X			X
Pharmavite	X			X
Philips North America	X			X
Sara Lee Intimate Apparel	X			X
Smith & Nephew		X		X
Union Pacific RR		X	X	
Whirlpool	X			X
Williamson-Dickie	X			X
TOTALS	14 (61%)	12 (52%)	8 (35%)	18 (78%)

*Continental Tire and Michelin's business is divided between OEM and replacement tire.

**Motorola's business involved wireless and pager business to consumers and business customers.

to participate in the audit research are companies that recognize their own deficiencies, this individual is the person who has been charged with initiating a forecasting re-engineering effort. The liaison helps coordinate the details of the audit, as well as choose the individuals to be interviewed in the data collection phase.

The next step is an analysis of all relevant documentation. Prior to on-site data collection, it is useful for the audit team to become

Figure 9.1   Forecast Audit Process

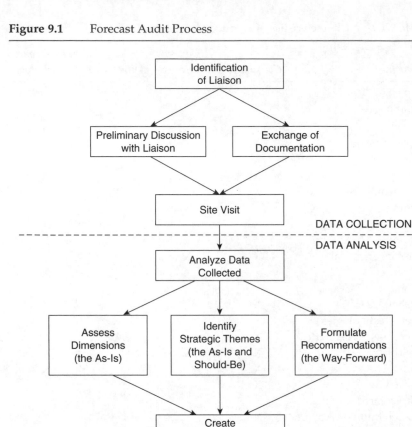

familiar with the forecasting process, as it is currently understood by those responsible for forecasting. Thus, any written documentation that describes information flows, reports that are available to forecasters or users, organization charts, hardware and software systems descriptions and documentation, historical accuracy figures and reports, and uses of the forecasts are analyzed by the audit team.

Of the 25 companies that have been audited to date, there has been considerable variance in the quality and completeness of the documentation provided before the on-site visit. At one extreme was a five-inch-thick binder containing an extremely comprehensive description of the current system—including detailed descriptions of what happens during each month and throughout the fiscal year of the forecasting process—along with hundreds of pages of reports that can be generated on demand by the forecasting system. At the other extreme was a photocopy of the software manual for the forecasting system that was installed, but never used, and no documentation of processes.

In addition to receiving information from the company being audited, the audit team provides a detailed interview protocol to the audit sponsor. This interview protocol is the same one used in Phase 3 of the research, and can be found in the Appendix to Chapter 8. This protocol presents detailed questions on the four dimensions discussed in the previous chapter, that is, how forecasts are prepared, the systems that are used to support forecasting, the techniques that are employed, what (if any) approaches are taken to measuring forecasting performance, and how the forecasts are used. The sponsor typically provides copies of this protocol to the interview participants to help them prepare for their interviews. The protocol is designed to help those who are to be interviewed understand the type of information that the audit team is trying to collect. It is never the case that any single individual is able to answer all the questions posed in the protocol. Rather, the protocol is meant to guide the audit team through the entire data collection process, and provide those interviewed with guidance to reflect on issues in preparing for the interviews. In other words, by the completion of the on-site visit, the audit team's objective is to have answers to all the various items in the protocol from the combined interview responses.

Although it is the responsibility of the sponsor to select the individuals to be interviewed, the audit team should communicate the critical importance to the success of the audit that an appropriate range of individuals be included on the interview list. The participant list needs to be both "broad" and "deep." Broad means adequate representation from all the different functions in the company that are involved in developing or using the sales forecasts. It is important that at least three different groups are represented: those who provide input to the sales forecast (e.g., the sales and marketing organization), those who actually prepare the sales forecast (i.e., the sales forecasting group), and those who are customers of the sales forecast (e.g., purchasing, production planning, logistics planning, and finance).

The participant list also needs to be "deep" in the sense that it includes various levels of the organizational hierarchy. If only senior-level managers are interviewed, there is a danger that they have inadequate understanding of the detailed issues and problems faced by the people who actually do the work. At the same time, if only "workers" are included, there is the danger that interviews will become little more than complaint sessions, and the audit team may be left with an insufficient understanding of the strategic issues surrounding the sales forecasting process. Therefore, it is up to the audit sponsor to select carefully and schedule the right individuals to participate in the interviews.

Following this preparation is the on-site visit, conducted by a team of four auditors. The team of four auditors splits into two subteams so that two auditors are present for each interview, providing the ability to assess inter-rater reliability, a crucial component of validity and reliability in interview-based research. Each auditor takes detailed notes, so any differences in interpretation can be resolved at the time of data analysis. Interviews typically include one subject and two auditors, although occasionally two or more subjects are present during a single interview.

The interview typically begins with one member of the audit team briefly describing the audit's purpose and giving assurances of confidentiality. The auditors then ask the subject to describe his or her role in the forecasting process. Probes include questions such as:

- "What do you do with that information?"
- "Where do you obtain that information?"
- "Is the information you obtain from that source credible and complete?"

While a considerable portion of the interview is spent gaining an understanding of the subject's formal role and responsibility regarding the forecasts, the auditors also probe to obtain insights as to the subject's satisfaction with the sales forecasts and the sales forecasting process. Focus is placed on understanding any frustrations or problems the subject has with the forecasting process and his or her role in that process. Each interview ends with a "wish-list" question, where one of the auditors asks the subject to describe what he or she would do to make the forecasting process more effective. Interviews typically last 45 minutes to an hour.

At the 25 companies audited to date, the number of interviews has ranged from 22 to 64, with an average of 32 per company. Following completion of the interviews, the auditors combine all interview notes, then distribute those notes to all audit team members. With data collection completed, data analysis begins.

The "As-Is State"

The purpose of the sales forecasting audit is to articulate for the audited company its "as-is" status, a vision of its "should-be" position, and a description of the "way-forward" process that will help the company improve its sales forecasting practices. The first step is for the research team to understand fully the current status of the company's forecasting practices (the "as-is"). As each member of the audit team analyzes the data, two primary objectives are foremost. First, the company's position on each of the four dimensions of sales forecasting management—functional integration, approach, systems, and performance measurement—is assessed. Each member of the audit team identifies characteristics of the company being audited, and compares those characteristics to the bullet points in Figures 8.1, 8.3, 8.5, and 8.7 from Chapter 8.

Initially, each research team member does this work independently, and then all members meet to compare the results of their analyses. When disagreements arise, the analysts talk through their reasons for highlighting a particular bullet point on one of the four dimensions, citing evidence from the documentation and/or the interview notes. Eventually, consensus is reached. The results of this process are a version of Figures 8.1, 8.3, 8.5, and 8.7, with various bullet points, or portions of bullet points, highlighted to identify characteristics of the audited company on each of the four dimensions of forecasting management.

It is important to note that during the analysis it is common to identify characteristics consistent with multiple stages of sophistication along a forecasting dimension. For example, it could be the case that on the functional integration dimension, a company exhibited one world-class, Stage 4 characteristic, such as "forecasting seen as a cross-functional process that serves the entire organization," while also exhibiting several Stage 1 and Stage 2 characteristics. The insight revealed here is that while well positioned organizationally to achieve a high level of functional integration, lack of a forecasting champion (Mentzer et al., 1997) has prevented this company from taking advantage of this organizational strength.

As discussed in the next section (the "should-be" state), this articulation of characteristics at different stages of sophistication helps a company identify and prioritize areas where improvement can take place. The audit process is not concerned with classifying the company solely within a single discrete stage of sophistication as much as understanding the relationships among the stage characteristics and the implications for improving performance.

The second objective of analyzing the interview notes is to identify "strategic themes" that emerge from the data. These strategic themes are issues that cut across multiple dimensions of forecasting management, and that are so pervasive or that cause such wide-ranging problems that they demand special attention and discussion.

Following is a discussion of those strategic themes that emerged at a majority of the companies:

• **Limited performance measurement and lack of performance evaluation.** Although this characteristic is discussed at length in the dimension on "Performance Measurement," it is such a pervasive characteristic that at most companies it has warranted special discussion as a strategic theme. One clear lesson learned as a result of this research is that companies do not seem to adequately measure forecasting performance, tie that forecasting performance to the evaluation of individuals, and then reward individuals for excellence in forecasting.

• **Blurred distinction between forecasts, plans, and goals.** This is a situation where a company does not recognize that forecasts are a projection into the future of expected demand, given a stated set of environmental conditions, although plans are managerial actions proposed by the organization to capture and supply as much of the forecasted demand as possible. Evidence of this theme can be found in these actual statements from audits: "we forecast up to plan," or "it would be suicide for me to forecast anything different than the plan." Such statements indicate these organizations are creating forecasts based upon plans or sales targets, rather than their best judgments about future customer demand. Recall that these issues are discussed in detail in Chapter 1.

• **Limited commitment to sales forecasting.** This theme was manifested by a number of different situations at audited companies, including: insufficient commitment of resources to training, documentation, systems support, or reward and recognition programs; relegating the forecasting function to relatively low levels in the organizational hierarchy; unwillingness to designate a forecasting champion; and lack of accountability throughout the organization for forecast accuracy. At one company, this theme was manifested by the failure to fill an open director-level forecasting position for more than a year. Because of this lack of leadership, the company's forecasting improvement efforts were unfocused and unsupported by other constituent organizations in the company.

- **Islands of analysis.** This is the situation where a company has non-standard, non-interfacing systems or procedures for performing similar tasks, or forecasting systems that fail to connect with other enterprise systems like production planning or finance. These "islands" can range from each forecasting analyst having his or her own "homemade" spreadsheet with unique characteristics and assumptions, to separate forecasting systems installed and operating in different departments of the company, to the manual transfer of data either into or out of a forecasting system. An extreme example of this phenomenon occurred at one audited company, where three separate forecasting systems had been installed over time: a mainframe-based legacy system, which was the "official" forecasting system, an AS/400-based system installed by production planning, and a PC-based system installed by logistics. These latter two were described as "black-market" forecasting systems, and were installed because the forecast user organizations did not trust the integrity of the "official" forecast, and so created their own forecasting systems.

From these two sources (dimensions and strategic themes), the portrayal of the audited company's "as-is" state of forecasting management practices is complete. The second stage of the audit process is the description of the "should-be" state of sales forecasting management practices for the company.

The "Should-Be" State

Although understanding the current status of sales forecasting management (the "as-is" state) is important, managers cannot take steps toward excellence without guidance on the directions to take. For this reason, it is important to provide a clear picture of the "should-be" state of forecasting management in the company. This "should-be" picture can be found in the figures that detail each of the four dimensions, in two different ways. The first is to provide broad targets at which managers can aim. Examination of stage four in each of the four dimensions describes the most advanced level of forecasting excellence uncovered in the sales forecasting benchmark research. Therefore, a "best practices" company would operate at Stage 4 on all four dimensions. Stage 4 characteristics provide managers with a long-term target toward which they can strive. However, because few companies have achieved a level of excellence near Stage 4, it is important that intermediate targets be set to move toward Stage 4. If, for example, a company's "as-is" status is primarily in Stage 1, then Stage 2 characteristics can be seen as intermediate targets that will improve forecasting effectiveness, and begin the company on the path to the excellence found in Stage 4.

The second way that Figures 8.1, 8.3, 8.5, and 8.7 from Chapter 8 provide the "should-be" picture is in a more detailed, tactical sense. Careful examination of these figures reveals that for many of the bullet points found in each dimension, there is a natural progression from Stage 1 (low level of forecasting sophistication) to Stage 4 (high level of forecasting excellence). In Figure 8.1, for example, which describes the dimension of Functional Integration, the first bullet under Stage 1 describes major disconnects between marketing, finance, sales, production, logistics, and forecasting. For one company that found its current "as-is" state described by this bullet, the immediate "should-be" target was found in the first bullet of Stage 2 (coordination [formal meetings] between marketing, finance, sales, production, logistics, and forecasting). In this more detailed way, a company can see where it should be going in each of the four dimensions of forecasting.

The benefits of achieving a Stage 4 level of sophistication along each dimension receives support from research in forecasting technique development and application, systems design and implementation, and management. The Functional Integration characteristics of communication, coordination, and collaboration reflect the benefits associated with team-based forecasting (Kahn & Mentzer, 1994), and are identified as one of seven keys to better forecasting (Moon et al., 1998). Maintaining a separate forecasting function is suggested as a means to reduce bias and support forecasting processes (Fildes & Hastings, 1994). Providing forecasts in formats that match the requirements of user functions helps improve understanding and input (Marien, 1999; Fliedner, 2001; Mentzer & Schroeter, 1994). Forecast development is also viewed as a consensus-building process, acknowledging the relationship between unconstrained market forecasts and the constraints associated with operating capabilities or requirements (Fildes & Hastings, 1994; Waddell & Sohal, 1994). Schultz (1992) emphasizes the need for multi-dimensional performance metrics, noting that "we must go beyond measures of accuracy and look to objective performance measures such as sales, costs, and profits" (p. 410).

Reviewing characteristics associated with a Stage 4 level of Approach, top down/bottom up forecast development has been identified as a means to improve forecast performance over either approach separately (Kahn, 1998; Fliedner, 2001). The need for forecast reconciliation between sales and operations (Fildes & Hastings, 1994; Waddell & Sohal, 1994; Nelson, 1987), and an understanding of the impact of sales force gaming (Galfond, Ronayne, & Winkler, 1996), whether internally or from customers, are also proposed to impact forecast accuracy. Forecast education that goes beyond technique development (Mentzer & Cox, 1984b) and top management support (Miller, 1985; Schultz, 1984) are also recognized as key elements of forecast success.

Characteristics associated with a Stage 4 level of sophistication along the Systems dimension reflect findings from case studies involving system development and implementation (Mentzer & Schroeter, 1993, 1994; Mentzer & Kent, 1999). Mentzer and Kent (1999) outlined the development and implementation of new processes and systems that helped The Longaberger Company establish a "system-centric" approach to forecast development. Their discussion addressed the need for companies considering forecasting systems to "make the tool fit the problem." Kahn and Mentzer (1996) discussed the benefits of incorporating EDI as a means to integrate supply chain demand information to improve data availability and accuracy, and subsequently reduce inventory costs. Their propositions are supported by studies evaluating the impact of forecasting information availability on variability in the supply chain (Chen et al., 1999). Chen et al. (1999) quantified the improvement in supply chain forecasting and inventory performance resulting from a shift in information availability from a decentralized to centralized model.

Performance measurement characteristics were supported by Fildes and Hastings (1994), who recognized that environmental factors influence forecasting practices and performance. Calling on managers to make forecasting important and to "measure, measure, measure," Moon et al. (1998) emphasized the need to implement measures of forecasting performance based on accuracy and its impact on operating performance.

While an understanding of the "should-be" state is critically important to the continuous improvement process, it is not very useful without an understanding of how to get to that "should-be" state. For that reason, we now turn to the third purpose of the forecast audit: the description of the "way-forward."

The "Way-Forward"

The audit process provides the audited company with a "way-forward" roadmap through a series of concrete recommendations. While the recommendations are unique for each company, based on the current status of their forecasting practices, these recommendations usually fall into four categories. Two of these categories, systems and performance measurement, directly match the dimensions previously discussed. The other two categories, process and training, are designed to help companies in both functional integration and approach.

Process recommendations refer to the way forecasts are created and used. One company, for example, was at Stage 1 on the dimension of Functional Integration, so process recommendations included instituting a consensus forecasting process, where different people from different parts of the company work together in a forum characterized by open information-sharing to create a consensus forecast. On the other hand, another company's forecasting practices were at Stage 1 on the Approach dimension, and statistical tools were not used effectively to uncover patterns in historical demand data. Thus, the process recommendations included implementation of a process where baseline forecasts are generated statistically, then distributed to knowledgeable experts, such as sales or marketing people, for adjustment.

Training recommendations refer to specific situations where company personnel who are involved in forecasting have inadequate skills or knowledge to perform their forecasting tasks effectively. For example, salespeople are usually in a position to provide forecasting intelligence, but in only one of the 25 companies in our database did salespeople have any training on why forecasting is important (Functional Integration), or how to make qualitative adjustments to baseline forecasts (Approach). Thus, in almost all companies that constitute the audit database, such training programs targeted at problems in Functional Integration and Approach were recommended.

Similarly and surprisingly, in 17 of the audited companies the people in the forecasting group had received no training on how time series and regression analysis can be used to create baseline forecasts, so training programs targeted at this deficiency in the Approach dimension were recommended.

System recommendations refer to the way computer and communication systems can be enhanced to develop and communicate forecasting information more effectively. For example, the "as-is" status of one company showed forecasting systems were not closely integrated with other corporate systems, in this case finance and MRP systems, resulting in manual transfers of data. Therefore, the system recommendations included creating electronic linkages that allow data transfers between systems. Also, in several companies where "island of analysis" existed, characterized by multiple processes or systems performing similar tasks, system recommendations included specific procedures designed to eliminate such islands and standardize on a single set of forecasting processes.

Finally, *performance measurement recommendations* refer to specific metrics that should be put into place to measure forecasting performance adequately. For example, in 10 companies the salespeople were asked to make adjustments to baseline forecasts, but the accuracy of those adjustments was not measured and communicated back to the salespeople. This resulted in a recommendation that such a measurement and feedback system be implemented. Similarly, in the 18 companies that had implemented some performance metrics, accuracy was the only metric used. Thus, other metrics designed to assess the impact of forecasting accuracy on overall supply chain costs and customer service were recommended.

❖ MANAGEMENT RESPONSE TO AUDITS

While recommendations have been included in each of the 25 audits conducted to date, there has been considerable variance observed in management's responses to these recommendations. Management reaction has typically fallen into one of three categories, which we can characterize as either "address the problems," "assign the blame," or "why should I care?" Companies that fall under the "address the problems" category tend to have an organizational culture oriented toward solutions, regardless of which department is "to blame." Companies in this category also tend to recognize that responsibility for complex organizational problems are usually shared across functions, and thus look for cross-functional solutions.

Companies in the "assign the blame" category tend to have an organizational culture oriented toward identifying the source of organizational problems, and when that source is identified, that department becomes responsible for solutions. Since forecasting problems tends to be cross-functional, it is usually impossible to identify a single source of forecasting problems. Thus, companies in this category tend to bog down in assigning blame rather than in pursuing solutions.

Companies in the "why should I care?" category tend to view forecasting as an unimportant activity. In these companies, there is no understanding at the senior management level of how forecasting improvements can dramatically enhance the company's key performance indicators.

One company in particular provides an excellent example of the "address the problems" response. This organization, which was in Stage 1 on all four dimensions of forecasting management, responded by assigning a cross-functional project team first to perform a detailed review of the recommendations, then propose a prioritization scheme, followed by an action plan. Three months after the conclusion of the audit, this project team met with the audit team to review their proposed priorities and action plan, and this was followed by a 2-year-long effort to re-engineer their approach to sales forecasting. As a result of that re-engineering effort, this company now approaches Stage 4 on all four dimensions of forecasting management, and their supply-chain costs have been reduced dramatically. In fact, the company estimates their entire implementation effort cost less than $1 million, but the savings in raw material purchasing costs alone (buying more on long-term contracts based on accurate forecasts rather than buying at the last minute on the spot market) during 1 year were in excess of $7 million. Thus, the return on investment from implementation has been considerable. It is important to note that this $7 million saving was seen by upper management as an accomplishment by all departments involved in the forecasting effort, not just purchasing.

Another company provides an example of the "assign the blame" response. At this organization, which was primarily at Stages 2 and 3 on two of the dimensions and Stage 1 on the other two dimensions, the auditors' final presentation to senior management degenerated into a heated discussion between executives over which department was at fault for the problems identified by the audit team. While these executives agreed that problems existed, none were willing to acknowledge that performance improvements were needed in their individual departments. As a result, no consensus could be reached on how to effect change, and no re-engineering effort was carried out. Over the next 18 months, this company experienced considerable disruption and customer service problems due to an inability to forecast demand hitting their distribution centers.

Finally, at an audited company that exhibited the "why should I care?" response, during the question-and-answer portion of the final presentation to senior management, the executive vice president of marketing rose from his chair and stated that all the company really needed was a new "killer product," and with such a new product, all this attention to forecasting improvement would not be necessary. At another company, the CEO spent the time during the final presentation to management doing other work and gazing absently around the conference room. At a third company, the audit team was told that because they had moved to a "just-in-time" environment, forecasting was no longer important (a naïve statement, since accurate forecasts are an integral part of just-in-time processes). None of these companies, to date, has made any changes in sales forecasting management and, thus, has not realized any of the supply chain cost savings and customer service benefits achieved at the other companies.

Schultz (1984) cites a number of factors that influence the success or failure of organizational efforts to implement new forecasting models. One of his findings is that the presence of top management support is the top-ranked predictor of implementation success, and lack of top management support is the top-ranked predictor of implementation failure. In the examples cited above, top management support was clearly present in the "address the problems" response profile, and top management support was clearly lacking in the "assign the blame" and "why should I care?" responses. Obtaining such top management support is one of the key contributions from a forecasting champion (Mentzer et al., 1997); this is discussed at greater length in Chapter 10. Consistent with Schultz, one conclusion from this auditing research is that the existence of a sales forecasting champion, along with the top management support for forecasting improvement such an individual can obtain, is critical to long-term organizational success in sales forecasting management.

❖ CONCLUSIONS

One important finding that emerged from this research is the realization that—as with other types of audits—an outside, unbiased analysis is critical to the success of the audit. Several companies in the study had attempted forecast process improvements on their own, prior to the audit study, and reported frustration with their inability to effect significant organizational change. In these companies, the use of external auditors was very helpful both in the articulation of the company's true forecasting process and in inspiring management action. Individuals who are directly affected by a company's forecasting processes will share their experiences and frustrations more freely with external auditors whom they perceive to be unburdened with preconceived ideas and free from any political agendas. This perspective helps to uncover elements of the forecasting process that may not be evident to those who are involved in the process day-to-day. This research reinforces Armstrong's (1988) call for the value of sales forecasting auditing. Academics and practitioners should develop the skills and knowledge base necessary to conduct such sales forecasting management audits.

The positive results companies obtained from the sales forecasting audits conducted to date provide encouragement for other companies to follow suit. The example provided earlier of one company realizing substantial savings in purchasing costs during the first year as a result of more accurate and credible forecasts provides an exemplar. Dramatic savings in supply-chain costs are typical when the audit recommendations are fully implemented.

From the 25 companies that constitute the database for development of the sales forecasting audit process, there are a number of lessons from which all managers can benefit. First, it is clear from this research that forecasting is a distinct and critical management function, and not just an exercise in technique or software selection. Technique development and selection have been the focus of much research, and this literature has made an enormous contribution to improving sales forecasting accuracy. However, this audit research has demonstrated that companies must look beyond techniques and software, and must pay close attention to overall management of the sales forecasting process.

A further lesson this sales forecasting audit research provides managers is that the four dimensions of forecasting management articulated in Chapter 8 are a useful diagnostic and prescriptive framework to affect sales forecasting improvement. A significant portion of the audit methodology described here makes use of this framework, and it has been very helpful for characterizing a company's current forecasting management status, as well as showing managers the "should-be" state to which they can aspire.

Finally, the benchmark phases of "as-is," "should-be," and "way-forward" developed by managers involved in this auditing research are an excellent way to examine the process of continuous improvement in sales forecasting management. These three phases have provided managers with a clear, concise way to think about the process of continuous improvement, not only in sales forecasting, but also in other business functions and processes. Without both a clear understanding of how a company currently operates (the "as-is"), and a vision of what world-class really is (the "should-be"), changes to core processes (the "way-forward") will be unfocused and ineffective.

10

Managing the Sales Forecasting Function

❖   ❖   ❖

We were trying to explain the intricacies of managing the sales forecasting function in his company to the new CEO of a large retail chain. This was a new CEO whose background was in marketing for a consumer products manufacturer.

"I don't understand why this is such a big deal," he said. "Just select the right technique and, where it needs adjustment, let my marketing folks make the necessary adjustments."

"That's fine at the product level," we answered, "but you have to realize the magnitude of the number of forecasts needed to run the stores. It doesn't help the stores at all if we accurately forecast the demand for men's white shirts, size 15–35 at the national level—the store manager needs to know the demand at each store for each shirt, in each style, in each size."

Recognition began to dawn on his face. "You know, my background is in marketing. I never thought about forecasting in terms of anything except the product. Just how many variations of our products do we carry in each store?"

The answer (given different products, sizes, and styles) was 62,000!

He gulped, "And we have 1,100 stores? Why, that means we have a DBN of forecasts to make each week!"

"A DBN?" we asked.

"Yea, a darn big number."

How should companies manage this DBN of weekly, or monthly, or in some cases daily, forecasts? That's what this book has tried to communicate. In this final chapter, we'll give some final summary thoughts about how the forecasting process should be managed, and why the CEO (or a company's shareholders, for that matter) should care about forecasting.

❖ INTRODUCTION

As we have discussed throughout this book, managing the sales forecasting function is a complex, yet critical, task in today's business enterprise. Most companies are beginning to realize that one key strategy for success is to effectively manage the entire supply chain—from raw materials all the way to the final end consumer, along with all the various support services along the way. Yet effectively managing a supply chain is nearly impossible unless there is a clear idea of demand, and that is the role of forecasting. To conclude this book, we offer this final chapter containing some concluding thoughts that all business executives should understand. If you are a forecasting manager, you might want to hand this final chapter to your senior executives, since it is designed to focus attention on a few key "take-aways" about effectively managing the sales forecasting function. We begin this final chapter with the critical role that leadership can play in both re-engineering a forecasting process and effectively managing it over time. Such leadership can be found in what we call "the sales forecasting champion." We then offer 7 critical points of sales forecasting management, which we call "The 7 Keys to Better Forecasting." We conclude with a discussion aimed directly at senior managers, with some thoughts on "Why the CEO Should Care."

❖ THE ROLE OF THE SALES FORECASTING CHAMPION

As we described in Chapters 7 and 8, in addition to studying several hundred companies through surveys, our research team has worked with more than 100 different companies, either understanding their sales forecasting practices and processes in detail (20 companies in Phase 3), helping them to identify their strengths and weaknesses

Table 10.1   Sales Forecasting Champion Characteristics

- Managerial Perspective
- Cross-Functional Perspective
- A Leader, Not a Clerk
- A Sales Forecast Developer and User
- Technique Perspective
- Systems Perspective
- Mentor/Trainer
- Ongoing Training

through sales forecasting audits (25 companies in Phase 4), or assisting with sales forecasting process and system implementations. One factor that consistently had a strong impact on the level of sales forecasting success at these companies was the existence of a **sales forecasting champion**. Whether the head of a recognized forecasting group, part of a loose collection of forecasters within different departments, or a user of the sales forecasts who does not actually develop them, we found that sales forecasting champions have several characteristics in common. These characteristics are listed in Table 10.1, and each is discussed here in turn.

Managerial Perspective

Successful sales forecasting champions have an appreciation of the managerial/planning role that sales forecasting plays within the corporation. This encompasses an appreciation of the iterative role of sales forecasting and business planning. For example, one company in our database begins its planning process by developing a market-based sales forecast. From this base, the annual business plan is developed. If the market-based sales forecast does not generate sufficient earnings for the business plan, the sales forecast is sent back to the champion with instructions on how much sales must increase in each market over the original forecast to meet the plan. The champion in this company then works with marketing and sales to determine the additional marketing resources that need to be budgeted to increase sales to the desired level. This revised sales forecast goes back to planning and continues to iterate until a realistic plan is finalized. The key to this iterative, forecast-to-plan-to-forecast-to-plan, process is a sales forecasting champion who understands and guides each step so that realistic, market-based forecasts and plans are developed.

Cross-Functional Perspective

To manage the process just described, the sales forecasting champion cannot have a business orientation planted in one functional area. Rather, the sales forecasting champion must understand the planning purposes for which the sales forecasts are used by the various business functions (i.e., marketing, sales, finance/accounting, production/purchasing, and logistics). Each of these areas has unique planning needs to which the sales forecasts are an input. Marketing plans usually involve projected product changes, promotional efforts, channel placement, and pricing—with consideration of the effect all these have on demand. Sales management is typically concerned with setting goals for the sales force and motivating those salespeople to exceed these goals—concerns that require accurate demand estimates. Finance and accounting are charged with the job of projecting cost and profit levels and capital needs, all based upon a given sales forecast. Production must concern itself with two very different sales forecasts—a long-term forecast for planning capital requirements such as future plant and equipment, and a short-term forecast for the production planning and raw material purchasing schedules. Since logistics is responsible for moving products to specific locations, sales forecasts are needed at the product by location level. To be effective, and regardless of where they are located in an organizational chart, the sales forecasting champion must understand these divergent functional needs and deliver a sales forecast that meets them.

In other words, the sales forecasting champion must successfully play the role of symphony orchestra conductor, striving to get the best information out of each area of the company. This individual must be a facilitator of communication across functional silos (as discussed in Chapter 1), and effectively convince each area in the company that spending time, energy, and resources in the cause of creating good forecasts benefits everyone.

A Leader, Not a Clerk

To accomplish these cross-functional, managerial roles for the sales forecasts, the sales forecasting champion must be a leader and an advocate who recognizes the importance of sales forecasting as a critical, company-wide management function. As we discuss in a later section, this role can take different forms depending upon the way sales forecasting is organized in the company. However, regardless of the form, the sales forecasting leader and advocate should possess two core characteristics. First, the sales forecasting champion must be able to clearly explain the role of the sales forecast in the planning processes of the various functional areas. Not only must the sales forecasts be credible (i.e., accurate and believable) over time, but the sales forecasting champion must be seen as a credible representative of these forecasts.

Second, this credibility must extend to all company areas and levels. The effective sales forecasting champion must have the organizational clout (either through authority or persuasive ability) to be taken seriously by top management and the management of all the business functions. This individual must have the ability to "pound on the CEO's desk" in advocacy for the forecasting function. Without such ability, this individual is more of a clerk than a leader.

A Sales Forecast Developer and User

The establishment of this credibility, advocacy, and understanding comes largely from the same source—the sales forecasting champion must be seen as someone who has experience not only in developing sales forecasts, but in putting them to use in the business planning functions as well. Experience in developing sales forecasts lends a technical and market-based credibility to the sales forecasting champion. Whether in marketing, sales, production, or logistics, experience in using the sales forecast lends an element of "they are really one of us" and they understand the planning needs to which the sales forecast is put—and the implications of inaccurate forecasts on the users.

This dual experiential background for sales forecasting champions gives them credibility with their constituents and provides the information necessary to develop quantitative forecasts and to qualitatively adjust them.

Technique Perspective

The dual experiential background just discussed also dictates that the sales forecasting champion *understands* the use of quantitative and qualitative sales forecasting techniques. The champion may or may not have strong statistical training, but they always have a strong understanding of the environment in which the company operates and an appreciation of the advantages and disadvantages of different statistical approaches. We call this latter trait *quantitative analysis strength*, rather than statistical strength, because it means much more than just the ability to analyze a stream of numbers with statistics. Rather, it is an appreciation of where certain statistical techniques do and do not work, and when qualitative (informed business environment) analysis is superior to, or can augment, statistics.

Systems Perspective

Similarly, the effective sales forecasting champion is not necessarily a "systems person," but has a clear understanding of the role systems play in the development of accurate and timely sales forecasts. It is surprising how many companies have no clear definition of the sales forecasting process or the systems that bind that process together. In the most effective companies, these processes and systems are well defined and are clearly understood and explicated by the sales forecasting champion.

Without such clear communication of how the process and systems interact, islands of analysis will develop within the forecasting process. As discussed in Chapter 8, when such islands of analysis exist, the resultant sales forecasts may be significantly different from forecasts developed elsewhere in the company (other islands), and these differences lead to conflicting plans.

Mentor/Trainer

Effective sales forecasting champions spend much of their time developing sales forecasting skills in others. The mentoring dimension of this characteristic is aimed at developing a similar appreciation in others of the role of the sales forecasts in the planning and management of various functional areas. Fostering an appreciation in each functional area for the forecasting needs of other functions within the organization is often a long and difficult process—one that requires considerable mentoring skills on the part of the sales forecasting champion. Many companies have staunchly ingrained planning processes that start with earnings estimates that meet the expectations of external financial analysts and work backward to a "sales forecast." Changing this process to one that starts with a market-based sales forecast, develops the financial plan from this base, and iterates back and forth between sales forecast and business plan until a plan is reached that takes into account marketplace and financial realities is not an easy task. Again, the sales forecasting champion role as a mentor is an integral part of bringing such a change to fruition.

The sales forecasting champion as a trainer recognizes the need for input to the sales forecast from multiple sources and the training requirements needed by each of those sources to ensure forecasting improvement. Sales forecasting analysts need training in the use of statistical techniques and the advantages and disadvantages of each technique (i.e., when and where each technique should and should not be used). Marketing personnel need training in how to turn their market-based knowledge into effective, qualitative adjustments to the sales forecast. Similarly, salespeople need training in how to turn their customer-based knowledge into effective, qualitative adjustments. Production and logistics personnel need training in how to bring their capacity planning perspectives into the sales forecasts. It is not necessarily the job of the sales forecasting champion to conduct all of this training, but it is their job to identify these training needs and help each group obtain the proper training.

Ongoing Training

Finally, sales forecasting champions as mentors/trainers recognize their own ongoing training needs. The state of the art of sales forecasting changes every year, and the effective sales forecasting champion attempts to stay current in these changes. Attendance and participation at conferences and seminars, as well as staying current in the sales forecasting journals and books, are all characteristics of effective sales forecasting champions.

As a career path, many forecasting champions become heads of forecasting groups, often with the title of Forecasting Manager or Director of Forecasting, and continue with this as a career for many years. Many in such a position move on to higher roles in the business planning functions of the company. Still others move into the more traditional business functions, while keeping their understanding and appreciation of the sales forecasting/business planning/demand management ability to leverage corporate effectiveness. Regardless of the eventual career path taken, however, the challenge to anyone reading this book is: Are you willing to become the forecasting champion in your company?

❖ THE SEVEN KEYS TO BETTER FORECASTING

In 1998, several members of the research team wrote an article to summarize what we had learned up until that point, and place it in a context that senior executives could appreciate (Moon et al., 1998). With another six years of working with companies behind us, we now revisit those "seven keys" and offer them as a summary of much of the learning from our experience with hundreds of companies.

Key 1: Understand What Sales Forecasting Is and Is Not

The first, and perhaps most important, key to better sales forecasting is a complete understanding of what sales forecasting actually is, and of equal importance, an understanding of what sales forecasting is not. Sales forecasting *is* a *management process*. Sales forecasting *is not* a computer program. Our research has found that it is important to view sales forecasting as a management function because it affects so many areas across an organization. Regardless of whether a company sells goods or services, it must have a clear picture of how many of those goods or services it can sell, both in the short and long term, so that it can plan to have adequate supply of those goods or services to meet customer demand. Thus, sales forecasting is critical to a company's production or operations department, and to supply-chain demand planning. Adequate materials must be obtained at the lowest possible price; adequate production facilities must be provided at the lowest possible cost; adequate labor must be hired and trained at the lowest possible cost; and adequate logistics services must be obtained to avoid supply chain bottlenecks in moving products from producers to consumers. None of these fundamental business functions can be performed effectively without accurate sales forecasts.

However, many companies with which we have worked consider the most important decisions regarding sales forecasting to revolve around the selection or development of computer software. These companies have adopted the overly simplistic belief that "if we've got good software, we'll have good sales forecasting." Yet our research team has observed numerous instances of sophisticated computer systems that have been put into place, costing enormous amounts of time and money, which fail to deliver accurate sales forecasts. They have failed because system implementation was not accompanied by effective management to monitor and control the forecasting process. For example, one company with which we worked has an excellent computer system with impressive capabilities to do sophisticated statistical modeling of seasonality and other trends. However, the salespeople, who are the originators of the forecast, use none of these tools because they do not understand them and have no confidence in the numbers they generate. As a result, their forecasts are based solely on qualitative factors and are often highly inaccurate. This, and many other examples, shows how some companies have focused on *sales forecasting systems* rather than *sales forecasting management.*

As we discussed in Chapter 1, another way that companies confuse what sales forecasts are from what they are not is the failure to understand the relationship between forecasting, planning, and goal setting. A sales forecast should be viewed as an *estimate* of what future sales might be, given certain environmental conditions. A sales plan should be seen as a *management decision* or *commitment* to what the company will do during the planning period. A sales goal should be a *target* that everyone in the organization strives to obtain and exceed. Each of these numbers serves different purposes. The primary purpose of the sales forecast (the informed estimate) is to help management formulate its sales plan and other related business plans (its commitment to future activity). The sales plan's purpose is to drive numerous tactical and strategic management decisions, such as raw material purchases, human resource planning, and logistics planning. The sales goal (the target) is primarily designed to provide motivation for people throughout the organization to meet and exceed corporate targets.

While the sales forecast and the sales plan should be closely linked (i.e., the sales forecast should precede and influence the sales plan), the sales goal may be quite independent. The objective of those who develop a sales forecast should be to make that sales forecast as accurate as possible. The objective of those who develop the sales plan should be to realistically factor in the constraints of the organization's resources, procedures, and systems. The objective of those who receive a sales goal should be to beat that goal. It is appropriate for a sales goal to be developed based on a sales forecast, plan, and motivation levels. However, since forecasters should strive for accuracy, it is *not* appropriate that a forecast be confused with the firm's motivational strategy.

Key number one—understanding what sales forecasting is, and what it is not—is a necessary beginning step for any company to improve its sales forecasting performance. Companies that focus only on the computer program, without accounting for the management issues such as motivation, cross-functional integration, and measurement, fail to significantly improve sales forecasting performance. And companies that confuse sales forecasts with plans and goals provide disincentives to sales forecast developers to forecast accurately.

Key 2: *Forecast* Demand, *Plan* Supply

One mistake that many companies make is that they forecast their ability to *supply* goods or services, rather than forecasting actual customer *demand*. At the beginning of the sales forecast cycle, it is important to create sales forecasts that are unconstrained by a company's capacity to produce. Take as an example a forecaster for a certain product who questions the company's sales force and learns they could sell 1,500 units per month. At the same time, current manufacturing capacity for that product is 1,000 units per month. If that forecaster takes that production capacity into account when creating initial sales forecasts, and forecasts 1,000 units, then nowhere is there a record of the unmet demand of 500 units per month, and the information on where to expand manufacturing capacity is lost.

This phenomenon often occurs when historical shipments are used as the basis for generating sales forecasts. Sales forecasting based upon shipment history only leads a company to repeat its former mistakes of not satisfying customer demand. Forecasting actual demand allows measurement of the difference between demand and supply so the difference can be reduced in future periods through plans for capacity expansion.

Unfortunately, forecasting actual customer demand is more difficult than forecasting a company's ability to supply. Systems and processes are needed to capture this elusive demand that was not fulfilled. Although more difficult, trying to forecast true demand helps a company make sensible, long-term, capacity decisions that can profoundly affect its market position. By identifying where capacity does not meet demand forecasts, the company has valuable information on where to expand capacity through capital planning. Such a long-term program of matching capacity planning to sales forecasts reduces the incidence of chronic under-forecasting and results in higher levels of customer satisfaction.

Key 3: Communicate, Cooperate, Collaborate

Another problem that we have observed in some companies with which we have worked is an unwillingness to work cross-functionally to achieve high levels of sales forecasting performance. Those companies that forecast most effectively consider it critical that inputs to sales forecasts be provided by people from different functional areas; each of these functional areas contributes relevant information and insights that can improve overall accuracy.

Such cross-functional sales forecasting requires a great deal of communication across department boundaries. As we discussed in Chapter 8 in the section on Forecasting C^3, communication, cooperation, and collaboration are critical to successful sales forecasting. Those companies that demonstrate world-class sales forecasting practices have succeeded at communicating, advanced to cooperation, and moved their culture to one of true cross-functional collaboration, through the use of consensus-based forecasting. One of the most important elements to effective sales forecasting is to have a mechanism that brings people from multiple organizational areas together in a spirit of collaboration. Such a mechanism, often organized by an independent sales forecasting group, ensures that all relevant information is considered before sales forecasts are created.

Our research team observed one such mechanism in place at a consumer products company, where regularly scheduled, half-day meetings were held that brought together representatives from national accounts (sales), product management (marketing), production planning, logistics, and finance. These meetings were organized by the sales forecasting group. Each participant came to the meeting prepared to discuss upcoming issues that would affect sales and demand over the forecast period. Formal minutes were kept, so that reasons for forecast adjustments could be documented. The end product of these monthly meetings is a consensus sales forecast, with numbers that sales forecast users have helped to develop. The result of this type of consensus-based sales forecasting process is elimination of duplicate forecasting efforts and a sales forecast that is trusted by users. The bottom line is a more accurate and relevant sales forecast.

Key 4: Eliminate Islands of Analysis

Islands of analysis are distinct areas within the firm that perform similar functions—in this case, sales forecasting. Each functional area maintains a separate sales forecasting process, thus performing redundant forecasting tasks and responsibilities. Because islands of analysis are often supported by independent computer systems with uncoordinated databases, information contained within different islands is not shared between different functional areas.

In our research, we have identified sales forecasting islands in logistics, sales, production planning, finance, and marketing. As discussed in the previous section, these islands usually emerge because of a lack of interfunctional collaboration between units, which leads to a lack of credibility associated with the sales forecast. Because the "official" sales forecast generated in a particular department may not be credible to sales forecast users, those users often take steps to implement processes and systems to create their own sales forecasts. The result is islands of analysis.

Islands of analysis are detrimental to corporate performance. Sales forecasts developed in this manner are usually inaccurate and inconsistent. Because each area maintains its own sales forecasting process and often its own computer system, data, if shared at all, are only shared through manual transfers, which are prone to human errors, and which contribute to forecast inaccuracy. When completely separate sales forecasting systems are used, the assumptions that underlie the sales forecasts, such as pricing levels and marketing programs, may differ from one system to the next. Furthermore, each area that forecasts independently does so with a unique bias, making separate forecasts inconsistent and unusable by other areas. The redundancy associated with each separate sales forecasting process costs the firm both money and valuable personnel time and energy. Islands of analysis often lead to employee frustration and an overall lack of confidence in the sales forecasting process.

To improve sales forecasting performance, management attention must be devoted to eliminating factors that encourage the development of islands of analysis. As discussed in the "Systems" section of Chapter 8, this goal can be reached by establishing a single sales forecasting process that is supported by investment in a sales forecasting infrastructure. Regardless of the particular forecasting software that is used, it should be able to develop, analyze, and distribute sales forecasts. The system must possess appropriate forecasting tools including a suite of statistical techniques, graphical tools, and the ability to capture and report performance metrics over time. A critical component of this sales forecasting infrastructure is its ability to access historical sales data from a centrally maintained data warehouse. It should be electronically accessible to all functional areas, and it should provide real-time data.

Once islands of analysis are eliminated, the firm can expect improved sales forecasting performance and significant cost savings. Forecasts will be more accurate, will better meet the needs of various departments, and will be more credible. When systems are electronically linked, the errors that result from manual data transfers can be avoided, and forecasting information can be accessible to all functional areas. From a cost perspective, a single sales forecasting process eliminates redundant efforts within the firm, thus saving valuable employee time and other resources. And because accuracy improves, all the well-documented cost savings in areas like purchasing, inventory control, and logistics planning can be tracked and realized.

Key 5: Use Tools Wisely

There is a tendency in many companies with which we have worked to rely solely on the opinions of experienced managers and/or salespeople (qualitative tools) to derive sales forecasts, ignoring quantitative tools like regression and time-series analysis. Alternatively, many companies expect the application of quantitative tools, or the computer packages that make use of these quantitative tools, to "solve the sales forecasting problem." The key is that both quantitative and qualitative forecasting tools are integral to effective sales forecasting. To be effective, however, these tools must be understood and used wisely within the context of the firm's unique business environment. Without understanding where qualitative techniques, time series, and regression do and do not work effectively, it is impossible to analyze the costs and achieve the benefits of implementing new forecasting tools.

Wise use of forecasting tools requires an acknowledgment of where each type of tool works well and where it does not, then proceeding to put together a process that utilizes the advantages of each tool within the company's own unique context. In terms of qualitative forecasting, for example, we have found that salespeople generally do a poor job of taking their previous experience and turning that into an initial sales forecast. However, these same people are generally quite good at taking an initial quantitative sales forecast and qualitatively *adjusting* it to improve overall accuracy. In terms of quantitative techniques, time series models work quite well in companies that experience changing trends and seasonal patterns, but are of no use in determining the relationship between demand and such external factors as price changes, economic activity, or marketing efforts by the company and its competitors. Conversely, regression analysis is quite effective at analyzing these relationships, but not very useful in forecasting changes in trend and seasonality.

To apply this key, a process should be implemented that uses time series to forecast trend and seasonality, regression analysis to forecast demand relationships with external factors, and qualitative input from salespeople, marketing, and general management to adjust these initial quantitative forecasts. This general recommendation for integrating quantitative and qualitative tools must be refined for each individual company by finding the specific techniques that provide the most improved accuracy. The consequences of addressing this key are a more cogent sales forecasting process, where the implementation of each tool is understood in the context of the overall process, and improved sales forecasting accuracy as each tool is wisely used to do what it was designed to do.

Key 6: Make It Important

As was emphasized in Chapter 2, *"What gets measured gets rewarded, and what gets rewarded gets done."* This management truism is the driver behind the final two keys to better sales forecasting. In many companies with which we have worked, sales forecasting is described by senior management as an important function. While in our experience this assessment is shared by individuals throughout the firm, few organizations institute sales forecasting policies and practices that reinforce the notion that sales forecasting is important for business success. There is frequently a gap between management's words and his or her actions, which are manifested in the way reward systems affect forecasting behaviors. In other words, companies frequently tell those who develop sales forecasts that "sales forecasting is important," while failing to reward forecast developers for forecasting well or punishing forecast developers for forecasting poorly. This leads sales forecast users to become frustrated by what they perceive as a lack of interest and accountability for sales forecasting accuracy on the part of developers. Such frustration often leads to user manipulation of existing sales forecasts, or in the extreme case, the development of separate islands of analysis, which duplicate forecasting efforts and ignore valuable sales forecast input.

One way that sales forecasting can be made important to those who are responsible for creating and using sales forecasts is to give all individuals involved in forecasting adequate training. In addition to other training objectives that have been discussed, sales forecast creators and users should understand where and how sales forecasts are used throughout the organization. In many companies with which we have worked, salespeople and product managers indicate they understand little of what happens to their forecasts after they have completed them. When forecasters become aware of all the downstream ramifications of inaccurate sales forecasts, the task takes on more importance to them.

Another action that management can take to communicate the importance of sales forecasting performance is to incorporate sales forecasting performance measures into job performance evaluation criteria. Clearly, salespeople, product managers, and others who are responsible for creating forecasts see sales forecasting as part of their job if there are important rewards associated with sales forecasting excellence. Even senior managers get very interested in sales forecasting when metrics of accuracy are worked into their personal performance evaluations and bonus plans. But focusing on senior management is not enough. One company with which we worked includes sales forecast accuracy as a meaningful part of performance plans of senior executives, but not of those on the "front line" who work with sales forecasts on a daily basis. The job has not been made important to those who do the job, and the effect is that the job is still not done very well.

This is particularly true of those people who are typically responsible for initial sales forecast input—the sales force. At nearly all the benchmark and audit companies, salespeople were critically important pieces of the sales forecasting puzzle, yet in almost all cases, salespeople who develop sales forecasts were neither provided feedback as to how well they forecast nor offered any types of rewards for forecasting well. In fact, many salespeople agree with the following sentiment that was expressed by a salesperson for a technology-based manufacturer, *"My job is to sell, not forecast."* Similarly, product managers, who also provide critical input to the sales forecasting process at many companies, often consider sales forecasting an extra burden that takes them away from their "real jobs."

In summary, a company can communicate that sales forecasting is an important management function if it understands the sales forecasting process, provides the necessary training that allows forecasters to do the task well, and provides significant rewards for sales forecasting excellence.

Key 7: Measure, Measure, Measure

In this section, we have presented a series of keys that, if implemented, help improve sales forecasting performance and, as a result, the performance of those functions that use sales forecasts to plan and manage operations. Without the ability to effectively measure and track performance, there is little opportunity to identify whether changes in the development and application of sales forecasts are contributing to, or hindering, business success. This key may be intuitive for most business managers, yet our research has identified surprisingly few companies that systematically measure sales forecasting management performance. In cases where measures have been implemented, they are infrequently used for performance assessment or to identify opportunities for sales forecasting improvement.

In cases where measures are collected and documented, there may still be insufficient detail or little understanding as to how such measures can help identify opportunities for sales forecasting improvement. Generally we have found that even when sales forecast accuracy has been measured over time, few individuals who contribute to the sales forecast development review the history and can determine whether their forecasting performance has improved, remained constant, or deteriorated. This last aspect reflects a complacency toward performance measures when such measures are not used to evaluate an individual's job performance or that provide little support to identify sources of forecasting error.

Very importantly, companies should assess sales forecasting accuracy in terms of its impact on business performance. Highly accurate sales forecasts should not be an end in themselves, but should rather be a means to achieve the end, which is successful business performance. Improvements in sales forecast accuracy require expenditures of resources, both human and financial, and these improvements should be approached in a return-on-investment framework. For example, in a distribution environment, maintaining or improving customer service may be a worthy corporate objective. Investment in more accurate forecasts may be one way to achieve that objective. However, if the investment required to significantly improve accuracy is very high, then alternative approaches to improving customer service, such as carrying higher inventory levels, should be considered. The resulting strategy for improving customer service is then based on sound business analysis.

Measuring and tracking forecast accuracy ultimately helps build confidence in the sales forecasting process. As sales forecast users realize there are mechanisms in place to identify and eliminate sources of error, they are more likely to use the primary sales forecast developed to support all operations in the company. Islands of analysis will begin to disappear, and the organization will be able to assess the financial return that comes from sales forecasting management improvements.

❖ WHY THE CEO SHOULD CARE

As we discussed in Chapter 2, no company was ever successful simply from more accurate sales forecasting. Unless these more accurate forecasts can be translated into higher levels of customer service and lower supply chain costs, the impact of improved forecasting accuracy is lost on corporate profitability. By the same token, "C-level" executives (CEO, COO, CFO, and so on) are not interested in investing corporate dollars to improve forecasting performance unless it can be translated into higher returns for the shareholders. After all, return on shareholder value is the primary concern of upper management. Although improved forecasting accuracy often has a profound impact upon corporate profit and shareholder value, it is seldom presented as such to upper management.

Given this reality of business management, what is the most effective way to demonstrate the impact of improved sales forecasting performance to the CEO? The answer lies in the translation of forecasting accuracy into improved operational plans and execution and improved service to customers. The former results in lower costs per dollar of sales, and the latter results in increased sales.

The example presented in Chapter 2 illustrates this point and, thus, is repeated here as Figure 10.1. This company originally had sales revenue of $2,000,000,000 and total costs of $1,900,000,000 (annual profit of $100,000,000), on a working capital base of $200,000,000. The fixed capital base (consisting primarily of plant and equipment and three distribution centers) was $500,000,000. This resulted in a return on shareholder value (RSV) each year of 14.29%.

Based on a sales forecasting audit, a number of areas for potential improvement were discovered. As a result, management authorized a series of actions to implement recommended improvements to these processes—actions that included a new sales forecasting package to provide a more accurate base forecast; a revised demand management process that included greater input from marketing, sales, and operations to the base forecast to arrive at a final revised forecast; a computer and communications system to augment this process; and a new performance evaluation system to measure and reward everyone involved in the forecasting process who improved forecasting accuracy or who used those improved forecasts to lower supply chain costs and/or improve customer service.

From the start of this effort, upper management insisted upon dollar measures of the impact of these more accurate forecasts upon lower operations costs and increased sales from improved customer service. It was quickly realized that the latter of these two could not be fully and accurately measured, so the company settled for documenting only when the more accurate forecasts led to improvements in inventory available to meet customer demand—in other words, when sales were made because the inventory was available, as opposed to a lost sale due to stockouts.

The results of this documentation are illustrated in Figure 10.1. Increased sales as a result of improved in-stock situations were $2,000,000, while the operating costs of meeting total demand decreased by $7,000,000, resulting in increased profit of $7,010,000.

The operating cost savings fell into three main categories. First, more accurate forecasts led to a reduction in the amount of inventory held by the company to meet uncertain demand variations (i.e., safety stock) in the amount of $45,000,000 (also note that the reduction in inventory resulted in lower working capital). This resulted in savings in the cost of money on those invested funds, lower risk costs on the inventory (obsolescence, shrinkage, and insurance), and lower facility costs. The total of these three cost components is typically referred to as inventory carrying cost, which was reduced $5,000,000 per year.

Second, more accurate forecasts led the company to buy more of its required raw materials on long-term contract from supply chain partners, rather than on the spot market. The reduction in price between these two methods of procurement led to a $1,000,000 annual savings.

Finally, the company often faced the situation of producing a certain product and shipping it to its East Coast distribution center to meet anticipated demand, only to find the demand was lower than forecast on the East Coast and higher than forecast on the West Coast. As a result, some of the inventory of that product that had already been

Figure 10.1   An Example of Forecasting Improvement Impact on
Shareholder Value

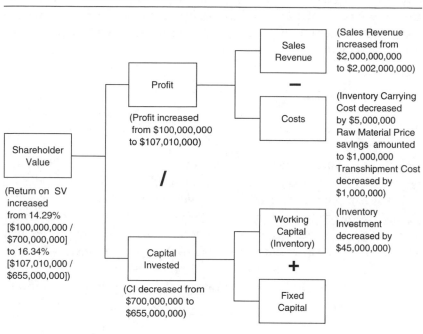

shipped from the production facility (located in the Midwest) to the East Coast distribution center would have to be moved (transshipped) to the West Coast distribution center. Improved forecasting accuracy by product and by distribution center lowered the incidence of this scenario and its accompanying costs in the amount of $1,000,000 a year.

Although fixed capital was negligibly affected by these changes, working capital (money invested in inventory) decreased by $45,000,000. This resulted in a decrease in capital invested in the company by the shareholders of $45,000,000. As we mentioned, whether this $45,000,000 is paid out to the shareholders as a dividend or kept in retained earnings for future investments is irrelevant to the financial impact being evaluated here.

The result of all these changes in forecasting performance was improvement in profit by $7,010,000 each year, the capital investment base went down by $45,000,000, and return on shareholder value increased from 14.29% to 16.34%. The total cost of all the improvements in sales forecasting management was approximately $1,650,000, for a return on investment result of 7,010,000/1,650,000 (425%)! All of this clearly shows that improvement in forecasting accuracy can have a dramatic effect on corporate profitability and shareholder value— precisely why the CEO should care.

❖ THE CEO SHOULD CARE AT TELLABS

To finish this point, one more example is provided. Tellabs is a large, global telecommunications equipment manufacturer that embarked on a several-year effort to improve sales forecasting performance. Tellabs partnered with Steelwedge, a demand management systems provider, to assess and improve their demand management processes and implement the Steelwedge software. The result of this partnership was not just a new software package, but a collaborative demand management process that was supported by a system customized to their process needs.

As Figure 10.2 illustrates, performance results were dramatic. Shorter cycle times and higher fill rates both resulted from a significant

Figure 10.2   Measurable Results for Tellabs

Results:	Before	After
Accelerate Cycle Time	12 Days	7 Days
Increase Actual Fill Rates	67%	74%
Improve Mix Accuracy	55%	76%
Increase Aggregate Accuracy	87%	94%

Savings Using STEELWEDGE:	
Inventory Savings Effects (annual)	$6.5 Million
Service Level Improvements (annual)	$750,000
Annual Logistics Cost Savings	$3.7 Million
TOTAL ANNUAL SAVINGS	$10.95 Million

improvement in accuracy. These higher customer service metrics resulted in $750,000 in annual revenue enhancements. Coupled with the inventory and logistics savings, the annual bottom line impact of the demand management improvement effort was $10.95 million! Although Tellabs did not share with us the total investment, such a significant bottom line impact must have resulted in a dramatic return on investment and certainly gave the CEO many reasons (10.95 million of them) to care.

❖ CONCLUSIONS

We began the Preface of this book by stating that this effort had been a labor of love. Well, sometimes love hurts. It was an enjoyable, yet gut-wrenching, process to bring together the experience of four decades of work with hundreds of companies, all between the covers of one book. We profoundly hope this effort assists you in better managing the sales forecasting function within your company and, as a result, better managing the demand management and demand planning functions in your company and your overall supply chains. If we have accomplished this, we have been successful.

References

Armstrong, Gary and Philip Kotler (2003), *Marketing: An Introduction*, 6th edition, Upper Saddle River, NJ: Prentice Hall.

Armstrong, J. Scott (1988), "Research Needs in Forecasting," *International Journal of Forecasting*, 4, 449–465.

Arter, D. R. (1989), "Evaluate Standards and Improve Performance With a Quality Audit," *Quality Progress*, 22 (9), 41–43.

Bienstock, Carol C., John T. Mentzer, and Monroe Murphy Bird (1997), "Measuring Physical Distribution Service Quality," *Journal of the Academy of Marketing Science*, 25 (No. 1), 31–44.

Bloomfield, Peter (1976), *Fourier Analysis of Time Series: An Introduction*, New York: John Wiley & Sons, Inc.

Bowersox, Donald J., David J. Closs, John T. Mentzer, and Jeffrey R. Sims (1979), *Simulated Product Sales Forecasting*, East Lansing, MI: (Michigan State University Bureau of Business Research.

Box, G. E. P. and G. W. Jenkins (1970), *Time Series Analysis: Forecasting and Control*, San Francisco, CA: Holden-Day.

Brown, Robert G. and R. F. Meyer (1961), "The Fundamental Theorem of Exponential Smoothing," *Operations Research*, 9 (No. 5), 673–685.

Chen, F., Z. Drezner, J.K. Ryan, and D. Simchi-Levi (1999), "The Bullwhip Effect: Managerial Insights on the Impact of Forecasting and Information on Variability in a Supply Chain," In: *Quantitative Models for Supply Chain Management*. Boston, MA: Kluwar Academic Publishers.

Churchill, Gilbert A. Jr., Neil M. Ford, and Orville C. Walker, Jr. (1993). *Sales Force Management*, 4th edition, Homewood, IL: Richard D. Irwin, Inc.

Cohen, J. and P. Cohen. (1983), *Applied Multiple Regression/Correlation Analysis for the Behavioral Sciences*, Hillsdale, NJ: Lawrence Erlbaum Associates.

Conference Board (1970), *Sales Forecasting*, New York.

Conference Board (1971), *Planning and Forecasting in the Smaller Company*, New York.

Dalrymple, Douglas J. (1975), "Sales Forecasting Methods and Accuracy," *Business Horizons*, (December), 69–73.

Dalrymple, Douglas J. (1987), "Sales Forecasting Practices: Results From a United States Survey," *International Journal of Forecasting*, 3, 379–391.

Davidson, Timothy A. (1987), "Forecasters—Who Are They? Survey Findings," *Journal of Business Forecasting*, (Spring), 17–19.

Dew, J. R. (1994), "The Critical Role of Auditing in Continuous Improvement," *National Productivity Review*, 13 (Summer), 417–422.

Drury, D. H. (1990), "Issues in Forecasting Management," *Management International Review*, 30 (No. 4), 317–329.

Fildes, Robert and R. Hastings (1994), "The Organization and Improvement of Market Forecasting," *Journal of the Operations Research Society*, 45 (1), 1–16.

Fildes, Robert and Edward J. Lusk (1984), "The Choice of a Forecasting Model," *Omega*, 12 (No. 5), 427–435.

Fildes, Robert and J.C. Ranyard (1997), "Success And Survival of Operational Research Groups—A Review," *Journal of the Operational Research Society*, 48 (4), 336–360.

Fliedner, G. (2001), "Hierarchical Forecasting: Issues and Use Guidelines," *Industrial Management and Data Systems*, 101 (1), 5–12.

Galfond, G., K. Ronayne, and C. Winkler (1996), "State-of-the-Art Supply Chain Forecasting," *PW Review*, (November), 1–12.

Gaski, John F. (1984), "The Theory of Power and Conflict in Channels of Distribution," *Journal of Marketing*, 48 (Summer), 23–41.

Granger, C. W. J. (1980), *Forecasting in Business and Economics*, New York, NY: Academic Press, Inc.

Hanke, John E. and Arthur G. Reitsch (1995), *Business Forecasting*, 5th Edition, Englewood Cliffs, NJ: Prentice-Hall.

Herbig, P., J. Milewicz, and J. E. Golden (1993), "Forecasting: Who, What, When, and How," *Journal of Business Forecasting*, (Summer), 16–21.

Hogarth, R. and Spyros Makridakis (1981), "Beyond Discrete Biases: Functional and Dysfunctional Aspects of Judgmental Heuristics," *Psychological Bulletin*, 90, 115–137.

Holt, C. C., F. Modigliani, J. F. Muth, and H. A. Simon (1960), *Planning Production Inventories and Work Force*, Englewood Cliffs, NJ: Prentice-Hall.

Hussey, D.E. (1995), "Human Resources: A Strategic Audit," *International Review of Strategic Management*, 6, 157–195.

Janis, I. L. and I. Mann (1982), *Decision Making: A Psychological Analysis of Conflict, Choice, and Commitment*, 2nd Edition, New York, NY: Free Press.

Kahn, Kenneth B. (1998), "Revisiting Top-Down Versus Bottom-Up Forecasting," *Journal of Business Forecasting*, (Summer), 14–19.

Kahn, Kenneth B. and John T. Mentzer (1994), "The Impact of Team-Based Forecasting," *Journal of Business Forecasting*, (Summer), 18–21.

Kahn, Kenneth B. and John T. Mentzer (1995), "Forecasting in Consumer and Industrial Markets," *Journal of Business Forecasting*, 14 (Summer), 21–28.

Kahn, Kenneth B. and John T. Mentzer (1996), "EDI and EDI Alliances: Implications for the Sales Forecasting Function," *Journal of Marketing Theory and Practice*, (Spring), 72–78.

Kahneman, Daniel and A. Tversky (1973), "On the Psychology of Prediction," *Psychological Review,* 80 (No. 4), 237–251.

Keith, Janet E., Donald W. Jackson, and Lawrence A. Crosby (1990), "Effects of Alternative Types of Influence Strategies Under Different Channel Dependence Structures," *Journal of Marketing,* 54 (July), 30–41.

Krueger, Richard A. (1994), *Focus Groups: A Practical Guide for Applied Research,* 2nd Edition, Thousand Oaks, CA: Sage Publications.

Lapide, Larry (2002), "You Need Sales and Operations Planning," *Journal of Business Forecasting,* 21 (Summer), 11–14.

Lowenhar, Jeffrey A. (1984), "Fortune 500 Firm Revamps System After 32% Forecasting Error," *Journal of Business Forecasting,* 3 (Summer), 2–6.

Makridakis, Spyros and Steven C. Wheelwright (1989), *Forecasting Methods for Management,* 5th Edition, New York: John Wiley & Sons.

Makridakis, Spyros, Steven C. Wheelwright, and Victor E. McGee (1983), *Forecasting: Methods and Applications,* 2nd Edition, New York: John Wiley & Sons.

Malhotra, Naresh K. (1996), *Marketing Research: An Applied Orientation,* 2nd Edition, Upper Saddle River, NJ: Prentice Hall.

Marien, E.J. (1999), "Demand Planning and Sales Forecasting: A Supply Chain Essential," *Supply Chain Management Review,* 3 (Winter), 76–86.

Mentzer, John T. (1988), "Forecasting with Adaptive Extended Exponential Smoothing," *Journal of the Academy of Marketing Science,* 16 (No. 4), 62–70.

Mentzer, John T. (1999), "The Impact of Forecasting Improvement on Return on Shareholder Value," *Journal of Business Forecasting,* 18 (Fall), 8–12.

Mentzer, John T., Carol C. Bienstock, and Kenneth B. Kahn (1999), "Benchmarking Sales Forecasting Management," *Business Horizons,* 42 (May-June), 48–56.

Mentzer, John T. and James E. Cox, Jr. (1984a), "Familiarity, Application, and Performance of Sales Forecasting Techniques," *Journal of Forecasting,* 3, 27–36.

Mentzer, John T. and James E. Cox, Jr. (1984b), "A Model of the Determinants of Achieved Forecast Accuracy," *Journal of Business Logistics,* 5 (2), 143–155.

Mentzer, John T., Daniel J. Flint, G. Tomas, and M. Hult (2001), "Logistics Service Quality as a Segment-Customized Process," *Journal of Marketing,* 65 (October), 82–104.

Mentzer, John T. and Roger Gomes (1994), "Further Extensions of Adaptive Extended Exponential Smoothing and Comparison with the M-Competition," *Journal of the Academy of Marketing Science,* 22 (Fall), 372–382.

Mentzer, John T. and Kenneth B. Kahn (1995), "Forecasting Technique Familiarity, Satisfaction, Usage, and Application," *Journal of Forecasting,* 14 (No. 5), 465–476.

Mentzer, John T. and Kenneth B. Kahn (1997), "State of Sales Forecasting Systems in Corporate America," *Journal of Business Forecasting,* 17 (Spring), 6–13.

Mentzer, John T. and John L. Kent (1999), "Forecasting Demand in the Longaberger Company," *Marketing Management,* 9 (Summer), 46–50.

Mentzer, John T., Mark A. Moon, John L. Kent, and Carlo D. Smith (1997), "The Need for a Forecasting Champion, *Journal of Business Forecasting,* 16 (Fall), 3–8.

Mentzer, John T. and Jon Schroeter (1993), "Multiple Forecasting System at Brake Parts, Inc.," *Journal of Business Forecasting,* 9 (Fall), 5–9.

Mentzer, John T. and Jon Schroeter (1994). "Integrating Logistics Forecasting Techniques, Systems, and Administration: The Multiple Forecasting System," *Journal of Business Logistics,* 13 (2), 205–225.

Miller, D. M. (1985), "Anatomy of a Successful Forecasting Implementation," *International Journal of Forecasting,* 1, 69–75.

Moon, Mark A. and John T. Mentzer (1999), "Improving Salesforce Forecasting," *Journal of Business Forecasting,* 18, (Summer), 7–12.

Moon, Mark A., John T. Mentzer, and Carlo D. Smith (2003), "Conducting a Sales Forecasting Audit," *International Journal of Forecasting,* 19 (No. 1), 5–25.

Moon, Mark A., John T. Mentzer, Carlo D. Smith, and Michael S. Garver (1998), "Seven Keys to Better Forecasting," *Business Horizons,* (September-October), 44–52.

Myer, Raymond H. (1990), *Classical and Modern Regression with Applications,* 2nd Edition, Boston: PWS-Kent Publishing Company.

Nelson, C.R. (1973), *Applied Time Series Analysis,* San Francisco: Holden-Day.

Nelson, P.T. (1987), "Viewpoint: A Forecast Is Not a Sales Plan," *Journal of Business Logistics,* 8 (2), 115–122.

Ott, Lyman (1988), *An Introduction to Statistical Methods and Data Analysis,* 3rd Edition. Boston, MA: PWS-Kent Publishing Company.

Pan, Judy, D. R. Nichols, and O. M. Joy (1977), "Sales Forecasting Practices of Large U.S. Industrial Firms," *Financial Management,* 6 (No. 3), 72–77.

Pedhazur, Elazar J. (1982), *Multiple Regression in Behavioral Research,* 2nd Edition. New York: Holt, Rinehart & Winston.

Pedhazur, Elazar J. and Llora Pedhazur Schmelkin (1991), *Measurement, Design, and Analysis: An Integrated Approach.* Hillsdale, NJ: Lawrence Erlbaum Associates.

Pritsker, A. Alan B. (1986), *Introduction to Simulation and SLAM II,* 3rd Edition, New York: John Wiley & Sons.

Pritsker, A. Alan B., C. Elliot Sigal, and R.D. Jack Hammesfahr (1989), *SLAM II: Network Models for Decision Support,* Englewood Cliffs, NJ: Prentice-Hall, Inc.

Reichard, Robert S. (1966), *Practical Techniques of Sales Forecasting,* New York: McGraw-Hill.

Roberts, S. D. and R. Reed (1969), "The Development of a Self-Adaptive Forecasting Technique," *AIIE Transactions,* 1 (No. 4), 314–322.

Sales Management (1967), "Sales Forecasting: Is Five Percent Error Good Enough?" (December 15), 41–48.

Schultz, R. (1984), "The Implication of Forecasting Models," *Journal of Forecasting*, 3 (1) 43–55.

Schultz, R. (1992), "Fundamental Aspects of Forecasting in Organizations," *International Journal of Forecasting*, 7, 409–411.

Shiskin, J. (1961a), "Tests and Revisions of Bureau of the Census Methods of Seasonal Adjustments," Bureau of the Census, Technical Paper 5.

Shiskin, J. (1961b), "Electronic Computers and Business Indicators," National Bureau of Economic Research, Occasional Paper 56.

Sparkes, John R. and A. K. McHugh (1984), "Awareness and Use of Forecasting Techniques in British Industry," *Journal of Forecasting*, 3, 37–42.

Stern, Louis W., Adel I. El-Ansary, and Anne T. Coughlan (1996), *Marketing Channels*, 5th Edition, Upper Saddle River, NJ: Prentice Hall.

Stevens, James (1992), *Applied Multivariate Statistics for the Social Sciences*, 2nd Edition. Hillsdale, NJ: Lawrence Erlbaum Associates.

Theil, H. (1966), *Applied Economic Forecasting*, Amsterdam: North-Holland Publishing Company, 26–32.

Trigg, D.W. and A. G. Leach (1967), "Exponential Smoothing with an Adaptive Response Rate," *Operations Research Quarterly*, 18, 53–59.

Tybout, A. M. and J. R. Hauser, (1981), "A Marketing Audit Using a Conceptual Model of Consumer Behavior: Application and Evaluation," *Journal of Marketing*, 44 (Summer), 82–101.

VICS (2004), www.vics.com.

Waddell, D. and A.S. Sohal (1994), "Forecasting: The Key to Managerial Decision Making," *Management Decision*, 32 (1), 41–49.

Wheelwright, Steven C. and D. G. Clarke (1976), "Corporate Forecasting: Promise and Reality," *Harvard Business Review*, 54 (November-December), 40–42.

Wilson, J. Holton and Hugh G. Daubek (1989), "Marketing Managers Evaluate Forecasting Models," *Journal of Business Forecasting*, 8 (Spring), 19–22.

Winters, P.R. (1960), "Forecasting Sales by Exponentially Weighted Moving Averages," *Management Science*, 6, 324–342.

Index

About the Authors

Tom Mentzer is the Harry J. and Vivienne R. Bruce Excellence Chair of Business in the Department of Marketing and Logistics at the University of Tennessee. He has directed all four phases of the Sales Forecasting Benchmarking Studies, served as a consultant for numerous companies in the area of sales forecasting management, taught a sales forecasting management course every year for more than 25 years, conducted numerous sales forecasting management seminars, and published six books and more than 180 articles and papers in the areas of sales forecasting, marketing, logistics, and supply chain management.

Mark Moon is an Associate Professor of Marketing at the University of Tennessee, Knoxville. He earned his Ph.D. from the University of North Carolina at Chapel Hill, and his MBA and BA degrees from the University of Michigan. Mark's professional experience includes positions in sales and marketing with IBM and Xerox. He has been a member of UT's sales forecasting research team since 1996, and since that time, has published numerous articles on best practices in forecasting. Mark has played a key role in Phase 4 of the Sales Forecasting Benchmarking Studies, and has worked with 25 different companies to audit their forecasting practices.